FOLLOWING ON

FOLLOWING ON

A year with English cricket's golden boys

David Tossell

Know The Score Books is an imprint of Pitch Publishing

Pitch Publishing
A2 Yeoman Gate
Yeoman Way
Durrington
BN13 3QZ

www.pitchpublishing.co.uk
www.knowthescorebooks.com

Published by Know The Score Books 2010

A CIP catalogue record for this book is available from the British Library.

10-digit ISBN: 1848187041
13-digit ISBN: 9781848187047

Printed and bound in Great Britain by Cromwell Press Group

CONTENTS

ACKNOWLEDGEMENTS

WRITING ABOUT a particular group of players becomes a much harder, less rewarding task without the support of the whole team. I am very lucky, and very thankful, to have had the cooperation of every member of the England Under-19 squad that won the 1998 World Cup: Ian Flanagan, Paul Franks, Michael Gough, Jamie Grove, Giles Haywood, Rob Key, Richard Logan, Graham Napier, Stephen Peters, Jonathan Powell, Chris Schofield, Owais Shah, Graeme Swann and Nick Wilton, as well as their coach, John Abrahams.

I am also grateful to David Capel, David Graveney, Paul Grayson, Ian Thomas and Simon Timson for their time and insight. Others who do not appear in the book have offered valuable assistance, including Jeni Crouch, Chris Kelly, David Morris, James Motley, Haydn Parry, Nathan Ross, Natasha Sutherland, Arlo White and Richard Whitehead.

Simon Lowe supported the project from the beginning and Paul Camillin at Pitch Publishing saw it through to its conclusion, while Graham Morris at www.cricketpix.com and the staff at Colorsport and Getty Images were most helpful in coming up with photographs.

My family were as supportive as always, especially my wife Sara, who managed never to sound too exasperated when turning down social invitations because 'David's going to be out watching cricket'. One day I'll surprise her by writing something she might actually read.

INTRODUCTION

THE BOYS OF '98

'The Under-19 World Cup was one of the happiest times of my life and I have got goose bumps now just talking about it. It was absolutely brilliant' – **Graeme Swann**

JOHN ABRAHAMS is a cheerful man who rarely talks for long without a chuckle passing his lips. He is also, should you ever need such information, the answer to a couple of cracking cricket trivia questions. If asked who was named Man of the Match in a Lord's final after being dismissed for a duck and not bowling a ball, remember that his captaincy was considered worthy of such an award in Lancashire's victory against Warwickshire in the 1984 Benson and Hedges Cup. At the time of this book's completion, Abrahams also remained the only coach to lead a male England cricket team to success in an official ICC global tournament, the 1998 Under-19 World Cup. Discussion of the latter of those achievements ensures a relentless current of laughter and happy memories.

'They were a great bunch of lads,' he recalled, squinting against the sun that pierced the windows at English cricket's National Performance Centre on the campus of Loughborough University. 'As coach on a trip like that you have to fill many roles and the last persona I want to take on is that of headmaster. But I can't remember any disciplinary stuff with them.' Either Abrahams has simply seen worse over the years or is being protective of his old boys because the players themselves admit they were hardly choirboys. 'I do know that they went out but they were sensible about it,' he admitted. 'But they were self-policing, they looked after each other and they knew when things went a step too far. And they came together as a team on the field when it counted.'

Born near Cape Town and arriving in Lancashire as a boy when his father Cec – a stalwart of the Cape Coloured cricketing community in the days of apartheid – accepted an offer to play league cricket in England, Abrahams's role as head of Elite Player Development for the ECB still includes hands-on involvement with the Under-19s in the capacity of team manager. Despite increasing sophistication in his area of work, some aspects remain unchanged from the ten winter weeks of 1997-98 when he and the likes of Graeme Swann, Owais Shah and Robert Key took on the world. 'If you have got some contact time with these kids you can start instilling in them the behaviour expected of an England cricketer. We remind them that people will know who they are if they are in an England blazer so the message is, "Don't let yourself down." You build a rapport and players come to know what is non-negotiable. That team knew the expectations.'

Before the players had a chance to pack for a tour that would take in Test matches and one-day internationals against their South African hosts, followed by participation in the World Cup, England captain Michael Atherton and coach David Lloyd visited them at their training base at the Lilleshall sports centre in Shropshire to give Nelson-like speeches. After all, there had not been a lot for English cricket to celebrate when Abrahams, team manager Phil Neale and the selectors sat down to pick their touring party in the autumn of 1997. In the previous 18 months, England had flopped at the World Cup, lost at home to Pakistan, been held to a drawn series in Zimbabwe and, finally, been beaten at home in the Ashes. Perhaps the brightest spot of the latest summer had been the mature, match-winning knock of 19-year-old Ben Hollioake on his one-day international debut at Lord's. Quite apart from the expectation it created around the player himself, it meant that the list of names comprising the Under-19 squad was scrutinised closely for someone else who might step up to the senior side so effortlessly. The players under the microscope were:

Ian Flanagan (Essex): Left-hand batsman.
Paul Franks (Nottinghamshire): Right-arm fast-medium bowler, left-hand batsman.
Michael Gough (Durham): Right-hand batsman, occasional off-spin bowler.

Jamie Grove (Essex): Right-arm fast bowler.
Giles Haywood (Sussex): Left-hand batsman, right-arm medium bowler.
Robert Key (Kent): Right-hand opening batsman.
Aaron Laraman (Middlesex): Right-hand batsman, right-arm fast-medium bowler.
Richard Logan (Northamptonshire): Right-arm fast-medium bowler.
Graham Napier (Essex): Right-arm fast-medium bowler, right-hand batsman.
Stephen Peters (Essex): Right-hand opening batsman.
Jonathan Powell (Essex): Off-spin bowler, right-hand batsman.
Chris Schofield (Lancashire): Leg-spin bowler, left-hand batsman.
Owais Shah (Middlesex): Captain. Right-hand batsman, occasional off-spin bowler.
Graeme Swann (Northamptonshire): Off-spin bowler, right-hand batsman.
Nick Wilton (Sussex): Wicketkeeper, right-hand batsman.

Having suffered a back injury, Laraman would return home prematurely without playing a major game on tour, leaving his 14 colleagues to contest the first youth World Cup to be staged since the inaugural event ten years earlier. 'We selected a side that could play four-day Tests but also compete in the one-dayers,' explained Abrahams, who had not long inherited his role from former Essex batsman Graham Saville. 'They were the best players anyway, so we thought they could perform at both forms. We had one or two with first-class experience and some had gone to Bermuda with us that year for an Under-19 tournament where we'd played what was basically our Under-17 team. The core group had been through our development system and then we obviously looked at performances during the season. We had quite a few all-rounders, so there was strength in depth and it was a fairly well-balanced side. The bowling attack was not threatening but accurate.

'One of the bigger calls is how a young player will cope being away from home and all you can do is suck it and see. Unless they have been on tour with you before you have no idea, although you try to communicate with county coaches to see what they are like. With that being such a long tour and being away for Christmas and New Year it was not easy, but to their credit all the players stuck together.'

Paul Franks, one of older and more experienced team members, recalled, 'Some of us had been hardened by county cricket, but we knew the challenge would be massive and we didn't underestimate the task ahead. The preparation was tremendous. We went away for about three training camps and we had the likes of Neil Foster and Geoff Arnold passing on their wisdom.'

According to Stephen Peters, 'Lilleshall was like a second home in those days. We used to go to the pub at the end of the drive and play pool. It was a great time and my memories of the whole thing are so fond. It was the best bunch of lads I have ever been with. Everyone got on fantastically well.'

Michael Gough added, 'The thing that sticks out for me is the early morning runs. At about half past six we would meet in the pitch black to jog down the drive and back, which was about two miles. It was character building and got your fitness up. Then we had a full day in the nets. We were miles from anywhere so there were no distractions and the guys used to show up bleary-eyed but in decent shape.'

Owais Shah, the captain, admitted that he did not exactly lead from the front in those sessions. 'I was not one of the fittest and I remember coming last in one of the runs that we did. I didn't really do much fitness as a kid because it was boring and I would rather bat or bowl or field. I didn't see a problem as captain coming last, as long as I tried my best. My attitude was, "When it comes to cricket I will be there for you."'

Once in South Africa, team morale was tested by events in the two Under-19 Tests either side of Christmas, both of which followed similar patterns. 'We were hanging on by our cuticles,' Abrahams smiled. 'We were outplayed in both games.'

In Cape Town, having given Test debuts to Gough, Richard Logan and Nick Wilton, England lost the toss and were sentenced to a long stretch in the field while their hosts rattled up 504 for 8 declared. Grant Elliott, two years before he would leave South Africa to forge an international career in New Zealand, made an unbeaten double century. Franks, captaining the team while Shah sat exams at college, was the most successful bowler with four wickets, while Swann's three victims cost 139 runs. In reply, England managed only 286, Swann making 75 from the number four position and Graham Napier striking 40 down the order. Following on, Peters (92) and Key (51) achieved a three-figure opening partnership but wickets fell steadily thereafter and England were dismissed for 256, just enough to achieve a draw.

Before the next Test at Fochville, Abrahams tackled the task of keeping morale high over the first Christmas many of the squad had spent away from home. 'We had a lunch that I organised in the hotel,' he remembered. 'I wrote a script for a *Blind Date* sketch and the guys had to act it out. Off their own bat,

Giles and Goughie had hired a couple of Santa outfits and organised a Secret Santa. It showed that by design or pure luck we had a team where everyone mixed in together.'

Back on the field, England's bowlers were hammered again, with only Swann (4 for 90) able to view his figures with anything other than contrition. Morne Van Wyk, a future one-day international player, hit 188 and South Africa again declared beyond 500. At seven wickets down and barely three figures on the board, England appeared doomed, only for Franks to arrive at the wicket and produce a remarkable unbeaten innings of 119. His partnerships of 75 and 88 with Wilton and Grove for the last two wickets lifted England to a respectable 291.

It still required a further rearguard to save the game, but Peters (55) and Key obliged with another good opening stand. Shah took over from there with an undefeated 104, an innings that remains one of Abrahams's most vivid memories of the tour. 'Jacques Rudolph was a leg-spinner and batsman back then and the way Owais played him was absolutely brilliant. Even at that age his ability to play against spin was fantastic. I have this mental picture of Rudolph delivering the ball and Owais seeing it halfway down and just turning away and starting to take his guard for the next ball. He knew there was no danger and psychologically it was a very positive action in his favour. He had total confidence in reading the ball.' At the other end, Gough reached a half-century in an unbroken fourth-wicket stand of 149 and the game was drawn comfortably at 247 for 3.

Unbeaten in the Tests, but hardly covered in glory, England's optimism for the World Cup took a further knock in the one-day series. After the first scheduled game fell foul of the weather, England lost comprehensively in the other two, with batsmen and bowlers equally culpable. Put in at Benoni, England lost five wickets for 26 and needed a Peters innings of 57 to claw them to 171 all out, a total South Africa passed with only three wickets down and more than 18 overs in hand. At Centurion Park, the home team elected to bat and set England a target of 253 to win. Again, the top order disintegrated – to the tune of 34 for 4 – and the only resistance was a seventh-wicket collaboration of 96 between Gough (56 not out) and Schofield (49). England were bowled out for 202 in a little under 45 overs.

However, Abrahams believes a turning point had been reached following the first of those defeats. 'They had been together a long time and the team cohesion was really good, as was the social side,' he said. 'But I remember a meeting at Benoni where we sat down with them and Phil and I said that we needed to improve. We said, "We have tried most things we know, so we are going to leave you for an hour to discuss how we are going to kick it on from here. Who is going to do what?" I never did find out what was said but I think it was the point when people started recognising their roles and accepting individual responsibility. Things soon started to change a little bit and I think Owais felt a bit more comfortable having had that meeting as they started geeing themselves up.'

Grove described it as an 'interesting' meeting and added, 'It was one of those honesty games, trying to find out what we were doing because no one really knew. It was a consistency thing. We could be brilliant in sessions. We had to decide where we were going to be batting because at that time we were just trying to get runs quickly and would lose wickets through stupid shots. We were trying to work out roles. Considering we were all hormonal 17 and 18 year olds it was a good, mature meeting.'

Shah recalled, 'Going into the World Cup, I don't think Phil and John really believed we could win. Phil was a very strict guy and I think they'd had enough of us. They thought we were not really interested in cricket. I reckon deep down the guys had had enough of the coaches as well. But we said, "We are going to show you how good a cricket team we are, and how we are such good a bunch of friends that we can pull together in big games."'

SPONSORED BY MTN, the South African communications company, the second Under-19 World Cup came a full decade after the likes of Brian Lara, Michael Atherton, Nasser Hussain and Sanath Jayasuriya had competed in the inaugural event in Australia. Jayasuriya had gone on to revolutionise the art of opening the batting in one-day cricket, blazing away from the first ball to lead Sri Lanka to an unexpected triumph in the senior World Cup in 1996.

On the basis of England's outdated and lacklustre performance in that tournament, few observers were including their junior team among the contenders for the title in South Africa. The smart money was on the host nation and India, whose squad included several players who had been part of the Under-15 World Cup success of two years earlier. Nor could the Australians, coached by the old fighter Allan Border, be discounted among the field of 16 teams. 'You know through experience that the teams from the sub-continent will be good in terms of skill and they will be street-wise,' said Abrahams. 'I don't think the Australians and South Africans yet had the infrastructure to indentify, select and prepare the best players, but you really don't know much about the opposition in those tournaments.'

Peters recalled, 'We didn't talk about the opposition at all, but we were well managed and we practised well,' although Abrahams explained that 'by the time of the World Cup we had to ease down physically because it had been a long tour'.

According to Richard Logan, 'Once the Tests against South Africa were done we re-evaluated and John and Phil kind of went easy on us. We had played a lot of cricket and now we had a few more days off. The work we had done early on held us in good stead and allowed us to get away from cricket a bit and then put our all into each game.'

Peters argued that it was little piece of player power that resulted in the squad being given more free time as the tour progressed. 'I remember there being a few issues. After three or four weeks we had not had a morning off and we were all getting a bit grumpy. We were getting up at 8.30 every morning and we wanted a lie-in until 10.30 every now and then. There were a few fall-outs, but at 18 or 19 there are bound to be a few itchy feet.'

Swann also contradicts Abrahams's benevolent memory of their conduct as tourists. 'John and Phil had the worst jobs in the world,' he laughed. 'They must have been pulling out their hair half the time. I had a few fall-outs with Phil but I absolutely love him now. I was a big cocky upstart of a teenager, so a man who is very anal about organisation – but unbelievably brilliant at what he does – was as far as possible from the way I was. We needed reminding why we were there because we felt we were on a lads' holiday most of the time.'

Key recalled that the release from the intensity of striving to impress employers aided the happy atmosphere among the young tourists. 'On a tour like that it's not like when you are vying for your position at your county,' he said. 'You all want to play and two or three have to miss out, but it's not like you are getting in the way of someone's job like you are in county cricket. There was no politics behind the scene, no senior old pro. When you are 19, you are all pretty much interested in the same things, which makes binding much easier.'

Franks remembered that Neale and Abrahams 'found it difficult managing us as a group because were away for so long'. He explained, 'The lads were looking for some relief and there were times when I felt we needed to relax and get away from it a little bit. We didn't do that perhaps as much as we could have, so there were times when the players and management became separated as a consequence. There were one or two underlying issues that got dealt with in a way that, looking back, might have been dealt with differently. It was more house-keeping stuff than anything. When you are 18 and 19 year olds away in foreign country there are all sorts of things you can get up to – whether that be curfews, or tidiness or rules you are expected to abide by. I am sure at times things got carried away, but when push came to shove we were together at the right times.'

It was the start of the World Cup that pointed everyone in the correct direction. 'It was a light at the end of the tunnel for the players,' said Abrahams. 'They were going to enjoy it. They weren't staying in one place for too long and getting bored and it was a really well organised event, starting with a big opening ceremony at the Wanderers.' Franks added, 'We had been away about eight weeks and the guys were starting to miss home, but the World Cup gave us some impetus. Winning that was what we set out to do.'

Any problems that might have existed in the England camp were nothing compared to those facing the West Indies. They arrived with seven players who contravened the age regulations due to the qualifying date being different to that of their domestic competitions. Their opening game had to be delayed for two days while reinforcements were flown in. One of them was Chris Gayle, whose 364 runs – including those in the 'Plate' event for teams eliminated in the opening stages – was the best total in the tournament. Meanwhile, Ramnaresh Sarwan, who would join him as one of the mainstays of West Indies batting for years to come, finished as the joint leading wicket taker with 16.

Drawn in the Sobers Pool with New Zealand, Namibia and Bangladesh, it would have been a surprise had England not made it to the Super League stage, but it was hardly the smoothest of passages. The opening game was at the St. Alban's College Ground in Pretoria against a New Zealand side that had recently given Australia a close contest. Spinners Swann and Schofield both bowled economically to restrict the Kiwis to 180, but the batsmen contributed to their own problems with three run outs. None of the England top four made it as far as 20 and, at 69 for 3, victory was in doubt until Swann and Haywood scored 39 each and the target was reached with four wickets and 6.4 overs in hand.

At the Nicky Oppenheimer Ground at Randjesfontein, Namibia's batsmen offered no sterner opposition than had been expected, limping to 161 for 9. Franks achieved two early breakthroughs and returned figures of 3 for 19 off seven overs, while Gough's spin produced 2 for 20. Key (35) and Shah (40), either side of 29 from Franks at the elevated position of number three, helped England to a winning score, but not before seven wickets had been lost. Abrahams recalled, 'I went into the dressing room when we were about six down and Phil was lying on the seats with a towel on his head, worrying that we weren't going to qualify.'

The picturesque setting of the Pretoria Boys High School should have completed England's unbeaten passage through the initial group stage, yet an unexpected reverse against Bangladesh left them grateful for the positive net run rate they had built up in their earlier games. It was a disgruntled England team that ended the day, with Shah complaining about various umpiring decisions in his official report and rueing the generosity of his butter-fingered fielders. England had appeared set for a big score after a hard-hitting 69 by Franks, supported by Key's 27. Yet a middle-order slump left Schofield (36) and Napier (24) to lift them to an all out total of 223. Bangladesh recovered from losing both openers to Grove, and a couple of wickets each for Napier and Gough could not prevent them winning with six overs remaining.

The tournament was now down to eight teams, with the winners of each group of four contesting the final. Pakistan, India and Australia formed England's opposition in the tough-looking D'Oliveira Pool. England batted first at Centurion Park against a Pakistan team that had won all three of their earlier games. Peters replaced the struggling Gough at the top of the order and responded with an accomplished 92 off 128 balls before being run out. Key contributed again, 35, and Shah, Schofield and Jonathan Powell all chipped in before England were dismissed for 251 in the final over. Imran Tahir, the leg-spinner who would play county cricket for Middlesex, Yorkshire and Hampshire, was the most successful bowler with four wickets.

Pakistan reached 46 before losing their first wicket when the dangerous Humayun Farhat, 34 off 23 balls, was caught by Swann off Napier. Hasan Raza, the only batsman in the tournament with Test match experience, was run out by Swann's quick thinking and Majid Jahangir took too long in scoring his 49. Pakistan finally succumbed in the 49th over, 18 runs in arrears. Napier finished with three wickets, while Swann and Schofield were economical once again. 'The game against Pakistan was one where we played really well,' Nick Wilton recalled. 'We posted a good score and bowled well. Everything clicked and Jon Powell took an absolutely outrageous catch on the boundary. Beating a good side with some good players meant we were feeling pretty confident.'

Peters added, 'When we beat Pakistan we started to think we could go on and win. There was a big team bath and after the game we sat in there for two hours with a couple of cans of beer and the stereo going. It was a great evening.'

After their most complete performance of the tournament, England faced India on a slow, low wicket at Benoni, where the opposition won the toss and reached 252 for 8. Franks, Haywood and Napier all took wickets early in their spells but none could derail skipper Amit Pagnis, who was eventually run out by Franks one short of his century. Rain reduced the victory target to 204 from 39 overs, according to the calculations of the Clarke Curve, a forerunner of the Duckworth-Lewis system. The innings was further disrupted by the weather on two occasions but that could not be used as an excuse for the collapse from 114 for 2, after Key made 57 and Franks 31, to 152 all out. Shah was one of three men to be run out, while Virender Sehwag, unsuccessful earlier with the bat, took three wickets.

It meant that victory against Australia, a convincing one at that, was now imperative if England were to have any chance of making the final. By the 11th over of the contest at Cape Town's Newlands ground, they were daring to dream after the accuracy of Franks and Logan produced a score of 29 for 4. 'Franksie set the tone early in the game because he was really aggressive,' said Abrahams. 'He was really loud, shouting to everyone, "Come on, boys. This is ours." He instigated that feeling of confidence.'

Napier continued, 'I remember Giles Haywood taking a superb catch early on at fine leg and that lifted us.' The fourth wicket, Franks's second, fell in controversial circumstances when even wicketkeeper Wilton appeared uncertain whether Marcus North's edge had carried. Yet umpire Nicholas Kock didn't even bother to consult his colleague at square leg before giving the batsman out. Logan delivered probably the best ball of the entire tournament, a fast yorker that skittled James Hopes, and it needed Michael Klinger's unbeaten 62 to get Australia to 147.

According to Franks, 'The bowling throughout the World Cup was a bit hit and miss. Conditions first thing in the morning tended to suit the bowlers and we lacked a bit of control at times, trying to take too many wickets instead of bowling in good areas. In the afternoon it could get flat quite quickly so you could cop some punishment. As a bowler your skills needed to be bang on. But we were hot when we needed to be – in the games against Pakistan and Australia.'

With England preparing to bat, the story became one of intrigue and cunning, as recounted by Abrahams. 'It was effectively a semi-final. We restricted them to a low score, but we knew that we needed to finish with a superior net run rate. Phil phoned a number in Johannesburg, the central point of the organisation, and asked how many overs we needed to score our runs in to be better than Australia. The first number we got was 33 and then they called back and said it was 36, so we went out with that in mind. We were sitting in the players' viewing area, which had a television. Just in case the commentators mentioned anything we said to Allan Border, "Do you mind if we turn it down so we can concentrate on what is happening?" So we turned the sound off. We have gone out all guns blazing and it is about 20 overs before they have realised what is happening and then there are frantic messages going back and forth.'

According to Grove, 'The Aussies should have twigged from ball one we were teeing off on every single shot, trying for a four or six every ball.' And Napier continued, 'Australia were that confident about beating us they had not even taken into consideration the possibility we might knock them out. They thought everything was dead and buried and suddenly they announced over the loud speakers what we were doing and by that time it was too late.'

A crowd of almost 6,000 saw Peters (51) and Key (25) put on 61 for the first wicket before Franks clubbed a pair of sixes in scoring 41 off only 34 balls. 'As a hit and miss pinch-hitter Franksie is probably the biggest miss going,' Swann recalled happily. 'But if he gets going he can belt it everywhere.' Shah hit the winning runs off the first ball of the 30th over and Australian captain Tim Anderson admitted, 'It didn't dawn on us that we could be caught and we didn't realise about the number of overs they needed to reach the total in. We'd have played differently if we'd known.'

Abrahams recalled the final comical episode of the day. 'The Aussies had this really bad outfit that someone had to wear if they cocked up during the day. Border, this great Test captain, had to wear it in the bar all night.'

Swann added, 'We went for a drink in a bar called the Green Man and the Aussies had named Border their "Dick of the Day". I remember us doing a pile-on – you know, when everyone jumps on top of someone – to him and thinking, "This is Allan Border for Christ's sake!"'

The result meant that India needed to improve their run rate against Pakistan the next day to deny England a place in the final, but after dismissing their great rivals for 188 they could not get home quickly enough to take first place in the group. The final table showed the top three teams tied with two wins each, while England had a net run rate of 0.494, compared to Australia's 0.174 and India's 0.046. Their opponents in the final in Johannesburg would be unexpected ones. Favourites South Africa surprisingly lost their closing game in the Pollock Pool to Sri Lanka, leaving them second on run rate to New Zealand.

ON THE day of the final, a 9 a.m. start in Johannesburg meant an early morning in a darkened Sky Sports studio for a fresh-faced Charles Colville, looking young enough to qualify for the tournament on which he was swotting up as transmission time approached. As Colville made a last-minute sweep of his notes and charts, former England coach Micky Stewart settled into a chair alongside him and the cameras began rolling. An uncomfortable-looking Owais Shah was shown explaining to an interviewer that his decision to insert New Zealand had been based on expectation of some early movement and then Stewart, who had watched these players progress through the age groups, introduced viewers to England's bowlers. Richard Logan, he advised, was 'still carrying a bit of puppy fat'; Chris Schofield would be an important figure in the long term because of the need to develop wrist spin at Test level; while off-spinner Jonathan Powell's recent growth spurt had hampered control of his deliveries. Once the action started, even Stewart was unable to address the most urgent question: Who had been distributing the bottles of colouring that had turned most of England's attack – Logan, Paul Franks, Powell, Giles Haywood and Schofield – into coppery blonds?

It was soon obvious that the occasion, as well as the dye, had gone to the bowlers' heads. With the ball apparently swinging too much, Franks and Logan had each bowled six wides in their first five overs, and Franks had added four no-balls. Then the dark-haired Graham Napier, who has waited until more recent times to add the highlights, bowled two wides in his first over. New Zealand were well beyond 50 without losing a wicket.

It was uncomfortable viewing for the England followers among the 8,000 in the cavernous Wanderers ground. They included several hundred 'Barmy Army' members, mostly ex-pats, who succeeded in upsetting the locals. Some got themselves kicked out of the Centenary Stand and were described by one writer as 'dishevelled, red-faced and pot-bellied boozers'. Yet they also gave England welcome support. 'There was a little section at one end of the ground where all the families and fans were,' Abrahams explained. 'There were St George's flags and they made a hell of a lot of noise, which was brilliant. We didn't allow ourselves the luxury of thinking it was going to be easy but we had the confidence of having beaten New Zealand already. We knew that if we played to the best of our abilities we should beat them.'

The mood of the match changed when Napier had both openers caught behind trying to cut. Haywood entered with his nonchalant medium-pace and had Jerrod Englefield caught at mid-wicket with his first ball. The Sussex youngster's first three overs were scoreless, contributing to a sequence of four successive maidens he shared with Napier. Having reached 50 in the ninth over, New Zealand laboured into the 27th before reaching three figures. With 15 overs remaining they were still only 122 for 5. Haywood had choked the middle of the innings, dismissing the dangerous Hamish Marshall and Lou Vincent on his way to figures of 3 for 18 off 10 overs. 'Giles was a medium pacer who bowled close to the wicket and just bowled it straight,' said Abrahams. 'If they tried a shot, it was a risk if they didn't get it quite right.'

Although Swann continued to bowl tightly, as he had throughout the tournament, Powell struggled to find a consistent length. Logan and Franks came in for more punishment towards the end of the innings as James Franklin and Peter McGlashan added 98, both reaching their fifties, and New Zealand closed on 241 for 6.

The inclusion of McGlashan's batting expertise had been at the expense of reliable seamer Richard Harkness. It meant that when Kyle Mills and Regan West were harshly dealt with for bowling too wide on either side of the wicket early in England's reply there was less back-up available. Peters was impressively keen to take advantage, whether it was cutting Mills to the off-side boundary or, with a Lara-like lift of the front leg, whipping consecutive deliveries through mid-wicket. Key, more watchful and timing the ball less well, was still only in the teens when Peters lifted Franklin over mid-off to pass 50 off 55 balls. Key hung in to help bring up the century partnership in the 20th over but, having survived one easy chance, one more difficult, and edged just wide of the keeper, he pulled lazily at Franklin and was caught off the top edge for 27.

After Franks was out for a frenzied 16, Shah played his most authoritative innings of the tournament, punishing anything slightly off line, although there were also a few occasions when he was left scurrying to make his ground. Peters overcame obvious tiredness to approach three figures with some calmly placed shots and eventually turned James Marshall to deep mid-wicket to reach his milestone, completing all three runs with his bat raised in the air. He and Shah had added 89 when he was caught in the deep for 107 with the score on 211, his 125-ball innings having included 12 fours. Only the formality of victory remained. 'A hundred in the final is everything to me,' Peters said after being named Man of the Match. 'I can't believe it has happened. The pitch was pretty flat and once I had passed 30 it became easier to score the runs.'

Shah went on to make 54 and, with teammates poised to race down from their balcony with St George's flags, he and Swann completed the win by running a leg bye off the last ball of the 46th over. While Shah turned to begin the diplomatic handshakes with the opposition, Swann, who had grinned and laughed his way through a flurry of thumping blows, grabbed a couple of stumps and charged off to help his friends begin the celebrations. Finally gathered in their blazers to watch Shah receive the trophy presentation, the players heard their captain conclude, 'It's a great feeling. Three weeks ago we weren't one of the favourites, but the boys done well. On paper we were a decent side but it didn't come together until the Pakistan game.'

HAVING GONE into the World Cup out of form, England had still been somewhat up and down throughout the tournament. Even Abrahams said at the time that the eventual success should not 'paper over the cracks' exposed by some of the earlier contests. England were said by some observers to have had an arrogance that was unmerited by their play. Among those of whom most had been expected, Franks had been an effective pinch-hitter but inconsistent with the ball; Shah had been largely disappointing until the final; Key had made a start in every innings but not gone on to make a big score; Swann had shown good control with the ball but his batting had fallen away. Yet, unlike the senior England team over the ensuing decade, they had shown the knack of winning when it mattered most, achieving outcomes greater than the sum of the individual parts. It was a good habit to have acquired along the long road through South Africa.

Back home, having participated in the kind of triumphant airport press conference that few English players have had the good fortune to experience, 14 young cricketers set out to secure their futures in the professional game. They'd had a taste of what it was like to represent their country and all would have said that they wanted more. But, as Abrahams pointed out, 'You have got to genuinely want it. There has got to be a real desire. It is all right saying "I want to play for England" but you have got to realise what that takes. You have to recognise the sacrifices you will have to make, commit yourself to the hard work that a lot of people don't see. Then luck plays a part, firstly in getting the opportunities to play for your county. But you have got have that desire to put yourself in a position where you could be picked.'

Perhaps the most remarkable thing about the careers of the boys of 1998 was the way that so many took a definitive route so quickly. Abrahams continued, 'Within three or four years, about half had gone on to play for England and as many were out of the game. It doesn't normally happen that the dividing line is so distinct in such a short space of time.' To be exact, within five years of the World Cup, five of the group – Franks, Key, Schofield, Shah and Swann – had played for the senior England team, while six – Flanagan, Gough,

Grove, Haywood, Powell and Wilton – had played their final game of first-class cricket.

In discussion with the players whose careers followed the latter route, I have asked them to offer an honest assessment of the factors, both in their game and their cricketing environment, that contributed to their failure to progress to a higher level. All have answered with honesty. None has whined and said 'I could have been a contender' and anything that might sound like an excuse has simply been an attempt to address that most difficult of questions. External factors and luck have played a part to varying degrees, but in the end most agree that cricket, being the revealing game that it is, probably delivers the rewards its participants deserve.

As 2009 began, the boys of '98 were either approaching or had just passed the age of 30, a good time to take stock of their achievements. It's an age when Test players should be at their peak and when county players are perhaps starting to look over their shoulders at young players threatening their livelihoods. It is also old enough for those who left the game prematurely to be establishing themselves in their new lives. Appropriately, the only members of the victorious Under-19 side on duty with the full England team as winter turned towards spring were the two players who had been at the crease when the World Cup was won. It is, therefore, with Owais Shah and Graeme Swann in the West Indies that this cricketing year begins. A year that held the promise of the Ashes, the World Twenty20 in England, a second Indian Premier League season, the inevitable questions about the structure and future of the game and, for the players, moments of invincibility and hopelessness, tales of conquest and regret.

01

THE KARACHI KID

'I remember a pre-season trip with John Emburey. I ran at him first ball and hit him straight over his head for six. I just thought that is how you play' – **Owais Shah**

SCENE ONE: February 6, 2009. A hotel meeting room in the Indian tourist destination of Goa. From an elevated position behind his lectern, the man with the expensive suit and Sotheby's accent scanned the gathering before him. Across India, five news stations beamed his face live into the homes of their viewers as, with the auctioneer's traditional 'going-going-gone' rhythm, he announced, 'One million. Five hundred. And 50 thousand. Sold to Chennai.'

The price tag applied to all-rounder Andrew Flintoff was, the room was reminded, 'the highest bid ever in the IPL player auction'. Seated behind and to the left of the podium, Indian Premier League Commissioner Lalit Modi stopped short of passing out in the manner of Del Boy on hearing that his ancient watch was worth millions in *Only Fools and Horses*, but his smile did betray the pride of a parent whose offspring is taking the lead in the school nativity.

At the circular tables packed tightly around the room, middle-aged Indian businessmen, moustaches bristling beneath bad comb-overs and above suits a little too tight, studiously entered the result on their scorecards and checked to see who was next up for grabs. Scarcely a minute later, Kevin Pietersen was purchased for an identical price to his England colleague by a goatee-bearded man in a loud shirt, who registered his bid with a mix of self-consciousness and lasciviousness, like someone raising his arm for a lap dance. Half an hour later, with considerably less fanfare, a somewhat less exalted teammate of Pietersen and Flintoff went under the hammer for $275,000 and was bound for the Delhi Daredevils.

Scene Two: Sabina Park, Kingston, 36 hours later. Ian Bell shuffled across his crease and allowed a delivery from Sulieman Benn to pass outside his off stump, practically turning his back to the West Indian slow left-arm bowler in contempt at his inability to make him play. There were three balls left before lunch on the fourth day of the first Test and England, already one wicket down, were trying to erase a first innings deficit of 74. Benn directed his next delivery a little closer to the stumps. Out of form and aware of his mortality as an England batsman, Bell could resist no longer, jabbing at the ball and edging into the wicketkeeper's gloves. As he departed the field, he glared at the bottom of his bat, accusing it of an involuntary action that seemed certain to have cost him his place, especially once England had been dismissed for a paltry 51.

Within these two episodes, the future of Owais Shah as a professional cricketer had been determined: England Test batsman and star of the Indian Premier League. Or so it seemed.

When the name of the 30-year-old Middlesex batsman had been presented to the group of perspiring representatives of the eight IPL franchises, the man himself was soundly asleep in Kingston's Hilton Hotel. By mid-morning in England, however, his wife Gemma could no longer contain the urge to call with news that the Daredevils had agreed to pay him double a decent annual county salary to join their ranks for their second season. 'My wife phoned at about 6.30 and told me that what had happened,' he said, standing in the shadow of the Sabina Park stands as his colleagues prepared for a day in the field. 'I knew there had been interest. I am looking forward to joining the Delhi Daredevils.' The last sentence was uttered as if training himself to remember the name of his team.

Significantly, when he spoke about the terms of his participation alongside the good and the great of the IPL, he didn't sound like someone expecting to be in the England Test team any time soon. He had, after all, been the 'spare batsman' on the last three tours and was once again stuck on the boundary edge. 'I am on an incremental contract with the ECB. I have to be back around the seventh or eighth of May, which allows me to play a few rounds of the Friends Provident Trophy before joining up with the one-day squad for the series against the West Indies.' He quickly added that 'there is pride and honour from playing in a Test match and there is no feeling that beats that', yet at the age of 30 – and with only two isolated appearances behind him – there was no disguising the resignation in his voice.

But then Bell had his rush of blood and everything changed. Ironically, the distraction of the IPL and the potential disunity it engendered in the team was thrown around by some as a reason for England's collapse to the third-lowest score in their history and defeat in the opening game of a four-Test series they were expected to win. That argument seemed little more than an opportunity for former players to create a sound-bite for media members frantic to squeeze as many angles out of the story as possible. After all, the potential for factions in the West Indies camp was even greater, given that only half of them had been fortunate enough to benefit from the $1 million payday offered by the Stanford Super Series in Antigua a few months earlier. They had seemed a pretty tight bunch as they jumped around in celebration of wicket after wicket.

There had been one particularly symbolic moment during the debacle. With Bell having given up his wicket off the last ball before lunch, Shah was into the nets immediately played resumed, a moment gleefully picked up by the TV producers. Viewers were apparently seeing the process of evolution before their very eyes. But if Shah had learned anything in the preceding 12 months it was to take nothing for granted. In the last year or so, Bell, Paul Collingwood, even new England captain Andrew Strauss, had scored significant runs when one more cheap dismissal would surely have seen Shah add to his Test portfolio. Even when his own weight of runs in the one-day team and the lack of form by the incumbents appeared to make him an irresistible selection, his name had been absent from the team sheet.

It was why, after scoring an unbeaten 125 in St Kitts the first warm-up game of the tour, he'd merely said, 'Whatever opportunity I get I want to keeping knocking out the runs. I will have to wait and see what happens.' Such equanimity was the result of having played only two Test matches, a year apart and each time as an injury replacement, despite banging out thousands of runs for Middlesex.

'I didn't get a go playing for England in 2004 to '06 and I don't think it had anything to do with my batting,' he explained in conversation later, referring to a period between June 2004 and September 2005 when he scored 13 centuries in English domestic cricket. 'The media said my face didn't fit but whatever it was Duncan Fletcher didn't think I fitted into his ideas.' The popular theory was that the England coach did not appreciate Shah's individuality, such as his own tested methods of playing spinners instead of adopting Fletcher's preferred 'forward press'. Shah added, 'That's life, but I feel that my game was good enough to play at a higher level and I was doing enough. I was the best batsman at the club, the most consistent, and had ticked all the boxes of where I wanted to be with my game.'

Even under a new England coach, Peter Moores, Shah had suffered the disappointment of watching the three-match series in Sri Lanka late in 2007 as a drinks waiter, while his friend Ravi Bopara was preferred to fill the batting slot vacated by the temporary absence of Strauss from the side. 'When I got picked for the tour to Sri Lanka, I sort of knew that I wouldn't get picked for the Tests because certain other people were preferred to me, but I was so grateful to be in the squad and you just don't know if someone might wake up ill and you might get a chance.'

It might seem natural for a player finding himself in such a position to wish a dodgy tummy upon a teammate or to be working out what level of failure from other batsmen could result in them being dropped. But Shah insisted that worrying about other players is both damaging and futile. 'That is not the reason you are not picked. It is because the captain or coach doesn't want to pick you. If you go down that route of looking at other players then you are saying it is a straight shoot-out between the guy who gets the most runs and the guy who gets no runs. But if the guy who doesn't get any runs still gets picked, then it is obviously nothing to do with how many runs you have both got. The captain and coach have in their mind who they want in the team and you are just there as an extra. You are not going to get in if you get a hundred today and the other guy gets nought, because that has happened to me and I still didn't get a game. You realise that the only way you are going to get a game is if someone gets injured and, because you can't control that, you don't worry about it.'

It was not meant to have been like this for the precociously talented kid from Karachi who had made his first-class debut at 17, gone on an England A tour at 18 and captained England's junior World Cup winners. Platitudes from captains and coaches about 'tough decisions' were wearing thin. But for once, the clamour for change was overwhelming and unavoidable. Typical had been the urging of cricket writer Martin Johnson in the *Sunday Times* to, 'Forgive Owais Shah for sleeping with the chairman of selectors' wife or whatever it was he did to warrant his continued exclusion.' On the morning of the second Test in Antigua, he was given the news that, for the first time, he was considered to be among the best eleven English cricketers rather than a stop-gap injury replacement. At last, his Test career was about to get going.

Perhaps the fact that it was Friday 13 February should have warned everyone. If not, then reports of the sandy, uneven outfield in the Sir Vivian Richards Stadium, built for the 2007 World Cup, ought to have done the job. International Cricket Council match referee Alan Hurst had declared the field as 'unsatisfactory but playable', yet when Jerome Taylor, one of the more light-footed members of the West Indies pace attack, pulled up on his first run-up, it was obvious what was about to happen. With sand kicking up from every stride, he tried bowling short of the crease and round the wicket before resorting to stamping on the ground, as much in frustration as in an effort to achieve any sort of repair. His new-ball partner, Fidel Edwards, bowled two balls each side of a break for rain but had three aborted deliveries along the way. After the last of these he implored his captain, Chris Gayle, to speak to the umpires and a few minutes of huddled deliberation involving Strauss and Hurst followed.

Whoever made the decision to construct an international cricket ground on reclaimed bog land had clearly never seen *Monty Python and the Holy Grail* with its cautionary tale of the king who built his castle on a swamp. 'Other kings said I was daft to build a castle on a swamp, but I built it all the same just to show 'em. It sank into the swamp.'

As the second Test was submerged in the sand, Shah was left standing in his pads on the pavilion balcony, drumming his hands to a song inside his head. The inevitable announcement that play was abandoned was the latest twist in a winter that had already seen the farce of the Stanford tournament, terrorism in Mumbai during England's tour, the dismissals of Peter Moores and Kevin Pietersen as coach and captain, and on-field trauma in the shape of a one-day whitewash in India, the failure to defend a 387 target in the Chennai Test in December, and the collapse in Kingston. Two years since his last Test match, Shah would be delayed a little longer.

MUCH OF cricket is, of course, about waiting. The batsman stands patiently while the bowler approaches, his colleagues in the pavilion awaiting their turn to take his place at the crease. Most of the spectator's day is spent in anticipation of what is coming in the next ball, the next over. That expectation, the growing tension, is the game's greatest appeal for many, allowing them to fully ruminate over every possible permutation of outcome. Owais Shah must have felt like he had been waiting for ever.

Having stood on a makeshift podium at the Wanderers ground in Johannesburg and lifted the ICC Under-19 World Cup, he had foreseen other glories in the shirt of the country to which his parents had first brought him to live at the age of eight, after he had already been introduced to the sport in the city of his birth. 'I started playing street cricket in Pakistan when I was about five. Then my dad got posted to London because he was working for the airline and I started playing club cricket here.

'I found I was able to do stuff different to the others because the kids here were very much taught basics. Sure, I was trying to learn the basics as well but I'd played the game a lot more than the kids in England. They were playing only a little bit at schools or for the club at the weekend, whereas I'd been playing every single day. I'd not had any coaching, so it was all very natural. You just tried to hit the ball for however many runs you had to score. It was a very different way of learning the game and I think it was an advantage that I was able to do that.' The wristy control he acquired playing cricket and hockey on the Karachi streets was supplemented by an ability to play with a straight bat, which he discovered partly out of necessity by playing in his grandparents' garage, with its unforgiving cement walls.

'I wanted to play for Pakistan because I didn't see England yet as my home. Javed Miandad was my hero for the simple reason that when I was six or seven I saw him hit this six off the last ball in a one-day tournament between India and Pakistan in Sharjah. They needed four to win and he hit it straight out the ground.'

In his young teenage years, Shah lived a dual existence. His parents, Jamshed and Mehjabeen, had moved back to Pakistan but would send their son to England during the summer to further his sporting education. Playing for Wycombe House Cricket Club in Isleworth, on the western outskirts of London, he lodged with one of the coaches, Ken Cross. 'He had a nice big three-bedroom house and I had friends here so I didn't mind coming over. I missed my parents but you got used to it and I was coming here to play cricket every single day. Back home you would be doing extra homework, now it was two or three months of solid playing. As a 12 or 13 year old, that is all I wanted to be doing. I was one of the top scorers at each age group and that success leads to more desire and hunger. I was one of the better players around so I wanted to play more. I was lucky that my dad could afford to send me and he saw it was improving my cricket.'

When the offer of a professional contract was forthcoming from Middlesex, the Shah family settled permanently in England. 'I was not qualified for England at that time, so my mum and dad thought about it and said, "He has a chance to play professional cricket and we are not going to stop him doing that." So they decided to move over so that I could have a career here. Hopefully, I have repaid their risk and their faith.'

Shah's first-class debut in 1996 brought him 53 runs against Nottinghamshire at Trent Bridge. By that time he had had already scored his first big hundreds for England Under-17s (at the age of 15) and Under-19s. Despite playing only a handful of first-team games, he was included in the England A team's 1996-97 winter tour of Australia. He started off with a pair of 70s against New South Wales's second team, prompting Peter Roebuck to describe him as 'a revelation, displaying qualities of concentration far beyond his years'. After a match-winning 43 in a later match he earned rave reviews from Rodney Marsh, who would soon be transferring from running the Australian academy to a similar role in England. 'If he keeps playing shots like that he won't go far wrong,' was the verdict of the former Australian keeper.

'I love the game, and that is the only reason I had success at an early age,' Shah continued. 'It wasn't because I spent ages working on my technique it was just the fact that I knew I could play. Still, to this day, I know I am a bloody good player – not that I want to go and tell the whole world about it. But I have a belief in my ability. I had that naturally as a kid. It was an attitude that rubbed off on me from my parents. They said, "Whatever you do, be the best." My father was like that; whatever he did he wanted to be the best.'

By the time Shah was named as captain for the England Under-19s' winter in South Africa in 1997-98, he had already scored a first-class century against Nottinghamshire and made an impact with his Middlesex teammates. 'I was just a young kid wanting to play cricket. I just wanted to go and bat and face John Emburey and Phil Tufnell in the nets and try to smack them out the ground. I remember a pre-season trip with John Emburey and I ran at him first ball and hit him straight over his head for six. After an over I did it again. By the end of that week everyone was saying, "Bloody hell, who is this bloke?" I didn't think much of it. I thought that is just how you play." Pausing and laughing, he repeated for emphasis, 'That is just how you play.'

Like the majority of that Under-19 squad, Shah's most vivid memory of the ten weeks in South Africa is the closeness of the players. 'We had late nights and really enjoyed ourselves but we performed when it mattered most. When you can get a team who does that, it is gold. We were really good mates and we played for each other and that was why we went on to win the World Cup.'

His own tournament featured several starts, but no major innings until the unbeaten half-century that saw England home in the final. 'We had some good games and once we ended up in the final we knew we were going to win,' he recalled. 'I said to the guys, "Just play your game and don't worry about anything else." As you get older there are times when you look at cricket as a job and think that it is tough, but there are times when I love playing cricket and I forget everything and just go and play. I absolutely love doing that. That group of guys just loved playing cricket and people would do extra practice because they enjoyed it, not to please the coach.'

Throughout the trip, Shah had been determined that the burden of captaincy would not detract from his ability to enjoy being away with his friends. 'I was used to going away throughout my life and it was just part of playing cricket. I didn't feel I had any extra responsibility and I don't believe in a captain having to be distant from the lads; that is one of the worst things you can do. You want all the guys to play for you and not have them think, "This guy thinks he has got the divine right to say what we are doing." I have played under loads of captains who are like that. The best captain I have played under is Adam Hollioake, who was very much with the lads. Everyone knew he was the leader. It is about how you carry yourself; it doesn't mean you distance yourself from the team.'

Teammate Giles Haywood recalled, 'Even at that age Owais was seriously talented; obviously the most talented of the team. So we looked up to him. He was a lovely guy and we always had a laugh. He was very relaxed but at the same time very focused on what he wanted to do.' According to Paul Franks, the tour vice-captain, 'Owais and I were sounding boards for each other. He was quite calm and relaxed, he trusted us as a group and he managed to get the best out of us. People had respect for him; when he talked, people listened.'

Jamie Grove added, 'Franksie had been captain of the age group team and I think people still looked upon him as captain. Owais was more of a symbol because he was the player people had been talking about since he was 12 and had more first-class experience than anyone else.'

Stephen Peters explained, 'Owais was a good captain but there were a lot of others who had cricket brains. It was a pretty easy job for him to be honest. There were no mess-ups on the field and it all ran really smoothly. We had our plans and everyone was pretty aware of what their role was. By time of the final we were a well-tuned side.'

Team coach John Abrahams's memory of Shah as a captain is that he was 'quite good'. He expanded on that by saying, 'He had not had a lot of experience so was a little bit formulaic to start with. As the tour progressed he recognised that occasionally you need to do something different and became a little more experimental and pro-active. You can only be so prescriptive because you have to react to changing situations, especially in the one-day game where things happen so quickly.'

Shah recalled that he 'listened to what the coaches had to say and rolled my eyes if I thought they were talking rubbish'. But he added, 'You do have to give the coach respect because he and the captain should be singing from the same hymn sheet regardless of whether they agree on everything.'

One of the more comical aspects of his captaincy that has lived with his colleagues was the post-final media interview that was hardly a lesson in international diplomacy. Graham Napier recalled, 'We had a briefing at Lilleshall from one of the media people, talking about making speeches and stuff like that, but I don't think Owais was there. His interview about the game was, "We dealt with them, innit?" I'll never forget that; it was fabulous.' Abrahams laughed as he confessed, 'It was something we should have addressed.'

And Grove had another memory of Shah's media technique. 'If you ever get a chance to see it, the most painful interview I have seen was when a morning show had all the team captains on. Some of the answers Owais was giving were hilarious. He was like this little cockney kid sitting there.'

Yet it was batting more than public speaking for which Shah had been taken on tour. And the batsman who journeyed immediately from triumph in South Africa to playing on a second England A tour is, according to Shah himself, almost unrecognisable from the modern-day version. The most obvious visible difference when watching the old footage is the absence of the heavy lean forward onto his front foot that is now a feature of his stance as the bowler runs up. 'There are certain shots I play the same but the majority I play differently. I looked up to Mark Ramprakash a lot in my younger days. He was the best batter at Middlesex and I was trying to see how he went about his game and I copied some parts of it. Then I had to find my own identity. I wanted to do everything just to become a good batsman. If that meant getting rid of my stance and batting side-on or batting left-handed then I would have done it.'

He pinpointed two turning points in his progress as a professional cricketer after returning triumphantly from South Africa. In 1999, *Wisden* had noted, 'Many thought the high praise lavished on Owais Shah meant that a little humility had to be added to his undoubted talent.' That was provided by a run in the second eleven over the final two months of 2000.

'After coming out of Under-19 cricket, I sort of got lost a bit,' he admitted. 'A lot of guys do. At Under-19 level I found it a lot easier to go out and play and it was almost a getaway from your regular stuff at Middlesex. After that, the reality hits that you need to perform day in and day out – here. No more one month away with England in an enjoyable form of the game, where you are playing with your mates and where you can hold your own. You are chucked into county cricket, where you are playing against proper bowling and you are expected to perform. You can almost lose your game. I didn't know how to react when I was dropped. I had never been dropped in any form of the game. They said, "You haven't performed," which I hadn't. I was down in the dumps and all sorts of stuff goes through your head. Have I let my parents down? What if they sack me next year? All that crap.

'I went away for a winter in Australia and said to myself that whatever happens I am going to come back a better batsman. I could get 700 runs a season and average 28 but that was not good enough. I couldn't cope with playing second team cricket – I just don't work like that – so I took control of my life. The best way to work things out is to fix it yourself. I did that and I came back from Australia to have the best six months of my life and play for England. Sure, I would take advice from other people and use it, but I took control of my mind, my technique and everything. People saw the results so I had done something right. It was probably from then on that people formed the opinion that I like to do things my way.'

That trait also led him determinedly down his chosen path away from cricket, marrying his schoolgirl sweetheart Gemma, despite his parents' initial uncertainty about a relationship with a non-Pakistani girl. 'I took on the responsibility of saying to my family that this was what I wanted,' he said. 'Mum and Dad came round to it and have supported me since.'

Having begun 2001 with three centuries in May and then played five games for England in the triangular NatWest tournament against Australia and Pakistan – scoring 62 in his second game at Lord's against the country of his birth – the next crossroads was reached in the winter of 2003-04, by which time he had been discarded by England. Again, the single-minded Shah was prepared to go via an unorthodox route in turning to former India captain Mohammad Azharuddin, at the time *persona non grata* with the cricket establishment because of links with bookmakers involved in alleged match-fixing activity. 'I came to a stage in my career when I wanted to go from a 1,000 runs per season player, which is OK but that is what you get paid for. I wanted to go for higher honours and stand out in county cricket, not be just another good batsman. I wanted to be one of the guys considered for playing for England regularly. A friend of my dad said I had certain faults in my game and I agreed. He said, "Why don't you go and speak to Azharuddin? He has an academy starting in India." So I rang him and he said, "Come over and we will do some work." I went over for a week and he picked me up every day and took me to the nets. He tinkered with my game and changed some things, like my stance, how I hold my bat, the areas I was looking to score. When I came back I became more consistent again. My game improved a hell of a lot and I scored 1,300 runs, then 1,700 the year after. Now I was standing out from the players in county cricket and chucking my hat in the ring for playing for England.'

At last, following illness and injury to the senior players in India in early 2006, Shah was summoned from yet another England A tour in the Caribbean to a Test debut in Mumbai. His composed first innings of 88, followed by 38 in the second, played a major part in a series-levelling victory. His disdain for the bowling of Harbhajan Singh earned him particular praise, yet it was another year – during which time England's batting had been routed in an Ashes whitewash in Australia – before he filled in unsuccessfully for the injured Michael Vaughan against the West Indies at Lord's and almost two further years before his Antigua call-up.

'If a guy gets 80-odd in his Test debut, why is he not playing in another Test match for a year?' he asked with the bemused look of someone who has given up hoping to ever find that particular answer. 'It is nothing to do with the runs. That happened to me and I accept it because it just how the coaches and captain are thinking at the time. "We don't want this guy in the team. We want the other guy, who might be out of form but we are still gonna go with him." So that is what I was saying earlier. You start realising you can't control how people think, only how many runs you get with the bat. You just go and do your best on a given day, perform consistently and keep knocking on the door.'

ANOTHER DAY. Another stadium. Another Test match, now officially the fourth of Shah's career. After giving up on the original venue as a bad job, the whole of Antigua, it seemed, had decamped to the Recreation Ground in the heart of St John's and had managed, in less than 48 hours, to get the venue ready for its first Test match in three years. Now primarily a football ground, the hastily-prepared wicket still had the halfway line running through it just back of a good length for anyone bowling from the Factory Road End and was reported by the England batsmen who had used it a few days earlier for nets to be fast and bouncy. No one could predict how it would behave after a couple of days of watering and rolling, nor was there any surprise when Chris Gayle asked England to bat after winning the toss for the second time in two days.

When Shah at last made it back to the crease in a Test match, he could hardly have asked for more comfortable circumstances. Fears about the wicket had proved unfounded, the West Indies bowlers had sulked their way through England's opening partnership of 125 and the new number three batsman was greeted by a couple of spinners. Having completed the stretching exercises he routinely performs at the crease, as much out of nervous habit than necessity, Shah eased back and cut his first ball from Gayle through the covers for four.

The innings he proceeded to play was a good crash course for anyone watching him bat for the first time. There was the usual collection of fidgets, physical jerks and facial ticks; the high backlift that gives the impression of an impending attempt to score off every ball and a couple of the 'strike a pose' moments that have got up some people's noses and led to accusations of arrogance. He displayed a repertoire of shots as well, driving Gayle with an open face to pass 13,000 first-class runs – more than any other England squad member – hitting cleanly down the ground and working the ball into gaps with the loose wrists that are a defining characteristic of his batting.

And then, having reached a patient 57, there was fatal evidence of his continued difficulties with running between the wickets, a fault that has dogged him in the way it did men such as Geoff Boycott and Nasser Hussain. He dropped a ball from Taylor in front of him, momentarily struggled with its whereabouts and belatedly set off down the wicket, whereupon he was justifiably sent back by Strauss and thrown out by the bowler. The wasted opportunity of a first Test century screamed from every muscle as he stomped off after an innings that was in many ways a microcosm of his career: much to admire, but in the end he had not quite delivered fully on the promise.

In England's second innings, looking to build quickly on a lead of 281, he lost his middle stump in trying to pull Powell into the mid-wicket stands for the second time. It left him with a return of 71 runs in the match for one dismissal by a bowler. It was enough, for now, to make him feel like an England player, yet the circumstances of his second knock allowed some criticism of his cricketing nous – not for the first time in his career. The fact that he had been stuck in the pavilion for the first hour of the fourth day, watching night-watchman Jimmy Anderson scratch around when England needed to get a move on, clearly irked the various former England captains in the media. When it emerged via coach Andy Flower that it had been Shah's own preference not to go in with ten minutes left the previous evening, Michael Atherton described it as a 'bone-headed decision'.

Perhaps the problem could have been solved if someone had simply given Anderson the old-fashioned 'hit out or get out' instruction when play resumed. Maybe the media's refusal to forgive Shah, in his comeback Test, the luxury of adopting a protectionist strategy when it came to his position in the team was somewhat hard-nosed. Especially considering the tortuous sequence of events by which he had come to be in possession of an England place.

02

DON'T LOOK BACK IN ANGER

'You realise that to play with a smile on your face is better than having a fight every game in the shower room' – **Graeme Swann**

THE THIRD morning of the Antigua Test match had dawned hot and sunny. Another day in paradise for the thousands of England fans who would happily grow more pink and drunk as the day wore on; consolation for the many who would be boarding flights home the next day, unable to revise travel plans around the rescheduled cricket. Their dollars would be missed by the locals, some of whom – while the Barmy Army were queuing to get into the Recreation Ground – were standing in line outside banks owned by Allen Stanford, formerly the benefactor and saviour of the region's cricket. The people of the island on which the tanned, smiling Texan had settled were rushing to rescue their savings from the clutches of a man now accused by US authorities of 'a fraud of shocking magnitude that has spread its tentacles throughout the world'. Back in England, the counties were beating a path to the embarrassed ECB's door, seeking reassurance that the Stanford money they had already received was not about to be snatched away.

Three months earlier Graeme Swann had claimed that he would buy a pink Cadillac if he won his piece of the $1 million per man on offer in England's 20-over crapshoot against the Stanford Superstars. On this day, while the inevitable storm was brewing over English cricket's rush to have accepted Stanford's money and hollow friendship, the Nottinghamshire off-spinner arrived at work with more down-to-earth ambitions and expectations. With temperatures running close to three figures, it was obviously not a day to be a fast bowler. Stephen Harmison would wander around the outfield fighting bouts of sickness, looking as though he would pass out at any moment. 'I thought I could be bowling 45 overs,' said Swann, having anticipated clogging up one end while the seamers took it in turns to home in on the football markings on the wicket.

But Swann, a gregarious character who accepts the vagaries of his profession with unfailing good humour, had already been caught out once in Antigua – simply by being selected to play. Initially, there had been no reason to think that the spinner's role would pass from Monty Panesar, selected for the first Test and the aborted second. But, explaining the unfolding of events, Swann recalled, 'I made it my mission to bowl to well at Andrew Strauss in the nets. As soon as he came out I grabbed the ball. The wickets were all turning and I caused him some problems. When you do that against your captain and then you see him talking to the coach, you think, "I have got a sniff."

'The night before the game, Straussy said, "Don't go out, get an early night, there is a good chance you will be playing." Everyone assumed it would be the same team so instead of going out for a meal with the missus and talking about cupboards and wardrobes he wanted me to get my head round the fact I might be in. You don't say that to someone unless they are going to play. I felt like a kid again, I was so excited.'

Strauss subsequently explained that the number of left-handers in the West Indies line-up had worked in Swann's favour. Of course, the same five southpaws had been present in the home team's top six two days earlier when Panesar had retained his place in spite of being unimpressive in the first Test. Those unaware of the problems Swann had posed his captain during practice wondered what foul deed Monty must have committed in the intervening 48 hours to fall out of favour.

The upshot was that the opening over of the third day, with England defending a first innings score of 566, fell to the twirly-armed off-spin of Swann. It was intended as a device to allow Harmison to swap ends but when opener Devon Smith's outside edge was beaten by flight and turn, Swann earned himself an extra over. 'It turned out of nowhere, which is always good because you know the captain has seen that and might bowl you more,' he said.

With the innings still in its infancy, the seamers were duly recalled, but as Smith and Ramnaresh Sarwan progressed comfortably in partnership for the second wicket, Swann was thrown the ball again. This time it was for real; not merely to facilitate another bowling change. In the way that this Test had seen Owais Shah's first opportunity to bat for England on merit, now it was time for Swann to be entrusted as England's premier Test match spinner. During the pre-Christmas tour of India he had played the first two Tests of his career, but that was ostensibly in the role of Noel Gallagher-type support to Panesar's Liam, the centre-stage presence. But as any Oasis admirer – and Swann is among the biggest – can testify, you can't always be sure what kind of performance you are going to get from Liam. It had become like that in recent months with Monty, who was outshone by Swann's consistency and creativity in Chennai and Mohali. It was, therefore, a curiosity to many when Panesar was still in the spotlight for the first Caribbean Test, with Swann unable even to get a place in the backing band.

'It was a surprise that I didn't play, but then it wasn't,' he revealed cryptically. By way of clarification, he continued, 'I must admit that, rather than thinking I would be the second spinner who didn't play and just thinking "this tour can pay for my mortgage", I'd gone out there thinking I had a chance to get in and show what I could do. But there is a lot of media pressure and a lot of politics that goes into who writes what and I genuinely think it has an effect sometimes. In this case Straussy was very honest with me. He said, "Look, you are the best spinner, you are bowling the best but we feel we owe it to Monty with his record. He didn't have a great tour of India but we still think he deserves it." I said, "Yes, I can't argue with that." I was disappointed, but one of the reasons I love Straussy so much is that he was so up front and honest about it.'

An hour into the third day in Antigua, with the West Indies having advanced to 109 for the loss of captain Chris Gayle the previous evening, Swann stepped back into the attack. Smith had reached an untroubled 38; a newsagent patiently marking up the morning's newspapers in preparation for the day ahead. But as he watched Swann's delivery drift towards leg stump he swished excitedly in the direction of mid-on and was bowled. 'He was playing really well but then decided to have a whack across the line, which obviously I was delighted with,' the bowler said. Night-watchman Daren Powell then edged a delivery that was leaving him in the air and Swann went to lunch with two wickets.

When Sarwan took on Swann in the afternoon with a four and six off successive deliveries, the ball was tossed even higher, tempting one big hit too many. Panesar's default response would have been to fire it in on a flat trajectory. But even Swann was starting to despair of removing a man who had already scored one century in the series. 'I said to Straussy that we might as well just give him a single and wait for the new ball because I didn't think we could get him out. Thankfully, on 94 he decided to hit me out the ground for six. It is something I would do so I applaud him for trying it, but I was overjoyed it went straight to Fred [Flintoff].'

It was shortly after tea when Sarwan made that injudicious hack to midwicket. One ball later wicketkeeper Denesh Ramdin chipped a full toss back into Swann's arms. Sulieman Benn thwarted the hat-trick, but a first five-wicket return in Test cricket was there for the taking. 'I went off to have a blister on my foot looked at and said to Andy Flower that milestones like that didn't really bother me. I was just lying to myself. Then I took the fifth wicket and I was running around like an idiot.'

Benn was the victim, failing to stretch his long leg far enough forward to escape Rudi Koertzen's lbw decision. Swann sprinted into the arms of the nearest colleague, Jimmy Anderson. 'I had to apologise for embarrassing him because I don't know why I did that. The seamers had been doing such a good job of reversing the ball I thought I might not get back on, so I was delighted to get the chance. Maybe the ridge played into my hands a bit. Everyone was expecting it to play havoc and people were preoccupied with it.'

Having declined to enforce the follow-on in order to save his tired and aching bowlers – Flintoff (hip), Swann (right elbow) and Harmison (sickness) – Strauss declared only when a 500 lead had been achieved with a day and a half to play. By the time tea arrived on the last day, England still needed five wickets to win the game in the 36 overs scheduled to be bowled. Swann had trapped a sweeping Gayle lbw, enticing him by leaving square leg open, and he was rewarded further when the dogged Brendan Nash was struck on the right pad, leaving the West Indies with only the bowlers left to bat. After Anderson picked up two more wickets, Swann, changing ends, appealed three times in quick succession against Benn, whose bat lagged too far behind pad to prevent the spinner earning his eighth wicket of the game. Even though it was clear that fading light would prevent all 14 remaining overs being bowled, just one more unplayable ball or rash stroke would win the Test and level the series. But Fidel Edwards got away with some ungainly groping and he and Powell eluded the clutches of the nine close fielders for 36 minutes, long enough to allow the light meters to have the final say.

'It was frustrating when the clouds got in the way,' Swann recalled. 'When the umpires offered the light it was quite a debilitating feeling because we'd controlled the game for five days. It was gutting really.'

GRAEME SWANN had never been one to let the fortunes of his sport get him down for too long. A couple of months shy of 30 when the tour began, if he had been known for anything throughout his career it was his cheerful disposition. His presence in the England squad gave the reporters a sure-fire quote when one was needed. 'I don't think he knows how to pass a microphone,' is the verdict of BBC Radio's Arlo White, who confidently predicts Swann graduating to a career in broadcasting. As early as 1998, *Wisden* was saying, 'The 19-year-old Swann was a refreshing presence, exuding breezy confidence while others around him appeared careworn.'

That teenage enthusiasm remains largely intact, although he is pleased that maturity has rid him of the less desirable elements of his embryonic cricketing personality. 'I think the cockiness and strut I used to have has gone out of my game now,' he explained. 'You get fed up with getting shouted at and abused. You realise that to play with a smile on your face and enjoy it is better than having a fight every game in the shower room. I am a happier cricketer now. It is easy to be happy when you are doing well but every game I play I pretend is my last. As you are getting older and wiser you realise you can't do this for ever.'

That cricket was the career he wished to pursue was never in doubt. With a father, Ray, who played for Bedfordshire and Northumberland and an older brother, Alec, who would play nine years of first-class cricket for Northamptonshire and Lancashire, he was almost literally delivered into the game. 'I was born at the end of March and in the second week of April I was at Old Northamptonians, where my dad played. I grew up not expecting to do anything other than play cricket. People like Geoff Cook and Wayne Larkins have told me my dad was good enough to play first-class. Watching him play club cricket, he was easily the best player and got his name in the newspaper all the time. We used to get free chips at the fish shop because they thought he was famous.

'I grew up thinking you did whatever your dad did. I'd played cricket in the garden growing up with Alec, who was two years older, and when we started playing club cricket and junior county cricket at 11 or 12 we realised we were head and shoulders ahead of everyone else. Kids who have not had that experience and been shown cricket from an early age don't have the know-how. We seemed years ahead of them – if not physically, then technically. From 12 or 13 I was saying I wanted to be a cricketer and the teachers said, "We get thousands of children saying they are going to be footballers or cricketers. What are you really going to do?" I had this firm belief I was just going to play cricket. I never found it hard to train or work on it.'

Having made his way through the usual progression of county and regional age-group cricket, Swann played for Northamptonshire's second eleven just after his 16th birthday and by 1997 had earned a one-day debut for the first team, taking two wickets against Worcestershire. That summer also saw him make his England Under-19 debut against Zimbabwe, scoring an unbeaten 156 at number seven on his home ground. A few days earlier he had played for the national Under-18s against the same tourists at Sleaford, hitting 142.

'The thing I remember most is that my A-level results were coming out that week. I got in a fight the night before they came out and woke up with a huge black eye and fat lip. I can't remember why that happened. I think a couple of us walked into the wrong pub at the wrong time and got a good shoeing for our troubles. I remember being on the phone to my mum in the morning, having been about 80 not out, with an ice pack to my face and finding out I had passed my A-levels like I promised her I would – despite having done no work whatsoever. The cricket just seemed to take care of itself at that time. I was just into professional cricket and loving it. I wasn't doing much bowling at that time. I think I was still hoping to be a top order batsman who bowled a bit.'

The winter of 1997-98 brought the Under-19 tour of South Africa, with Swann recalling that the World Cup was tucked away at the end like a bonus feature on a DVD. 'It didn't really hit us that we were having that World Cup because we played South Africa first and that seemed a bigger thing. Besides, I have never been one to look forward to something too much because I get too excited. When I was a kid, December the first was the worst day in the world because it meant there were 24 more days to go before Christmas. I remember loving every minute of the tour, despite us playing some very average cricket. It was the first time I had been away with my mates and we were having the time of our lives, like any 19 year old would. It was the first winter I had not been in school. This was like freedom, the start of my life. Instead of going back to school and hating it I was going on tour and rooming with my best mate, Richard Logan. I have still got some great mates from that squad. And the World Cup just topped it off.'

Swann's contribution to the two drawn Test matches was seven wickets spread over two South African innings, in which he bowled 43 and 42 overs respectively, and a quick-fire 75 in the first game, batting fourth in the order. Wicketkeeper Nick Wilton recalled, 'Swanny was a brilliant tourist, the life and soul. There was a gag a minute and a string of impressions. And he was the one I thought was going to play 100 Test matches. He batted, bowled and fielded brilliantly – the complete package.'

In the opening match of the World Cup, Swann hit 39 against New Zealand and then sat out the next two traumatic matches. 'Against Namibia, they said it was the game I could have off. They came close to beating us and I remember laughing with whoever I was walking round the ground with saying, "This is another bollocking coming." Then I had food poisoning from a fish restaurant in Port Elizabeth – or was it a hangover? – and couldn't play against Bangladesh. I was holed up in this hotel room and I remember Graham Napier popping his head in the room and looking ashen-faced. When I asked what had happened he said they'd lost. I said, "No you didn't." This was before anyone had heard of Bangladesh. He said, "No, we lost. These little kids kept smashing us everywhere." After that we were thinking there was no way we were going to win it.'

After victory over Pakistan and defeat against India, came the infamous match against Australia. 'They were brilliant,' Swann recalled. 'We had seen them on TV and we were thinking that it could be ugly. But then we bowled them out for next to nothing. We got Marcus North caught behind; not on the half-volley but to a catch that bounced about three yards in front of Nick Wilton. I remember one of their guys getting really shitty, getting caught behind for nought and not walking and then being run out by Owais at gully. I remember running past him and telling him in no uncertain terms to go fuck himself because he was stood there moaning about it. It was a whirlwind of a game.'

And so to the final, the excitement of which was evident in the breathless manner of Swann's delivery of his recollections. 'We didn't bowl particularly well and 240 in those days was considered a great score, but Stephen Peters smacked it everywhere. That was the best I played all trip. Second ball I faced was a long hop and I pulled it for six – off the mark in a World Cup final with a six! I middled everything, got 20-odd in about 13 balls and the next minute we were scampering a leg bye and I was picking up a stump. I have got a great picture of me in mid-air punching and screaming. It was a brilliant shot and it was in the local paper. You can see the unbridled joy, almost a look of shock. I have got a red face because it was so hot; just a sun hat on, no helmet. It just sums up everything about that trip.

'I made my first-class debut later that year and then played Yorkshire in my second or third game. Darren Gough bounced me and said, "You haven't got a fucking sun hat on now, have you?" It was the first time I realised that anyone else in cricket might have watched us out there. I thought it was on TV for our mums and dads.'

Swann's first match, against Surrey, had already helped bring him down to earth. 'County cricket was the first I played where I was a little bit in awe of the guys I was up against. Jeremy Snape was our off-spinner but John Emburey, who was the coach, said, "We want you in the team as quick as we can because you are a better spinner and you had a good winter. I was in from the start of the season and did really well – especially with the bat. But I remember the first time I bowled in the Championship getting absolutely destroyed by Ali Brown. That was the first wake up I had in cricket. I thought, "Shit, this is going to be hard," and the first season was the steepest learning curve I ever had. Everyone was ten miles an hour quicker and batsmen would maul you and try and intimidate you.'

The famous Swann cockiness, however, was not going to let him back down from any challenges. 'From playing league cricket when I was 14 or 15 I learned very early how to answer back and fight back,' he remembered. 'I did that in first-class cricket and it was only when Craig White bowled me a bouncer at about 95 miles an hour after I had a go at him that I thought, "This is a mug's game." Ever since then I have probably had one or two fall-outs a year and it is with the same people. On the whole I tend to avoid confrontation. But if someone really winds me up or I don't think they should be playing the game I will let them know.'

As well as being introduced to first-class cricket in 1998, Swann took 19 wickets to bowl England to victory in the first two Under-19 Tests against Pakistan, earning a place on the England A tour to Zimbabwe and South Africa. He returned to take 57 first-class wickets the following summer and average more than 31 with the bat. Having been added to the senior England squad for the final Test against New Zealand at The Oval, he was then selected for the tour of South Africa. It proved to be a frustrating few months, even if it did present him with a debut one-day international appearance at Bloemfontein, where he bowled five wicketless overs.

'I remember very little about the tour apart from drinking a lot and playing very little cricket,' he admitted. 'We were staying in hotels where the Virgin

Atlantic air crews were staying and I was in the bar for ever, chasing women but not enjoying a second of it. It was the first time I had been involved in cricket and not been picked for the team. I was not good enough to be playing, but obviously I thought I was. It was three and a half of the longest months of my life and I hated every minute. It was the first time I had my own room on tour so I was lonely, with no one to talk to, but I had a few quid in the pocket so I was doing what anyone else would have done. I looked for a way out and that was sitting at the bar having a few drinks and looking for any excuse to go out at night. Looking back I don't think I would do it any differently. It made me realise that touring when you are not playing is one of the worst things you can do. You can't feel more out of it or useless.'

Swann stopped short, however, of wishing ill-fortune on those in the team ahead of him. 'I have never bought into that. If you are not picked, you just deal with it. It is never the other bloke's fault. There might be players who root for people to play badly or get injured, but I have never been like that. If I knew anyone in my team was doing that I would knock them out.'

His most infamous contribution to the tour was incurring the wrath of the management by missing the bus to the stadium during the final Test match at Centurion. 'I got a call from the hotel manageress saying, "Do you want me to organise you a taxi?" I told her not to worry as I would get in the bus. She said, "It left 20 minutes ago." That was just being stupid and ill-prepared. I don't think it endeared me to Duncan Fletcher particularly, but I was not good enough to be there in the first place. I am all for picking guys when they are young if they are good enough, but I would have got smashed as a bowler and that probably would have been the end of me. It has made me a better cricketer to go the long way and get there in the end.'

That journey, which included further England A and Academy tours, continued at Northampton until the end of 2004. By then he was keeping a young Monty Panesar out of the team but feeling as though he should be somewhere else. 'It was mainly because Kepler Wessels, who was the coach there, didn't like me at all and I didn't particularly like him. I wasn't getting any better. I had got to the point where the wickets were almost too easy to bowl on at times and at other times almost impossible to bowl on. They were doctoring the wickets and the club had changed from the happy, friendly club I used to play for. Laughter and enjoyment was seen as the last thing you wanted in professional sport. The other players were banned from laughing at my jokes. It was so alien I had to get out.'

Current Northants head coach David Capel, who was on the staff under Wessels, agrees that Swann's relationship with the club had deteriorated to the point where it could not be restored. But he pointed out, 'I had to see it from both sides. I saw what was happening during that period of time and Graeme's behaviour and the way he was going about his business as young professional could have been improved. There are ways he could have handled things better, been more mature, read the situation better. He needed to look at people like Duncan Fletcher and Kepler Wessels, see who they are, look at what they are looking for from individuals and actually deliver some of that. Be aware of what needs to be done and can be done. That doesn't mean cutting out all of your personality; it's just a case of delivering what needs to be delivered. As a young man maybe he overlooked that.

'In life, we have to accept there are these learning areas. It is a shame from my point of view that that it couldn't be got through and the whole thing could not have been managed so Graeme could continue to play at Northamptonshire. But it became an untenable situation where it wasn't really bearable for Graeme and it was difficult for other people around him. The right decision was made and it has done him a world of good. I have been delighted to see his progress. His hard work and the way he has performed his role at Notts has resulted in him getting to where he needed to be.'

According to Swann, 'Moving to Nottinghamshire was the best thing I ever did. It made me a better bowler because I was happy again. Also, bowling on a Test pitch, you have to be a better bowler because you are always playing on the edge of the square, so you have a short boundary.'

In his first season at Trent Bridge he contributed to the team's first County Championship triumph in 18 years, but still believed his England days were in the past, referring later to seeing 'everyone who has ever attempted to bowl spin in the world playing ahead of you'.

He expanded on those feelings by explaining, 'I honestly didn't think about the Test team. I knew I was the best one-day spinner for a few years, mostly because when I got to Notts they told me that was why they had signed me. I would play against the guys who were in the team and out-perform them. But I had given up the ghost of ever playing for England again and was just having a great time playing for Notts. Test matches seemed a different sport. They were all my mates but the Test team seemed like an entity in itself, nothing to do with English cricket. It was like watching England play football. I knew I was never going to play for them.

'I only started thinking about playing for England again when Ryan Sidebottom phoned me up from Lord's and said, "Keep it to yourself, but you have been picked for the one-day squad in Sri Lanka. You haven't heard it from me." I thought he was taking the piss but I got a call later that night and sure enough I was in the team.'

As well as eventually cementing his place as the premier spinner in the one-day team, Swann was selected as the second slow bowler on the Test tours of Sri Lanka and New Zealand, but was left watching as Panesar bore those responsibilities alone. 'I wondered if I would get a game here or there. I was convinced I would get a Test in Sri Lanka and then didn't and that was like, "Here we go again." Subconsciously, maybe I thought I would never play Test cricket, but perhaps could eke out a one-day career. I thought they were never going to play two spinners so I could just get a bit of money for every tour I went on and pay the mortgage off by sitting on my arse. When we went to India at the end of 2008 it was such a massive bonus to play in those Test matches.'

Picked alongside Panesar in the first of the hastily re-arranged Test matches in Chennai, Swann made the most dramatic of starts, dismissing Gautam Gambhir and Rahul Dravid in his first over. His two wickets in each innings of England's defeat compared favourably to Panesar's failure to achieve a single breakthrough. It was notable that captain Kevin Pietersen appeared happier to throw the ball to Swann in the second Test at Mohaili, where he picked up another four wickets. Almost a decade after coming close to his first experience of Test cricket, Swann was finally discovering what he had been missing. 'It was only in India when I was the go-to spinner that I started thinking, "Hang on, this is brilliant. This is what I have wanted all my life."'

AFTER SWANN'S eight wickets in Antigua, the media's constant need to move the story forward brought inevitable questions about whether he was the man to take on the Australians in the summer. His more immediate concern, though, was whether he would be fit for the fourth Test. He arrived in Bridgetown, Barbados, with an aching right elbow, the legacy of a long-term condition caused by a piece of floating bone. Explaining that a few days' rest would provide a short-term cure, he also accepted that an operation – not his first – would be needed in order to achieve more permanent relief. 'There are bits in there that shouldn't be and they need taking out at some stage, but finding time to do it is a bit tricky these days,' he said.

In the end, Swann – along with every other bowler – might have wished he'd missed a back-breaking draw in which more than 1,600 runs were scored for the loss of only 17 wickets. At least he emerged with credit once again, capturing three wickets on the third day as the West Indies set about piling up well over 700 in reply to England's 600. All three were lbw calls against left-handers; two via referrals after his original appeal was turned down. Swann was asked about the experimental system that allowed players to call for a review of the umpire's decisions until they had used up their two unsuccessful challenges. 'While it's there we intend to use it to our advantage,' he said candidly. 'It's a system that will have people arguing, but people have always argued about lbw. I have been complaining for years about lbws I don't get.'

The following day he completed his second five-wicket haul – as many as Andrew Flintoff had managed in 75 Tests – in a more clear-cut manner, bowling Jerome Taylor and Ramdin, whose 166 was overshadowed only by Ramnaresh Sarwan's monstrous 291, his third century of the series. The final day was spent with feet up, watching England bat out time, and discussing the state of his elbow with England's medical team. The outcome was a decision to have the operation after the final Test in order to be ready for the return series against the West Indies in May. His disappointment at missing the series of one-day games in the Caribbean was outweighed by the clear indication of the importance that was now attached to his presence in the Test team. Even with Monty Panesar making a promising return as part of a five-man attack in the fifth Test in Trinidad, Swann's stock continued to rise, with three wickets in each innings and the opinion of the BBC's Jonathan Agnew that on the final day he had delivered 'the best spell of off-spin bowling by any Englishman for years'.

Port of Spain's Queen's Park Oval saw another massive England batting effort in the first innings, matched by a West Indies team showing a clear determination to win their first Test series in five years. Early in the home team's reply, Swann had become visibly frustrated at some of his captain's suggested field placings. At last, however, he got Ryan Hinds stumped. Then Chris Gayle, returning with a torn hamstring and a hundred to his name, was brilliantly caught on the drive by Strauss and fast bowler Lionel Baker was adjudged lbw without playing a shot.

A frantic century by Pietersen left the West Indies needing 240 to win in 66 overs, a target that most commentators felt betrayed a lack of daring by Strauss when a gambler's instinct was most needed to extract a series-saving victory. Coming on as first change, Swann delighted in seeing Devon Smith heave across the line once again, leaving his back leg in front of the stumps. On 58 for 2, Swann induced Sarwan to edge to Paul Collingwood at slip. His first ball to Chanderpaul produced the same result, but this time dropped agonisingly short of the fielder. By the time tea was taken, Swann had bowled 12 overs for figures of 2 for 8. He was getting enough turn from the pitch to unsettle every batsman, while Hinds, in particular, appeared bamboozled when he held the ball back in its flight. Soon after play restarted, he beat Chanderpaul with an arm ball – undercut in its delivery so that it slid on towards the stumps – and earned yet another lbw. It was his 19th wicket of the series, considerably more than any other bowler managed and taken at an eventual average of a shade above 24. There were to be no more, however, as Ramdin and Edwards stubbornly refused to budge. The game was saved and England were 1-0 losers in a series they had been expected to win comfortably.

Disappointed at the result, Swann nevertheless recalled, 'Things went really well for me. I was bowling well and had a lot of left handers to bowl at. The wickets were flat so I got a lot of bowling, which all helped. Apart from my elbow feeling like it was going to snap off it was great fun.'

03

THE THIRD MAN

'I knew I was battling with the bat but didn't really know what I had to do to get better' – **Nick Wilton**

JUST OFF the High Street in the Sussex village of Robertsbridge an unimposing collection of buildings represents the place of origin for many of the runs scored in cricket's history, from W.G. Grace to Shivnarine Chanderpaul. The local boast of being 'The Home of Modern Cricket' may be stretching the point a touch, but inside the converted house and series of sheds and workshops across the road from the Robertsbridge Club (established 1892; 'Quiz Nights Back on Tuesdays') is the headquarters of bat manufacturers Gray-Nicolls.

Up a photograph-lined flight of stairs and beyond piles of kit and equipment is the office of the company's brand manager Nick Wilton. 'Sorry about the mess,' he offered, manoeuvring himself round a row of bats and stacks of cricket magazines to sit behind his desk. On the bookshelves opposite him, files recording the Test and one-day international performances of the men using the distinctive red-striped blade waited to be updated. 'The bonuses in our contracts, like how many more bats the players get, is based on how many runs they score, so obviously we keep track of everything,' explained Wilton, who a decade earlier harboured ambitions of being one of the men in those files.

He described the current Gray-Nicolls clientele as 'pretty strong worldwide', although a couple of Indian players would be a nice addition. 'They are quite expensive,' he said ruefully. 'They are a little like gods and a bit out of our league financially.' The combined eight centuries scored in the West Indies-England series by Andrew Strauss, Alastair Cook, Chanderpaul and Ramnaresh Sarwan were, he explained, good news for the company. It is those players who provide the publicity from which Gray-Nicolls can conduct the heart of its business: selling bats and equipment to club players around the world. 'It is important for our marketing to promote how well our players do,' he said. 'A lot has got to do with the player using the gear, but performances speak for themselves. It generates good coverage.'

Wilton's curiosity at events in the Caribbean, however, extended beyond professional concern over those near the top of the respective batting orders. Of great personal interest was the drama that had unfolded around two men whose arrival on the professional scene had ushered his own career towards a premature end.

Mother Nature's failure to pay attention to the ICC's Future Tours Programme had meant a rethink for England's management. Their original plan had been for wicketkeeper Matt Prior to miss the fifth and final Test to be at home with his wife, Emily, for the birth of their first child. But when Prior junior decided to begin his innings as England were preparing for the fourth Test in Barbados, the proud father returned early, allowing Tim Ambrose to take his place.

Unreconstructed traditionalists like Geoff Boycott posed inevitable questions about Prior's right to return to the team in Trinidad. Used to touring for months on end with barely a phone call home to loved ones, Boycott couldn't understand why today's mollycoddled players were allowed to flit backwards and forwards when they were supposed to be on national service and when the family was healthy and happy. But even more modern minds that Boycott's wondered whether Prior could not have waited until after the series and disappeared for a few days before the one-dayers. Team captain Strauss admitted that Prior had taken 'a risk', one that was compounded when Ambrose scored a frisky 76 not out and performed tidily behind the stumps during the draw at the Kensington Oval.

The fortunes of Prior and Ambrose, former county teammates, had always been intertwined. Hove had proved to be not big enough for both of them, forcing Ambrose to leave in 2006 for Warwickshire, where he developed into an international candidate. When Prior, following a debut Test century against the West Indies at Lord's in 2007, was jettisoned after increasingly sloppy glovework in Sri Lanka later that year, it was Ambrose who was called up. He too made a flying start, a hundred in New Zealand in his second match, but once bowlers began denying him any width outside the off stump the runs dried up and the call went out for someone who could score more heavily at number seven. It was why Prior was back as first choice for the tours of India and the West Indies and why he earned instant reinstatement at the Queen's Park Oval in Port of Spain for the fifth Test, despite Ambrose's performance on his reappearance.

Forgotten by all but the most dedicated followers of Sussex cricket was the fact that there had originally been a third man in the club's wicketkeeping triangle: Nick Wilton, a player who had won the junior World Cup with England and had forced his way into first-class cricket long before Prior and Ambrose came along. Still only 30, he had been out of the game for more than seven years as he reflected on the way in which Prior had marked his recall in Trinidad: an unbeaten first-innings century, but also an ugly total of 35 byes conceded in one innings and an expensive drop of Chanderpaul en route to a big hundred.

'What I do think is good is that wicketkeeping has been highlighted as a key area,' said Wilton, whose own playing expertise had always sat more firmly behind the stumps than in front of them. 'There was a time when you could simply have a stopper and that frustrated me because I always felt that if a Lara or Tendulkar nicked it on nought and went on to score a double hundred then the keeper already had 200 runs to make up. The keeper's skills are being shown to be important. I think Prior's keeping is improving all the time and as long as they give him a run and don't keep chopping and changing he will turn out to be OK. But I probably would go for a keeper first because I am sticking up for the keepers. I would probably look at Timmy Ambrose.'

That Wilton is able to speak generously about his former Sussex teammates is commendable, given that they effectively put him on the dole. Having earned the occasional first-team appearance in the two seasons that followed his World Cup adventure, Wilton finally thought his time had come when he was given a run in the side in the second half of the 2000 season following the release of one wicketkeeping rival, Andy Patterson, and the discarding of previous first-choice Shaun Humphries.

'I thought they were my gloves at the start of 2001 because I was the man in possession,' Wilton recalled. 'We went to Grenada on a pre-season tour and Matt did really well. When we came back Matt was announced in the first squad of the season and they decided to give him a run. He was an outrageous talent, but in that first year he probably wasn't averaging more than I would have averaged in first-class cricket and I felt I was a more solid option as keeper.'

The statistics back up his memory, Prior averaging 19.68 over the season with only one half-century, compared to the 16.66 Wilton had achieved in his eight Championship games the previous season. But the only first-class appearance Wilton was given in 2001 was against the touring Australians. 'There was an opportunity when Matt went to play for the England Under-19s. A space came up for a couple of one-day games but you know your days are numbered when you miss out on that one. They decided to give Timmy a go. I remember watching that game and thinking, "If it goes well, I am struggling." He got 70-odd and kept like Alan Knott.'

The fact that Wilton was unlucky enough to find himself at a club that had two eventual England keepers battling for a place can be put down, he believes, to the presence of future England coach Peter Moores, who had kept wicket for Sussex for a decade and been involved in coaching young players throughout that time. 'It was definitely down to Peter,' he said. 'Having someone who was a wicketkeeper and was coaching at the same time made a big difference. It meant I had regular contact with a wicketkeeper coach from age 10. There was always a keeper coming through the age groups and more recently there has been Andrew Hodd and Ben Brown.'

Wilton's own early contact with Moores came as a result of his club, in his home village of Crowborough, nominating him for a place in the county colts set-up. 'I progressed steadily through the age groups and at 17 was invited to train with the professionals,' he remembered. 'As a kid I used to try to do everything – bat, bowl and field – and I was a pretty good catcher. One of the coaches asked me to keep for a bit and I loved it. My heroes were Ian Healy and Jack Russell and I liked to watch footage and hear stories of guys like Alan Knott and Bob Taylor. Also, I spent a lot of time watching Sussex play when Mooresy was the keeper.'

Former Sussex and young England teammate Giles Haywood described Wilton as someone who 'worked very hard, was very focused and never drank' but no one was more surprised than the young keeper himself when he was selected for the England Under-19 trip to South African in the winter of 1997-98 after being out of cricket for several months with an injured shoulder. 'Earlier in 1997 I had gone to the MCC Young Cricketers at Lord's because there was a bit of congestion with wicketkeepers at Sussex. It meant I could play cricket every day but I got injured and came home early. How I got on that tour I don't know.

It was bizarre. I had played for England Under-17s the year before but when my shoulder popped out I had written off the '97 season. Then I got a letter to say I had been picked in a provisional squad of 25 and asked to go to Lilleshall to train. Stuart Eustace and Stephen Guy were also asked, but I got the nod and was the only keeper selected. If anything happened to me then Steve Peters would have taken over.

'It was a big trip for me. We had players in the squad who had a wealth of experience and played regular first-class cricket, then others like me who had played only a handful of second-team games. But the majority of us had grown up playing cricket with each other. We had excellent preparation, but we had a slow start and didn't really do ourselves justice in the Test matches. Maybe we thought we had a team of superstars and sat back a little bit.'

Batting low in the order, Wilton's biggest batting contribution in the two drawn Tests was scoring 33 to keep Paul Franks company on his way to a century. 'Knowing I was playing in every game meant I could relax a little and not look over my shoulder. I saw myself as a keeper so I spent all my time getting ready for that. Looking back, maybe that didn't help. My training was always keeper-orientated and I probably left it too late to work on my batting. My sole focus was to catch every ball. As a keeper you go through stages when you are in and out of nick, but an outsider might not see it. Even the guy at first slip might not realise you are battling like hell to get through the day. You do it all on your own because no one else has that experience of what it is like. If a batsman has a rough trot there is someone to pat you on the back or work with you in a partnership. I got better as the tour went on because I was playing regularly and was relaxed in the environment. I had a few bad days but in general I felt I got better.'

Coach John Abrahams's description of the softly-spoken Wilton was no great surprise, remembering him as 'a calming influence – a lovely lad that everyone liked'. He went on, 'He was a very capable keeper, sound defensively with the bat without a great array of shots. As the only keeper on tour he had to keep wicket every day, which was a feat in itself. He was not a great shouter but he was the focal point of our fielding and if he said something people listened.'

Wilton recalled that his poorest performance on tour was in the important win over Australia, the match that effectively secured a place in the final. 'It was a bizarre day. We sung our national anthem and theirs came out as "Lady in Red" by Chris De Burgh, which they weren't happy about. We just bowled brilliantly and blew them away, but it was my worst game. I dropped one of their guys when

I dived in front of first slip. I dropped two more off Graeme Swann and Chris Schofield and missed a stumping. Then Marcus North nicked one and it bounced. I dived forward, rolled over and didn't really know what had happened. He was given out but it hadn't carried, so I got a bit of stick. It was the best of days for the team but a bad one for me.

'We'd gone into the World Cup thinking that South Africa was a nice place so it would be nice to win a few games and stay a little bit longer. By the end of the group games we were all getting into form. In the final, everyone was a bit pumped up and the bowlers ran in and tried to bowl as fast as they could. Graham Napier and Giles Haywood then bowled brilliantly, but New Zealand rallied a bit at the end and we walked off thinking they had got too many. But then the run chase happened so easily, it was like it was always going to happen. I remember feeling massive elation. It was fantastic. It was a massive boost for me. I felt I kept well and was desperate to get back and stake a claim for a full-time contract with Sussex.'

Wilton made his first-class debut that summer, but within four years was playing Minor Counties cricket, with moderate success, for Berkshire in the vain hope of finding a way of prolonging his professional career. He continued, 'Mooresy retired and moved into a coaching role so I ended up playing a year of second-eleven cricket. I was not particularly successful but eventually [in 2000] I got a bit of a run. It didn't go as well as I hoped. I never doubted my keeping but the buzzword was that keepers needed to score hundreds. The side was struggling a bit at the time and every player was under scrutiny.'

By the time Wilton felt he had figured out how to improve his batting, Prior and Ambrose had moved ahead of him in the Sussex hierarchy, a situation he doubts the modern-day teenager would be allowed to get himself into. 'I wasn't as aware as players are now of what they need to be doing and working on,' he suggested. 'It was only in my last year at Sussex that I stripped everything back and learned how to bat again. I came up with a method that was pretty successful, based around knowing I couldn't play every shot, knowing what shots were risky for me, working out my strengths and how to get bowlers to bowl into areas that were good for me. Looking back, one of my frustrations is that it took me that long to work out a method that was successful in the second team and, having done that, not then been able to test it at first-class level.'

Wilton has also concluded that, like so many sportsmen, his technique failed him partly because of mental issues. Having had it 'pretty easy' as he progressed through age group cricket, scoring runs and taking catches, he was unprepared for the pressure he would feel when his progression chart began to plateau. 'I ended up with a massive fear of failure when I batted. People had always said I could end up as a pro or play for the England age group teams, so it was not until I was 19 or 20 and playing first-class cricket that I was seriously questioned for the first time. I found it hard to know what to do. The big thing now, with academies, is that guys are prepared mentally and are being challenged all the time to get better. When I got found out I had no idea what to do because I hadn't had to think about it before.

'By the time I was released after the 2001 season, I felt as though I was playing as well as I had ever done but it took me too long to get there. I gave myself a year to find another county and played Minor Counties to keep my hand in but there were no wicketkeeping vacancies. I didn't want to try to keep living the dream and, five years down the line, not have got anywhere. I was about to get married so I decided it was time to do something else. But I was a little bit lost for a while. I didn't know what I was capable of.'

Having discarded him a year earlier, Sussex came to his rescue by offering him a coaching position, working with the club's young wicketkeepers and acting as development officer in local clubs and schools. He retains good memories from that time of Moores, who led Sussex to their first County Championship in 2003. 'He was always a very impressive as a coach. He would always challenge players and get the best out of them.'

Three years later, a call to Gray-Nicolls to order some kit for his young players led to the discovery of a job opening and, one interview later, the position was his. 'I was ready for a change,' he admitted. 'I am lucky now in that I struggle to think of anything else I would rather do. Cricket is all I know, so it's nice to stay within it and this role has exposed me to all sorts of things that will hold me in good stead for the future.'

Wilton described his job as 'looking after the cricket products, building the range, looking after the players – from Test down to juniors – marketing and advertising'. He still finds time to assist in the coaching of Sussex's keepers and works occasionally with Essex's James Foster.

Among the biggest developments in the bat-making industry in recent years has been the entry of some of the world's major sports brands into an already cluttered market. Wilton explained, 'There are the established brands who have been around a long time, like us and Gunn and Moore, then the fashion brands like Adidas, Puma and Reebok are in. Nike are flirting with it. We like to think we have the expertise but they have big budgets so can source the best. But it is just a brand exercise for them; something else where you can switch on and see the three stripes or the swoosh.'

As he offered one of Michael Atherton's old bats for comparison with the much chunkier model of the 21st century, Wilton stressed the importance of remaining at the forefront of bat technology. His company's latest innovation has been the T20, which has a flat area on the back – the closest yet to a double-sided bat. 'The game is evolving all the time, so the technology has to keep up with it. Different shots are being played and we are trying to keep moving in the right direction. Of course, we are limited with what we can do. We can't touch the blade, which has to be 100 per cent willow, and we experimented with a hollow handle a few years ago, but now that has to be made of cane with only five per cent of spring or rubber, or whatever you use. We are pretty restricted but there is room to play around with shapes and profiles.'

Wilton explained that Gray-Nicolls sales were achieving satisfactory results, even though, inevitably, they were down somewhat in an economic climate that was persuading club players to hold on to their bats for a little longer. And, looking forward to the coming months, he confessed that for all the scientific research, the most important factors for his company would be matters completely out of their hands. 'We want the sun to come out. People playing cricket is what generates sales. With the summers we have had the last couple of years, club cricketers probably still have pretty new bats. And this is a massive year for cricket so a successful England side always helps.'

It promised to be the kind of year that Wilton, now married with a young son and daughter, once dreamed of being an integral part of. Instead he would be logging sales graphs and perhaps, after a gap of five years, playing the odd club game with friends. 'I am not regret free,' he said, 'and there are definitely things I would have done differently. My biggest regret is that in the games I did play I had that fear of failure and it took me too long to want to explore how I could get better. Deep down, I probably wasn't good enough so I am quite happy knowing I probably got out of cricket what I was supposed to. Occasionally there is the odd "what if" situation, but mostly that is long gone now and I'm quite happy with where I am.'

04

HOME AND AWAY

'It was disappointing not to get another crack [with England] because I didn't think I had done anything wrong. I remember feeling quite deflated' – **Paul Franks**

'The bigger the expectation, the worse I did. I needed to relax' – **Ian Flanagan**

DESPITE HAVING a major cricket ground squeezed into their town centre, between various municipal buildings and the dual carriageway, the people of Chelmsford, like those around most of the country, appeared unconcerned that the first-class season was creeping up on them. For some, however, a two-day friendly against Nottinghamshire was a comforting prospect in a world that seemed very different to that which had bidden farewell to the previous summer six months earlier. Back then it had been easy to shut out talk of the credit crunch; to simply change channels when it was hinted that the global banking system might soon be collapsing more dramatically than England's middle order. Now, news of jobs being lost, homes being repossessed and household trading names going bust were arriving in a barrage as unavoidable as the West Indian bouncers of the 1980s.

Arriving in front of the players' pavilion and noticing the holdall of an old friend placed on its familiar seat, one Essex member, his tweed cap a perfect match for the identical overcoats worn by him and his wife, looked around the County Ground and sighed contentedly. 'Nothing at all seems to have changed during the winter,' he beamed. 'It's quite reassuring.'

Yet there is no doubt that the opening of a new domestic season is not quite the ceremony of renewal it once was, even for the committed cricket follower. In years gone by, even if the county champions' game against the MCC did not pack them in at Lord's and the university matches failed to bring Oxbridge students flocking to the boundary edge, the search for scoreboards in the newspaper marked, for many, the arrival of spring. It brought the hope of a dry, hot summer and the promise that it would not be long before their fix of televised cricket was on its way. But in the weeks leading up to the first action of the English season, cricket fans with satellite television had been able to watch England in the West Indies, Australia in South Africa, India in New Zealand and had several weeks of frantic activity in the Indian Premier League coming up. The days of barren winter months without cricket are long gone. Modern winters mean more action than there are spare hours to watch it.

A momentous opening is just one of the traditionally recognisable characteristics of the English season that has been eroded by the 21st century cricket calendar. With more games taking place elsewhere in the world, England is no longer the only country playing during the months of May to September. That has meant that overseas players, instead of being signed on multiple-season deals and becoming recognisable local personalities, are now flying in and out on two- or three-week contracts for specific competitions or filling in time between international commitments.

Rather than having a discernible beginning and end, the English season has become something of a merry-go-round, with various jumping on and off points for players (according to their contractual commitments) and for fans (depending on their attention span). Can't commit to a full season? How about four weeks of Twenty20? Suits you, sir.

The County Championship, once a constant companion throughout the course of the summer, has been increasingly ushered to the front and back ends of the season, hidden away like the unwanted relative at a wedding. Despite that, however, the ECB were able to report a 30 per cent increase in attendance at Championship matches in 2008 – to 558,900. And the importance of the four-day game would be stressed in 2009 via the award of a £500,000 prize to the county champions, five times the amount earned by Durham a year earlier.

The Twenty20 Cup was, of course, the biggest crowd-puller; its 593,000 attendees in 2008 propping up what some people believe is a creaking domestic system in the same way that the arrival of the John Player Sunday League brought crowds back on a weekly basis to county grounds in the 1970s. Meanwhile, the Friends Provident Trophy, this generation's successor to the once drama-filled Gillette Cup and NatWest Trophy, saw crowds diminish by seven per cent, not altogether surprising for a competition that would be all but over before the end of May, prompting *Wisden* to remark in its 2007 edition, 'The destruction of the once-beautiful knockout cup should be used as a case study of blithering administrative idiocy. In Washington, politicians get impeached for less.'

There is plenty of evidence, however, to suggest that all forms of county cricket continue to attract interest from many times more people than have the opportunity to attend games in person. In these days of ball-by-ball internet updates and daily video highlights it is arguable that more people than for a very long time are following Championship matches as they happen.

Even so, as the new season approached, Michael Atherton, a renowned county cricket reformist, bemoaned 'a calendar designed not to produce decent cricket or decent cricketers but to milk as much money as it can'. It was this situation that led William Buckland to write the thought-provoking book *Pommies: English Cricket through an Australian Lens,* in which he suggested that the whole structure of this nation's game was back to front, with the preservation of the counties given unmerited precedence over the fortunes of the national team.

It was not a book that would have sold many copies among the faithful on a bright and breezy April morning in Chelmsford. 'I will stick up for county cricket all day long,' said Essex head coach Paul Grayson, taking a break from helping Ravi Bopara slog a few IPL warm-up shots in the nets. 'I think there are some excellent county players out there and some good young talent. We are not far from getting the structure right. Having two divisions works and has raised the level of competition levels. I have been involved for 15 or 16 years and I love it. This time of year is great, preparing players for a long season. Hopefully you get some silverware at end of it.'

At times, however, the players are made to feel – albeit on a more frivolous level – like those soldiers who attract public opprobrium because no one can understand why the battles to which they have been dispatched are even being fought. It is a state of affairs accepted with a puzzled shrug by Chelmsford product Stephen Peters, whose campaign for Northamptonshire would be his 12th full season in the county game. 'Everyone still talks about that Ashes winning side of 2005,' he said. 'Well, 95 per cent of that side came through county cricket. At that time county cricket was a great breeding ground, but a few years later we are not playing so well and county cricket has got issues again. It is just cycles. It makes me laugh, some of the things I read.'

No less bemused was Paul Franks, who made an immediate impact on the county game after returning from the 1998 Under-19 World Cup and, in 2007, became the first of that band of brothers to earn a benefit season. As teammates Alex Hales and Mark Wagh descended from the Chelmsford players' balcony to begin Nottinghamshire's innings, Franks sat at a clubhouse table defending his profession. 'I think county cricket is in a good place, with some great competitions going on. There are good players at the moment and I would like to think it will continue to grow. Whenever the England team doesn't do particularly well, it is county cricket that is to blame and people want change. I don't know what the answer is. Next year will be interesting when we start having two Twenty20 competitions. I would like to think we are not going to kill it; we don't need to bleed it dry. What was important about the second tournament was that it was going to different, with lots of money, razzmatazz and players from all over the world. Now that doesn't seem to be the case.'

Born in Sutton-in-Ashfield, Franks had entered the junior system of his home county at the age of 10, for which he gives great credit to the time spent playing in the garden with his father, John, a committed club player at Farnsfield. A powerfully-built right-arm seam bowler and a handy left-hand bat down the order, Franks remembered his advance through the age groups and into the England junior set-up as 'Roy of the Rovers stuff', adding, 'I have always had decent hand-eye coordination, but I also feel I have worked pretty hard for what I have got. I have never felt I could just wander out and do what I pleased.'

Franks was already relatively experienced in first-class cricket by the time he travelled to South Africa with the England juniors late in 1997. His county debut had been more than a year earlier at Southampton, where the cracking bats of Hampshire offered a rude awakening. 'I got three wickets and was happy with how I bowled,' he recalled. 'My first wicket was Giles White. I appealed for an lbw and it had gone through and bowled him. The lads were all round me and I didn't realise what had happened. But I also remember Robin Smith hitting the ball harder than I had ever seen in my life. It was phenomenal. The whole thing came round quickly and I don't think I really appreciated it until afterwards.'

Having gone to Pakistan with the England Under-19s in 1996-97 and taken a Championship hat-trick against Warwickshire the following summer, Franks was considered one of the senior players and was given the vice-captaincy of the team in South Africa. 'I was still very much a bowler who batted, who relied on enthusiasm and energy and bowled a lot of overs. I was a work in progress batting, but on good pitches I felt I could hit the ball, although I didn't have much of a gameplan. We didn't play well for about six weeks and it was tough for me because I was captain early in the tour while Owais was doing his studies. Being captain and the senior bowler was hard physically. We became a bit reliant on me and Swanny. We didn't deserve to draw the Test series but showed some character to get through it.'

Franks described his century at Fochville in the second Test, having gone in to bat at 117 for 7, as 'the turning point for me on the road to becoming an all-rounder'. He continued, 'It confirmed in my head that I wanted to be able to play as a batter or a bowler and it raised a few eyebrows. I had never been anywhere so hot and you could see for miles. Me and Nick Wilton tried to hang in there for a little bit and hoped it would get a little easier. I became a little more free with my batting as we lost wickets, but I basically just tried my best to bat out some time. It gave the lads a chance to regroup and showed that somebody could bat on that wicket.'

That innings led to the suggestion that he should bat at number three in the World Cup. 'Phil Neale came to me before the one-day series and said that they saw me as a good option as a boundary hitter. I was to express myself and I had license to go after the ball if it was there to be hit. I got 40-odd in a warm-up game in Port Elizabeth but after 0 and 0 in the two one-dayers I thought they were going to bomb me out.' Having begun the World Cup with 12 against New Zealand, he recalled preparing for the next game against Namibia. 'You know that feeling where you think you have got one more chance? The night before I was thinking, "I need to make this count." I didn't get a massive score [29], but helped us get a good start and never looked back after that.'

In the next game he took Bangladesh's bowlers for 65, before hitting an important 41 in the pivotal Super League game as England chased down Australia's 147 quickly enough to eliminate their arch-rivals on run rate. 'I don't think Australia even contemplated losing,' he said with obvious relish. 'Phil was very up to speed and said "These are the rules. If we can do this at this rate then we are in the final." After 10 weeks away we were tired but that was the stimulant we needed. Me and Richard Logan bowled well with the new ball and they were three or four down in no time. How they didn't realise we were in contention is beyond comprehension. We knew exactly where we needed to be at what point and I was probably a bit more attacking in that innings because I knew what was at the end of it. There was no panic and we ticked along quite nicely. When I got out I think we only needed about 20. That was when they realised the shit was about to hit the fan. It was one of the most special days of my career and we still talk about it when we see each other years later.'

Franks's contribution to the final victory against New Zealand was, he admitted, undermined by being 'a little too pumped up. I didn't get much sleep the night before and I was probably a bit over the top'. Wicketkeeper Wilton, who was forced to dive around as his teammate struggled to find his line and length, said, 'Franksie was in a zone of his own when he ran in to bowl.'

Dismissed for 16 in the run chase, Franks recalled doing his bit by following a typical dressing room ritual. 'They had lovely bucket chairs at The Wanderers overlooking the ground, but I sat in the corner and couldn't watch because this was everything I had wanted for the last three years. I had given my opportunity away, but when things started going well I thought, "Right, I am not moving now." It was not until we were cruising that I came out and had a look.'

Unlike those of his colleagues who found their careers stalling on their return from South Africa, Franks made another significant step forward in 1998, when he became Nottinghamshire's leading wicket-taker with 52 first-class victims. 'I had come back from the World Cup and I was really tired, but Notts wanted me to go and work with Dennis Lillee at his academy in India,' he said, breaking off to sign a tentative youngster's autograph book. 'It was a fantastic idea. I learned some great stuff from him and he made my action a little more efficient. I have been back quite a few times to see him. I came back to Notts and hit the ground running.'

And he didn't stop until selected for England for the first time in 2000, when he was named as a member of the one-day squad for the triangular tournament against Zimbabwe and the West Indies. It was the first full summer of Duncan Fletcher's reign as coach and the series that saw the introduction of Marcus Trescothick as a force at the top of the England order. But while the Somerset batsman used the games as a springboard to more than 200 England appearances, Franks, the other newcomer in the squad, saw his full international career begin and end with a solitary game against the West Indies at his home ground of Trent Bridge, a meaningless contest at the end of the group stages.

'The indications were that I was going to get a game earlier in the series against Zimbabwe at Old Trafford. I was quite disappointed when I didn't. As it was, the game I played was a dead rubber, right before the final. It was quite surreal because I had a routine where I would go out on the balcony about 15 minutes before play and put my boots on. The ground was quite full and there were people I knew wishing me well. They were announcing the teams and just as I stood up from tying my boots they called my name. I felt there were about 5,000 pairs of eyes on me and there was a nice round of applause and cheers. I thought, "Whoa. Where did that come from?" I walked back to the dressing room and had to get my thoughts together.'

Franks was given the new ball and finished with figures of 0 for 48 off nine overs, before being run out for four as England lost by three runs. 'I think I was still in a dream world for the first 45 minutes but I didn't think I bowled too badly, although it would have been nice to take a wicket or two. It was disappointing not to get another crack because I didn't think I had done anything wrong. I remember leaving Lord's after we won the final on the Saturday feeling quite deflated. I felt there was not a lot more I could have done.'

A third consecutive winter with the England A team persuaded Franks that he was still part of the England selectors' plans. But few seamers make it through their careers without at least one serious injury and in 2001, instead of pushing for an England place during an Ashes summer, Franks found that it was his turn to suffer. 'I started to feel discomfort in my right knee in South Africa with Notts in the pre-season. It was just grumbling away, nothing serious, but as the county season workload got heavier it got worse. I had to come off in a game at Oakham School against Leicester.'

A scan revealed severe tendonitis, for which rest was thought to be the best cure, but every time he attempted to resume bowling the pain returned. 'By this time it was the end of the season and I didn't think I was getting anywhere. They finally admitted that surgery was only way forward and I had an operation two weeks before Christmas. The potential rehab was six months and by then I had wasted seven already. They found that the source of the problem was a bone fragment that had caused extensive damage.'

Graeme Swann, now a Nottinghamshire teammate, recalled marking down Franks for future stardom during the World Cup tour and believes that his injury undermined a potential England career. 'At that time Franksie was carrying the Notts bowling and he was one of the best in the country. I genuinely believed he could have had 50 or 60 Test matches. Unfortunately he had a horrendous knee injury and never quite got his bowling back. He is still a very good cricketer and probably his batting is his number one thing now. At 19, I would watch him and think, "Jesus, this guy is good." Bowling-wise I had not seen anyone like him at my age. He was quick, put it in the right place and moved it around. I thought he was brilliant.'

Owais Shah recalled sharing high expectations of Franks's career. 'He was an outstanding player and he really kicked on after that tour. But then he went a little bit sideways after playing for England.'

Franks returned in the second half of the 2002 season, his action seemingly intact; a fast approach, a flurry of arms and a square-on position at the point of delivery. He helped Nottinghamshire to promotion in what was by now the two-division County Championship by taking 32 wickets at a little over 25. The disappointment of a less successful season with the ball in 2003 was tempered somewhat by a maiden first-class century at Leicester, followed by a 43-wicket haul in 2004 that earned selection for another England A tour. Since then, however, his appearances and contribution have been curtailed by injuries and his county's vast resources in the seam bowling department, although he approached the 2009 season with a new two-year contract in his pocket. 'The only way I will ever leave the club is if they tell me they don't want me,' he said. 'Trent Bridge is a fantastic place to play.'

Renowned in the Notts changing room for being methodically and painfully organised in the area of his locker, Franks, married with two young daughters, believes that fatherhood has 'given me perspective'. He said, 'Cricket is not the be-all and end-all and I like to think I can manage my time to suit my family to get best out of myself as a father and a player.' Yet his optimism and abiding enthusiasm for the game were obvious as he prepared to go and 'throw a few balls at Old Man [Mark] Ealham' in the Chelmsford nets.

'My game has not changed drastically in the past ten years but I am more experienced and I try to make as few mistakes as possible,' he suggested before heading off to assist his teammate and then score a bright 69 runs of his own. 'My role as a senior player is different to what it was when I was in my 20s. Now I try to pass on advice. I have always been an in-your-face player and a bit heart on sleeve – perhaps sometimes to the detriment, but I think more often than not to the good. When the going gets tough I don't hide away and I put the team first. My dad is very much that character. He would always just tell me to go and get stuck in. I have gone past the stage of setting targets for wickets and runs. When I get my chance to play I want to put in some match-winning performances. I think we are capable of winning some silverware in the next two years and I want to be a part of that and for a few more years yet.'

NINE YEARS after being released by Essex, Ian Flanagan was making his first return to Chelmsford. 'I have never been back here. It feels quite weird,' he admitted as he walked round the boundary. The surprise was not that he'd never felt like making what could have been a painful visit, but that three years of trawling around second eleven cricket with five different counties had never brought him back to the County Ground.

Were contracts earned by persistence alone, Flanagan, a dogged left-handed batsman, would still have been in the professional game. Instead, he had spent the last two and a half years working in recruitment in Australia. If the rising inflection at the end of his sentences betrayed his residence, so the various surfing brands on his clothing hinted at a new-found sporting passion, one that had just helped persuade him to retire after three summers of grade cricket in Brisbane. 'Trying to work 55 hours a week and then train two nights a week and turn up on a Saturday, I lost a bit of motivation for it,' he explained. 'I am enjoying the lifestyle over there. I want to go down to the beach, go surfing and do other stuff besides cricket. I have been doing that every weekend since I was ten.'

Having started his Australian cricket career at Redlands, the club that produced Australian all-rounder Shane Watson, Flanagan moved after one season to Northern Suburbs, which includes illustrious names such as Ray Lindwall, Ian Healy and Craig McDermott among its old boys, along with current internationals James Hopes, Mitchell Johnson and the West Indies' Brendan Nash. After averaging more than 45 in his first season at Norths, including a top score of 133, his output plummeted to an average of 14 in the season that finished only a few weeks before his trip home to Essex. 'I went over to prove I could play at that level and not be a useless Pom. I had a pretty decent first season at Norths and became an all-rounder but this last season I had an absolute shocker; a nightmare.'

The hard school of Australian grade cricket is often thrown in the faces of supporters of county cricket. Flanagan confessed that he had been converted to the benefits of a club system that produces battle-hardened players for Australia's six state teams over an English structure that supports roughly 400 professional players. 'Grade cricket was as intense as any pro cricket I played in England. I don't think the set-up here is focused on producing good players for the England team. Every level in Australia is based on producing people to do well in the national team. English cricket has the tradition and is an awesome set-up, but I don't think the ultimate goal of everyone involved is the benefit of English cricket.

'We play far too much cricket and there is not enough time to prepare. In Australia they don't think they play enough, but every game becomes such a pinnacle and a focal point. When you are in good nick here it is brilliant because there is another innings round the corner but when things are going badly it is the worse thing possible. You are in bad nick, low on confidence and you have to turn up and play another game. There is no time to sit back, practise and rebuild confidence.'

It is a point with which even county advocates such as Paul Grayson would not argue. 'We will have 26 days of cricket in the first month of the season,' he said. 'It is too much for professional sportsmen and that is how you get injuries. In an ideal world we would play 12 Championship matches per season and as a coach I would like a little more preparation time with the players. I feel like it is always a bit of a rush. You go from one competition to another and don't get enough time to prepare individually or as a group.'

There were, of course, no such considerations in the mind of the young Flanagan when he decided that cricket was where he wanted to spend his professional life. 'From about ten years old, a cricketer was all I wanted to be,' he recalled. Born and raised in Colchester, his ambition seemed poised for realisation when he scored 71 on his debut for the Essex second eleven against Kent at 16 years of age.

'It was quite intimidating being involved with some of the senior players. As a club we had a lot of strong characters and you had to be bullet-proof to survive, while I am quite shy to begin with. But it was such an adventure.' As was an England Under-19 Test debut in Pakistan, followed by a couple of first-class games for Essex during the summer of 1997. Then came selection for the Under-19 trip to South Africa. 'My first call-up for the Under-19s was a complete bolt from the blue. Andrew Flintoff was there, David Sales had just got a double hundred and I was really in awe of them. I was hoping to get on the South Africa tour, though, as a slightly more senior player. Everyone went over with a clean slate and everyone got a fair opportunity in the warm-ups.'

As the trip progressed, however, Flanagan was left in the invidious position of so many touring players, torn between the success of the team and his own failure to produce the performances he'd anticipated. Left out after two low scores in the first Test, it was a similar story in the World Cup: single-figure scores in two of the early games and the rest of the tournament spent watching from the pavilion.

He recalled, 'The first Test was the longest I have ever fielded; it felt like about two and a half days. Their batsmen were so disciplined that we couldn't get them out. Mentally, I was very fatigued by the second innings. Owais Shah came back after that and I was the batsman left out. Come the World Cup, I was batting myself out of contention and I was probably more suited to the longer games anyway. I was the kind of batsman who occupied the crease, strong off my legs, but my off-side play became more limited when I was in a period of self-doubt. I was better against faster bowling, which was why I liked to open or bat number three.'

Under-19s coach John Abrahams recalled Flanagan as a player who 'really put pressure on himself'. He continued, 'He was quite aggressive, gutsy and brave and he stuck it out against the quick bowlers, but was maybe a little limited in number of shots he could play. He was literally up for the fight every now and again but a good lad to have in your team.'

Flanagan went on, 'Once I didn't get runs against the weaker teams I let my hair down. The team started building momentum and people found their roles. I knew that unless there were a few injuries I wasn't going to get a game. It was hard being on the outside. I wanted them to win every game because after so long away we were all very close, but I felt like a peripheral member so I decided to enjoy myself. Maybe I didn't show the dedication required, and maybe that is why I am not playing now. The great thing about that tour was that there were a few breaks in the cricket when we got to travel and do things, like visiting Sun City for Christmas, playing golf and going to Table Mountain. But I think the tour regressed me as a player. I came back disappointed and felt I had a lot to prove in the following county season.'

Flanagan is certainly not the only member of the tour party who recalls struggling to make sense of all the advice he was being given at that stage in his career. 'When I was in form I played more naturally and didn't think about technique or analyse my game too much. In the end, I was over-coached. I tried to look at things too much. I felt I had a natural talent, but I batted my way out of it. I had a lot of advice, but the hard thing is to have the maturity to identify what works for you. When top coaches like Keith Fletcher here at Essex say something, you feel you have to listen to it. I tried to muddle together a lot of different ideas that coaches had, that I had, that my father had. It didn't really work.'

A quickly-acquired knowledge of one's own game and the ability to effectively filter that flow of advice is, of course, one of the milestones on a young player's career path. Abrahams commented, 'Robert Key could do that very well, although that is a fair point from Flanners and something we are very aware of these days. It is why good communication between us and county coaches is so important.'

Northamptonshire coach David Capel, who played alongside and was later in charge of several members of the victorious Under-19 team, said that a young player's recognition of good advice, as opposed to bad, was 'paramount' to his development. 'There are people who might have been successful with their own game but might not have the kind of advice or professionalism that is going to help a young player. A gift that young people need is to see that everybody has their different strengths that you can bring into your life and not take everything from one person. You need to pull out the best from people and ignore the lesser attributes. But that is a key ability to have.'

His head full of different theories, Flanagan's big scores proved to be as sporadic as his first-team opportunities over the ensuing three seasons. His continued presence in the England Under-19s produced the occasional half-century but by the end of summer 2000 he had played only 18 first-class matches and made only three fifties.

Yet Essex teammate Jamie Grove recalled, 'Flanners was a terrific player of fast bowling. I remember his first-class debut, when Allan Donald was bowling it around his ears and he made some very good runs. It was against the spinners that he struggled. He was having a tough time against Phil Tufnell on a dust bowl wicket and Keith Fletcher asked him why he was not scoring more runs. He went out after lunch and got himself out trying to hit out. I thought that was unfair on him.'

It turned out to be Flanagan's final first-team game for his county, although he admitted, 'I didn't see the end coming. I had not had a great season and was run down by constant second-team cricket. I would have one first-team game if we had an injury or a Test match call and I would be trying too hard. I played against Middlesex at Lord's and there were only one or two games to go before the end of season. I was released before the last game. I went from being in the first team to being released within a week or so, which I found difficult to take. I was only 20 years old; not that long in the tooth. They said I hadn't developed as hoped and they didn't think I was going to make it. I thought that was a tough call to make at that stage.'

Over the next three summers, Flanagan played second-eleven cricket for Nottinghamshire, Somerset, Gloucestershire, Kent, Leicestershire and Derbyshire, often appearing for different teams in consecutive weeks. Despite several centuries in Kent colours, the offer of a full-time contract never materialised and a 2003 ruling of the European Court of Justice made life even tougher for him. Slovakian handball goalkeeper Maros Kolpak was told he could continue playing for his German club because his country, not then in the European Union, had an associate trading relationship with Germany. That allowed numerous South Africans, and a few from other countries, to enter county cricket without having to count as an overseas player, eventually convincing Flanagan that it was time to give up his professional ambition.

'There were not many teams I didn't trial with, but my timing was a bit unfortunate because I was competing for jobs with experienced South Africans. I felt I was in the mix with Somerset and Gloucester and then I trialled with Kent for two seasons on a contract where I was paid expenses if I played. I was living with my parents and they were supporting me. During 2003 I injured my wrist and played through it but it got worse and worse and I was having cortisone injections every six weeks. On the day Kent signed Muttiah Muralitharan they said, "We are not going to sign you next year so you may as well try to get a go with another county."

'I played the following week for Derbyshire seconds at The Oval and got 152 and I was hoping that would be enough for them to sign me. All they could offer was an extended trial the next summer. At the end of the season I had an operation on my wrist and started working for a friend in the recruitment business and realised it wasn't all that bad. I couldn't face living out of a suitcase for another six months and I thought, "Stuff it." I was getting sick of cricket by that point. Every game was an away game for me. I had met a girl I was in love with and I didn't want to spend extended time away from her. I was offered money to play club cricket and Cambridgeshire offered me some money.'

After a couple of seasons in the Minor Counties game and spells in club cricket for Colchester and Hornchurch, Flanagan travelled with his Australian girlfriend to Brisbane, where he found sponsorship for a work visa. The relationship has since ended, but not the love affair with life Down Under. 'Now I can watch Test cricket as a fan, without wishing I was there playing with them,' he said.

Current Essex coach Grayson, a senior professional when Flanagan was trying to find a place in the team, agreed with the player's own assessment of his shortcomings. 'Flanners was always very workmanlike; strong at top of the order with a sound technique. He lacked a few shots, but he was a hard working lad and he put himself under too much pressure. When you are a young kid it can be quite difficult to deal with making a few low scores.'

Flanagan's departure from Essex contributed to the statistic of only one of the county's World Cup winners of 1998, Graham Napier, remaining at the club beyond 2001. It is a phenomenon for which Grayson said the explanation is the mental development of individual players and the creation of the right opportunities. 'By 18 or 19 you hope players have sound technique and after that you are looking to work with them on mental side. Can they cope with playing first-class cricket five or six days a week? We have got a similar group at our club now – Adam Wheater, Jake Micklebrough and Tom Westley have all played England Under-19s in recent times. We are not scared to play them if we think they are ready. A lot of times in the past, lads who are very successful in that age group go back to the counties and play too much second-team cricket. They get stale and their careers stagnate.

'As a club, we are always pushing and promoting players to the first eleven if they are ready. Then it is a case of creating the right environment as a coach; getting some senior players to look after them a little bit. But boys mature very differently. I played with Darren Gough when he was in the Yorkshire first team at 17. He was ready at that age, but maybe some do need two or three years in the second team. But you don't want the lads to play too much of it and get in bad habits so that the next jump up is too big for them.'

A look through the records of those boys of '98 whose careers ended early reveals an awful lot of second-eleven cricket. What is difficult to gauge, of course, is whether the progress of those players was actually hampered by an extended amount of sub-standard competition, or whether being condemned to the reserves was simply a reflection of deficiencies in their game. Perhaps it was a bit of both, with that mental fortitude Grayson referenced playing an important role in the ability to step up to a higher level.

Certainly, it was a jump that Ian Flanagan, shy, quiet and full of self-doubt, attempted to make on numerous occasions over the course of four years; yet one that the confident, boisterous Paul Franks, in his 'Roy of the Rovers' phase as a developing cricketer, rarely had to worry about. So while Franks was feeling the growing excitement of yet another new season, Flanagan was walking away from Chelmsford once again, the call of bat and ball no longer able to compete with that of sun and surf. It looked like being a long time before he returned.

05

OPENING UP

'I was at the point where I hated cricket; absolutely hated it' – **Stephen Peters**

HE HAD made the journey more times than he could remember. Down the external staircase that flanks the County Ground pavilion and out across the Chelmsford outfield; this was the route that had led Stephen Peters into professional cricket almost a decade and a half earlier. More than seven seasons after leaving Essex, the walk still held a special meaning for him. In 2006, his first year as a Northamptonshire player, it had led him to an innings of 178, the best of his career. Now, on the morning of his team's opening Friends Provident Trophy match of 2009, he was retracing those steps once more.

A decent crowd was gathering, eager to take advantage of a blue sky whose clouds offered fluffy decoration rather than the threat of rain. Essex's continuing expertise in the one-day game kept them coming. This match was the first in their defence of their trophy, while later in the summer they would embark on a bid to follow up on the previous season's Division 2 title in the NatWest Pro40 and attempt to improve upon the semi-final place they'd achieved in the Twenty20 Cup. From Keith Fletcher's team of the late '70s, through the eras of Graham Gooch and Ronnie Irani, Chelmsford's tight boundaries and enthusiastic support had become something of a fortress within the shorter game, with ten major one-day trophies to add to six Championships in the past three decades.

As a teenage batsman, Peters had played an important role in one of those successes, making a half-century in the quarter-finals of the Benson and Hedges Cup in 1998. But as he went out to take on his former team's opening bowlers, he knew that many of the Essex crowd held strong opinions about him; not for that innings against Middlesex, but for a departure from Chelmsford that had created 'real animosity'.

This was his second competitive knock of the season, his 31 in a rain-affected LV County Championship opener against Leicestershire a few days earlier having ended frustratingly after a brisk start. 'I find now that some days those first three or four balls come down and you see them nicely,' he said. 'On other days you think "I didn't see them – sharpen up!" But even on good days you can get to 30 nice and quickly and then get a great ball or play a rash shot. But as an opener your job is to see off the new ball. Sometimes you are not going to get the stats, but if I build an innings and give my team good starts I have done my job. Last year we averaged about 50 for the first wicket, so I had done my job most of the time.'

Against Essex's experienced David Masters on a wicket with an early-season tinge of green, there was no chance for Peters to settle. With a quick single against his name, the third ball he faced moved a little in its flight, nipped further in off the seam and hit the top of his middle stump. The familiar walk back had come sooner than he had planned, as it had on too many occasions during the period when it had returned him to the home dressing room.

In an accent unmistakeably Essex boy, Peters recalled the manner in which he and the county had parted company in 2001 after he'd spent three years trying to live up to the expectations of a century on his first-class debut against Cambridge University and his match-winning hundred in the junior World Cup final. His relationship with the club first came under strain in the winter following the victory in South Africa, when he missed out on an England A tour place that he thought had been earmarked for him. 'Essex wanted me to go away and play cricket, but I was a bit disillusioned and didn't want to go,' he recalled. 'I ended up working with my mate as a painter and decorator for the winter. Confidence-wise, I didn't recover for many years from that. I got heavily criticised for not wanting it enough and the coaching staff were disappointed with me.'

Having been unsettled by such disapproval from his employers and made to feel left adrift by the lack of moral support that was forthcoming at a difficult time, he had then been forced to contend with unhappiness over the role he was asked to play in the Essex team. 'I was batting at six and I hated it. I don't enjoy waiting to go in. I like getting in there first. Yes, it is tough opening at times, but you turn up to every game and know you are going to face the best bowlers with the newest ball on the greenest wicket and you get on with it.'

After following up his maiden Essex century as a 16 year old with another against Cambridge a year later, he had played four more seasons for the county without reaching three figures again. His most memorable competitive innings, the Benson and Hedges fifty, was three years in the past. 'I was in last year of my contract with Essex and they offered me another year,' he recalled, declaring his intent to air his side of what has remained a somewhat cloudy story from a miserable period in the club's history. 'To be honest, I was at the point where I hated cricket, absolutely hated it. It was nothing against Essex because they stuck with me and played me when I was doing poorly. Actually, what I needed in that last year or two was to be left out so I could go back to the second team and score runs. I got into a spiral of low scores batting at six and I didn't like it. I was waking up most mornings and saying to my girlfriend of the time, "I don't want to go in today."

'I contemplated giving up but then Stuart Law came to me at Cardiff one day and said, "Tom Moody is at Worcester, he sees you batting in the middle order and wonders if you fancy going there and having a crack up the order." I met him and thought I would give it a go for a year to see if I started enjoying cricket again. I remember going in and telling Essex that Worcester wanted me and I wanted to go. I wrote a letter to the chief executive, David East, and coach, Keith Fletcher, thanking them for the offer but saying I needed a fresh challenge. David East asked me, "Would you change your mind and stay if we had a change of coach?" Basically, he was telling me they were about to make a change. I said, "No, it has nothing to do with the coach or captain, it is about me hating cricket. I am going to give up if I don't have a crack somewhere else." He said, "Fine."

'Next thing I remember was the captain, Ronnie Irani, ringing and going absolutely berserk at me on the phone. I was due to play a first-team game the next day and I was told in no uncertain terms that I wasn't welcome at the ground and to sod off and play in the second team at Manchester. I was devastatingly upset at home that afternoon because I felt I had been betrayed. The chief executive had asked me if my decision was anything to do with coach or captain and I had categorically said no. Apparently that wasn't the story the captain ended up receiving. I drove back to the ground and lodged my disappointment with David and Ronnie about how I had been misconstrued. I don't know how that happened – I have got my own ideas – but my intention was to leave to resurrect my career, not because of anyone else. I cannot tell you how devastated I was. I had been at that club since I was eight years old and I just wanted to leave on good terms with everyone and enjoy my cricket somewhere else. That was ruined.

'Keith Fletcher drove up to Manchester and I will never forget it because I have got a lot of respect for Fletch. He had heard it was because of him that I wanted to leave and asked if we could have a chat. I said, "Fletch, it categorically had nothing to do with you. I need to leave, I am going nowhere." We had a great chat and we have seen each other on friendly terms numerous times since.'

The exit of Peters was just one part of a turbulent late summer that saw Essex's relegation from Division 1 of the County Championship, followed by the departure of disgruntled Australian batsman Law, former England off-spinner Peter Such and ex-skipper Paul Prichard. Writing in *The Independent*, Stephen Brenkley described one Essex performance as 'another exhibition of indolent mediocrity masquerading as first-class cricket'.

Peters continued, 'It is important for people to know about that time in my career. I remember an article in the *Romford Recorder* and it said that the new coach, Graham Gooch, had spoken to me and offered me a new contract to try to get me to stay. I can tell you categorically that I never spoke to Goochie in that time. I asked to leave on my terms and I did a piece in the paper a week later saying I had not been contacted by the new coach.'

Recalling that 'Ronnie and I didn't speak for a few years and whenever we played each other he would be very off with me', Peters described the disappointment at his former club as having 'worn off a little bit – I have some fond memories of playing there'. Time has also healed the rift between him and Irani, now a popular radio presenter. 'The last few years we have got on fine and if I saw him this afternoon in the pub we would have a beer and laugh and joke about winning the Benson and Hedges in 1998. I am sure he feels exactly the same. At the time he felt it was a personal matter but that was because he was told the wrong thing. I was just trying to save a career that was going down the pan. I was a decent player who was wasting away.'

Former teammate and current Essex coach Paul Grayson described Peters as an 'exciting young player with a lot of shots all around the wicket', but supported his decision to get out of the club. 'There was expectation for Steve to come through and be the next Essex boy to hit the heights for the next 15 years. I am not sure whether he could handle that expectation, so it was the right time for him to move on.'

AT A time when senior English cricket was hardly overflowing with match-winning heroes, it was not surprising that the scorer of a century in a World Cup final, albeit at Under-19 level, was burdened with the anticipation of more heroics to come.

Born in Upminster, where his father played for the local club and his mother and sister made the teas, Peters had switched to the more renowned youth set-up at Gidea Park and Romford. 'I played a bit of Under-19 cricket for Essex when I was 16, but I was tiny. Then I had a real growth spurt one winter and they took me on. I remember sitting round a table in the board room with my parents and someone mentioned a YTS scheme. I told my parents that night I wasn't interested in that; I wanted to play full-time.'

Typically of a small left-hander – even now his 5ft 11in. listing in the *Cricketers' Who's Who* seems optimistic – his greatest batting strength was off the back foot. 'I was a short arse who cut and pulled a lot,' he laughed as he looked out on a drizzly morning at Northamptonshire's County Ground. 'Essex is still a bit of conveyor belt for young talent and we had a great set-up. Alan Lilley was prominent in that and my second-team coach was Alan Butcher. I learned a lot from him – more than anything about not being too eager and wanting to get where I was going too quickly. I wanted to be playing first-team cricket as soon as possible.

'It was a great time because I played a full season of second-team cricket and scored quite heavily. You had to earn your second-team cap, which got you a little bit more in your wages, and then you made the first-team squad and got in the pre-season photos, was given a car parking space and didn't have to change down in the indoor school any more. There was always something to strive for.'

A big hundred for the England Under-19s against Zimbabwe ensured that Peters was among the players chosen to tour South Africa, where he scored a half-century in each of the two Tests and another in the first one-day international. Off the field, South Africa was also proving to have much more to offer than Pakistan, where Peters and his teammates had played a year earlier. 'Eight weeks in Pakistan was tough,' he admitted. 'The food was crap, you were ill a lot and most of us couldn't get home quick enough. This was different. We were eating Nando's and big steaks for absolute peanuts, the beer was cheap and there were a lot of attractive girls. We had expenses we could spend every night and were getting sun tans.'

After three low scores in the opening World Cup games, Peters was moved back to the top of the order and responded with an impressive 92 against Pakistan at Centurion. 'We changed things around and, for me, it changed the whole thing. I was run out backing up.' Another fifty in the run chase against Australia meant that Peters was still in top form when he and Rob Key set out to overhaul New Zealand's total in the final.

'We were a bit disappointed to have let them get 240, even though the wicket was good and the outfield was like glass. We had not chased a total of that size in the tournament so we would have liked it to be 20 or 30 less. I had got a lot of confidence from those two innings before so I was feeling in good nick. We just batted normally. We backed ourselves to put away bad balls and I can't recall us playing a rash shot or slogging one over the top. It was just proper cricket shots along the ground and in the gaps. I remember thinking at about 30 or 40 that they were really bowling balls I could put away. I had cut a lot, my confidence was growing and I thought it must be my day.

'It was an awesome feeling to win. We'd been getting phone calls from people at home after we reached the final telling us they were getting together to watch the final on TV and Doug Insole flew over as a representative from Essex. That all made us realise how much we were being talked about. The great thing is that we were just a very close bunch of mates by this time. With people like Swanny and Keysy there was always great banter and a lot of laughing and everyone had something to give to the group.'

After a holiday in Australia, where he unexpectedly got to see a televised re-run of the final in a bar in Brisbane, Peters returned to three years of trying to live up to the expectation he had created around himself. Even during the final, commentator Mike Procter had confidently announced, 'Remember the name Stephen Peters. We have seen enough of him today to know that he will play for England one day.'

John Abrahams ventured, 'After he didn't get selected for Essex when he came back he drifted around a little bit. At back of his mind I don't know if he was expecting to come back and be part of the first team. As with most cricketers, if you have a strength then people in the county game will recognise it and not bowl at it. I don't know if he tried to work enough on his weaknesses.'

Peters continued, 'When I realised how much profile we had received I started to feel the pressure. I was also targeted by the opposition and they got stuck into me – lots of short pitched deliveries and jibes. But I wasn't a naïve 19 year old so it didn't bother me.'

What was of concern, though, was the eventual downward spiral of his Essex career, leading to the move to the picturesque setting of Worcestershire's New

Road ground. 'There was the freshness of a different place every day, a new outlook, new coaching, new players, new everything,' he said. 'We had a few new players and Tom Moody integrated us brilliantly into the set-up. It was a great place to work and play.'

Peters had to wait only until the second game of the season to be given his chance to open the batting, rewarding Moody's faith with a score of 146 at Northampton. 'I'd batted five in the first game but we wanted to play two spinners so Tom asked me if I wanted to open. I have been opening ever since and my stats have improved dramatically. I have changed a few things technically over the years and reined things in a bit. Sometimes I feel I have lost a bit of flair, but it is not easy to go out and crash it everywhere when you are opening.'

Peters entered the 2009 season with a career batting average of just under 33 and a total of 18 first-class centuries, including seven in his first three seasons at Worcester. In 2005, though, he had discovered that he did not feature in the plans of new coach Steve Rhodes and 'put out some feelers', discovering that there was interest from Northamptonshire. 'I was not going to sit on my arse and not play, which I could have done because I had 18 months left on my contract. I had made a great home at Worcester but they were signing Phil Jaques, and Stephen Moore had done well. I wasn't going to play much. I felt I had progressed, but had one bad season. I went back and scored a lot of second-team runs but I was frustrated that I couldn't get back in. Then [coach] Kepler Wessels wanted me here to open the batting.'

Three centuries in each of his seasons at Wantage Road and an average in 2008 of more than 41 made him a fixture in the side as the new season began. 'I fell just short of 1,000 runs last year, but we missed a few innings,' he said. 'I was happy with my season because I felt I'd done my job. The coaches appreciated my efforts and I feel like an important and valuable member of the team.'

It is that search for acceptance and approval, the constant need to prove oneself, that Peters believes is unappreciated by anyone who has not played the sport professionally. It appears to be no coincidence that – as has been explored in books such as David Frith's *Silence of the Heart* – the suicide rate among cricketers is almost twice as high as the national average. 'Cricket has this dreadful, hidden burden,' said Frith, who urged the sport to 'answer the very serious question of whether it gradually transforms unwary cricket-loving boys into brooding, insecure and ultimately self-destructive men'.

While most team sports, football for example, offer a hiding place within the collective effort, cricket – with its individual duels, its judgemental averages and that lonely walk back to the pavilion – exposes every flaw or weakness. Several of England's junior World Cup winners have spoken of periods when the professional game got too much for them. Some, such as Ian Flanagan and Giles Haywood, chose to leave it behind, while Peters, who has experienced his share of cricket's vicissitudes, was lucky enough to find salvation via changes of location at critical moments in his career.

Of course, the cruel fact of life as a batsman is that even the best ones are merely those who keep the inevitability of failure at bay most often. Anyone who averages 40 over the course of a season is considered to be doing well yet, given that in order to reach that figure he has probably scored three or four centuries, it means that more often than not he will have left the field with a sense of underachievement. Few professions have such a low expectancy of success. Perhaps the batsman's American cousin in baseball, where the most proficient manages a hit only three times in every ten visits to the plate, is best placed to empathise. Even when runs are scored, there is no guarantee that it will be at a meaningful time. Any batsman will tell you that a century in a heavy defeat or in a second innings against part-time bowlers as a game meanders to draw is given less than full value. The most insecure of minds, those who believe the fates will only permit a certain amount of successful innings, may even end up cursing the fact that part of their allocation of form and luck has been used up when it didn't matter.

'County cricket is a great life and I love the constant cycle of games,' Peters reflected. 'But I think what people misread is how much the game messes with your head. I have seen a lot of grown men sat in tears in the dressing room when they have made five noughts on the trot. I don't think people fully understand the mental pressure of playing for your career every year. Other people can dictate your career and you are in their hands. You can get a run of bad decisions or a coach might change his opinion about you.'

Meanwhile, there are the practical issues associated with following such a precarious employment path, concerns against which top footballers are largely shielded by the vast sums of money they earn. For players who had earned a county cap, wages for the credit crunch season of 2009 ranged roughly between £40,000 and £100,000 – a typical week's pay packet in the Premier League. At Northants, coach David Capel had to plan for the campaign with a player budget of only £700,000, less than half that of some of the bigger counties with Test grounds. From that pot he had to find flights and accommodation for any imported players, as well as the weekly wages.

There is obviously a limit to how far the smaller counties can stretch their annual gift from the ECB. With clubs such as Worcestershire suffering the loss of their club sponsor of 10 years' standing, county professionals like Peters now bore the additional fear that future contracts would be based more on financial expediency than batting averages.

Since 2003, many clubs have found a new way to get the most value for money from the playing pool by virtue of the Kolpak ruling – further destabilising the career of the English professional. Despite the ECB withholding a percentage of its payment to counties for every non-England qualified player they field, Peters began the 2009 season with four South African teammates, skipper Nicky Boje, Riki Wessels, Andrew Hall and Johan van der Wath.[1]

With such uncertainty pervading many country dressing rooms, Peters continued, 'It is hard to plan your life when you never know if you can settle down and live in one place. I thought I was going to play the rest of my career at Worcester but I moved on again. Those things can affect your personal life as well. I have a lifestyle I wouldn't want to change, but there is an awful lot of stuff that comes with it that people don't appreciate.'

Two days after the Essex game, Peters batted beyond lunch on first morning at Kent before being caught by Geraint Jones for 32, another start that did not lead to a big score. But when Northants batted for a second time, looking to make up a first-innings deficit, there was no stopping him. After just under five hours at the crease, he clipped a four off his legs to reach his first century of the season. Even though his innings ended after 224 balls at 107, caught by his old England teammate Rob Key as he tried to clear mid-wicket, Peters had clearly established that he was on top of his game at a pleasingly early stage of the season. 'You do set a small target of three or four hundreds in a season, so to get one that early is nice,' he said later. 'It has been a few years since I got one that early. It can be tough opening the batting early in the season.'

Next day, however, he was dismissed second ball for a single in a Friends Provident Trophy game against Lancashire and suffered a broken thumb that would keep him out of action for two months. The gods of the game were, as always, reminding their disciples that success, form and luck were gifts only fleetingly bestowed.

1. The ECB has sought to address such situations with a new Memorandum of Understanding that, from 2010, gives the counties £2,000 for each England qualified player under 22 who appears in a Championship match and £1,600 forevery one under 26, to a maximum of five players. A tightening of Kolpak regulations has also made it harder for overseas players to qualify on that ticket.

Owais Shah and Graeme Swann celebrate after running a leg bye to win the Under-19 World Cup final against New Zealand in Johannesburg. (Duif Du Toit/Gallo Images)

Members of the victorious Under-19 team pose with the trophy on their return to England. Back, left to right: Graham Napier, Chris Schofield, Nick Wilton, Paul Franks, Rob Key, Giles Haywood. Front: Richard Logan, Graeme Swann, Owais Shah, Stephen Peters. Missing from the picture is Jonathan Powell. (Graham Morris)

Former keeper Nick Wilton outside the home of bat manufacturers Gray-Nicolls, where he now monitors the performances of players such as Andrew Strauss and Alastair Cook.

Nottinghamshire's Paul Franks, who endured a frustrating season, sends down a delivery in the Twenty20 game against Lancashire at Trent Bridge. (Getty Images)

Former batsman Ian Flanagan on his first return to Chelmsford's County Ground since his release by Essex in 2000.

Stephen Peters finds the boundary on his way to a welcome early-season century for Northamptonshire against Kent. (Getty Images)

Robert Key hooks during the England Lions' game against the West Indies at Derby. The Kent captain struggled to find form early in the season before forcing his way into Ashes contention with a string of centuries. (Getty Images)

Richard Logan celebrates a wicket for Nottinghamshire, one of four counties for whom he has appeared, but had to be content with Minor Counties cricket for Berkshire in 2009. (Getty Images)

Surrey leg-spinner Chris Schofield celebrates a wicket against Middlesex in the Twenty20 Cup, part of a fast start that made him one of the country's leading early-season wicket-takers. (Getty Images)

Giles Haywood at the London office where he focuses on property investments instead of batting averages.

Michael Gough (left), inspecting the ball at Grace Road with fellow umpire Trevor Jesty during his first season on the full first-class list, has recaptured his love for cricket by donning the white coat. (Getty Images)

Essex's new hero Graham Napier earned his first senior international call-up for the World Twenty20, but his only opportunity to bowl in England colours was in the nets. (Getty Images)

Jamie Grove poses happily outside the pavilion at Exning Cricket Club, but memories of the end of his county career can still provoke anger.

Jonathan Powell, dogged by injuries and loss of confidence, played only three first-class games after being picked out for future stardom and was one of the first of the boys of '98 to leave the game.

Graeme Swann fulfilled a childhood dream by helping England win the Ashes. Here he celebrates in the The Oval dressing room with Alastair Cook, who took the series-clinching catch off Swann's bowling. (Getty Images)

Owais Shah swings one of his six sixes during a match-winning 98 against South Africa in the Champions Trophy, arguably his finest innings for England. Two matches later he was dropped. (Getty Images)

06

THE KEY ISSUES

'The selectors and powers that be in the England set-up were after a certain type of cricketer and someone who went about their work in a certain way. Unfortunately I don't fit that mould, whereas the Ian Bells and the Paul Collingwoods seem to' – **Robert Key**

NO SOONER had the bell sounded to summon the players down through the Long Room than a rotund member, decked out in a garishly striped MCC blazer of yellow and red stood up very conspicuously from his seat in front of the Lord's Pavilion,. 'Blimey,' chirped a quick-witted chap in the general admission seats, 'Rob Key's put on even more weight!'

Key, who admits that he is 'never going to look like an athlete', was down the steps a moment later, the thick sweater he wore as protection against a damp and chilly morning doing little to discourage further banter. Following behind him among the MCC players picked to face Durham in the season opener were one former England captain, Michael Vaughan, and several players on the fringes of the national team.

Scorer of a double hundred against the West Indies on this ground in 2004, Key was beginning the season as a contender for England's number three position. Yet as the outsider behind MCC teammates Vaughan and Ian Bell, the incumbent Owais Shah and IPL-bound Ravi Bopara, you speculated on whether the Kent skipper had been selected less for his Test potential than for his captaincy. Over the previous four years it had befallen Key on a regular basis to lead shadow national teams, usually in the guise of the England Lions or England A, either on tour or against visiting overseas sides. Most recently he had taken charge on the winter tour to New Zealand, where he had averaged 66 in the two drawn 'Test' matches.

Having made the last of his 15 England Test appearances four years earlier, the Kent captain must sometimes have felt feel like the club cricketer given the 'honour' of captaining the second eleven as a veiled way of being told he was not good enough for the firsts. A couple of weeks after this Lord's contest – a rain-affected game in which Key, Vaughan and Bell were all dismissed cheaply in their one innings – he was at it again; leader of the Lions team facing the West Indies tourists at Derby, with national selector Geoff Miller commenting that he had 'captained the team outstandingly well in New Zealand'.

By the time the game began under moist, grey East Midlands skies, which served to remind the visitors how far they were from their sun-kissed home, Key was among those mentioned in connection with a more meaningful leadership role. Spoken of as a potential England captain before Andrew Strauss was named to replace Kevin Pietersen prior to the West Indies tour, there were whispers that Key could lead his country in the World Twenty20, for which he had been named in the provisional squad of 30. Strauss, who had not even had his own Twenty20 shirt in the Caribbean – he'd worn Matt Prior's – had agreed with the ECB that he would not participate in the June tournament. Key, who had led Kent to the last two domestic 20-over finals days and proved himself a resourceful opening batsman in the format, was this time more than a mere wild-card option. 'I've never really spoken to the selectors about the job but it would obviously be very nice,' he said, knowing that the issue would be resolved during lunch on the third day of the Derby game. 'It's always nice to get recognition and to hear people saying that you are good enough to captain England, but I have no idea where I stand in the pecking order.'

Turning 30 early in the new season, Key might not have worn a full England shirt for more than four years, but he was still by far the most experienced Test player of the 1998 youth World Cup winners, having made his debut against India in 2002 after two domestic seasons in which he'd scored eight first-class centuries. The 2002-03 Ashes series saw him win general approval for his temperament under fire, particularly from the home players, even if it was not reflected on the scoreboard in his four Tests. His 47 on a lightning-fast pitch in Perth prompted Aussie captain Steve Waugh to remark, 'He doesn't give a shit about much and is real relaxed. I like that in a bloke. It stops him getting overawed.'

Key admitted, however, 'I probably played for England a little too early. I had absolutely no idea of what type of cricketer I was or how I scored my runs. I would just see it and hit it. I developed a much better understanding of batting itself from that point on. If I'd had that I might have succeeded earlier.'

Discarded after low scores against Zimbabwe, he began the 2004 summer in the form of his life. By the first week of June, he had scored six centuries, including five in a span of seven innings. 'I was growing up as a cricketer. Being left out of the England set-up forced me to look at my game. I addressed it and learned more about it and it made a big difference. It was a mixture of having had a tough time and a winter of bloody hard work. I took a punt with some technical changes, in particular a trigger movement, and it all paid off. I got on a roll early and scored a hundred in the first game.'

Key reached 1,000 first-class runs by 2 June, faster than any player for 16 years. He was included in England's one-day squad, despite showing no great form in the limited overs game at the time, and when Mark Butcher was ruled out of the first Test of the late-summer series against the West Indies after a car accident Key was recalled to bat at number three for England.

Perhaps as much because of his build as any deficiency in his stroke play, Key's batting has never earned particularly high style marks. Phrases such as 'solid and workmanlike' have been used far more than 'flamboyant and flashy' in connection with his occupation of the crease over the years. Reporting his innings of 221 at Lord's, *Wisden* commented, 'The signature shots were chunky straight drives,' – the kind of description never applied to, say, Michael Vaughan.

An unbeaten 93 later in the series helped secure his prestigious selection as one of *Wisden*'s Five Cricketers of the Year and ensured a place on the winter tour of South Africa. Yet after passing 50 only once in six Test innings during England's series victory he found himself out of the side at the beginning of the most memorable of Ashes years. 'To be the man in possession and then get dropped was soul destroying,' he admitted. 'But that year was the birth of Kevin Pietersen as an England cricketer and Ian Bell had come on the scene and they felt they were the people for the job as opposed to me.'

Key was left feeling that, like his former Under-19 teammate Owais Shah, perhaps his approach to the game and his personality simply didn't fit the requirements of England captain Vaughan and coach Duncan Fletcher. 'When you are captain, you have certain people that you want around and certain people that you don't,' he commented. 'There are people who don't fit in with you and for some reason the way they do things doesn't fit what you want. Unfortunately that was the case the case with me, and I imagine it was the same for Owais. The selectors and powers that be in the England set-up at that stage were after a certain type of cricketer and someone who went about their work in a certain way. Unfortunately we don't fit that mould, whereas the Ian Bells and the Paul Collingwoods seem to.' He paused, chuckled and added, 'Hopefully we can fit the mould at some stage.'

Key went on, 'They want a multi-skilled cricketer in this day and age and if you don't have that you have got to score a lot of runs to make up for it. But the thing about cricket over a lot of the team sports is that it is about skill. If you are the most skilful rugby player or footballer but you are unfit or slow, you are not going to be playing higher than second or third division. If you are the most skilful batsman in the world but you are slow and not particularly fit you are still potentially the best batsman in the world. Probably that is why there has been a market for people like me and Owais in cricket because of a high skill level, which has taken over from the other attributes. But at the end of the day more people seem to want players with both.'

Thus began Key's life as England's second-team captain, a role that offers a unique set of challenges. As the man holding the England hopes of others in his hands, you can't simply get your head down and worry about your own chances of selection. Nor can you go hell for leather to win the game as there is a need to make sure everyone's skills are given a thorough testing. Once again, it's like being a club captain: everyone has had paid their subs and therefore deserves to either bat or bowl.

'Lions matches are often about people having their own agenda, which isn't always a bad thing,' he explained before the West Indies contest. 'If you go and perform you've got a good chance of getting in the England side. You obviously want to go out and win, but every player is thinking that it's an opportunity to show people what they can do. If there are people wanting to stake a claim, the captain's job is all about making sure they get that opportunity. I'm in the same boat as those people. I suppose I could actually shaft some of them, but I don't believe you can live your life like that. If somebody bowls two bad overs you can't whip them off and say, "Sorry, mate, that's it for the day." By seeing these games like that it's a pretty easy thing to manage.'

It is a job that Key approaches with dignity and professionalism, but away from the role later in the year he admitted, 'It is frustrating more than anything. Sometimes you feel there is not much you can do to get back in the England team. When you get older and you see your peers and people younger than you playing for England, then it is not much of a consolation prize. It's just one of those things you do to try and move a step closer.'

BORN IN Dulwich and raised in Beckenham, Robert Key came from a sports-mad family, his mother Lyn having played cricket for Kent Ladies and his sister Elizabeth once taking a hat-trick. He played for Kent as early as the Under-11 age group and was pushed through the older sides under the watchful eye of former Kent batsman Alan Ealham. 'I played a fair bit of second-team cricket early on. I was thrown into adult cricket and did pretty well. I developed quite quickly from age 16 and 17. You grew up by playing in a better standard of cricket and it gave you confidence. I believe that if you are good enough you will get there in the end, even if you get thrown in there and struggle.'

Early in the summer of 1997, having not played for younger England teams, Key was chosen to lead an inexperienced England side in an Under-19 tournament in Bermuda. 'I had been playing for Kent and gone along to the England nets but never quite made it into the national set-up until that tour. The team was made up of everyone who had not been playing for England Under-19s.' Coach John Abrahams recalled him 'doing a reasonable job' as skipper, but when it came to appointing the captain for the 1997-98 tour it was Shah who was given the job – a decision that looks incongruous viewed at the distance of more than a decade and with the knowledge of their leadership record since.

Abrahams explained, 'At that time, once Keysy stepped over the line he was absolutely, brilliant, totally switched on, especially if he had a bat in his hand. The other side of his game back then was not brilliant. He worked hard at his own game, but there were other parts he didn't totally buy into. I am not suggesting he was a bad lad but as a captain and role model he was not necessarily the type you wanted, especially on a long trip. Owais was also a little more experienced in first-class cricket.'

Key recalled, 'Owais was a schoolboy wonder. We both went to the Under-14 trials and didn't get in and then he went on to the Under-15 trials and got into that and scored a double hundred or something. He was by far our most experienced player. He was the big gun, the name player in the whole tournament.'

Graham Napier recalled it being 'a natural thing for Ace to be captain as he was older and experienced'. But, having played under Key in Bermuda and since for the Lions, he added, 'I thought he was very good captain. It is difficult being in charge of players on the verge of being first-class or international cricketers, seeing what they can do and also trying to win games at the same time. There is a very simple quality about his captaincy. You all know what you have got to do and you can just get out there and do your job.'

Graeme Swann said, 'At that level, whoever has the reputation from playing against each other growing up tends to be seen as the senior player, which was why Owais was captain. He was a horrendous captain in real terms but he was perfect at that time because everyone respected him as a player. He would probably be the last choice of captain now. He's a space cadet.'

Shah was entrusted with the Middlesex job for only a month after Andrew Strauss's England call-up in 2004 before the club apparently concluded he was making a pig's ear of it and offered it to Ed Joyce instead. Meanwhile, Key has become a skipper of some renown since taking charge at Kent in 2006. Abrahams believes that Key's rebellious streak has ended up helping his development as a captain. 'He was quite a mature and strong character and the players looked up to him. He tested authority all the time, which is brilliant. He even tested Rod Marsh at the Academy, but from a mental point of view it keeps him alert and thinking and stops him getting bored.

'I remember a game at Chelmsford where I told our strength and conditioning coach, Dean Riddle, to get them ready for 15 minutes and then send them across to the nets. As they got started, Keysy said to Dean, "Why are we doing this?" Dean spent 15 minutes explaining, at which point Keysy says, "Right, that's it. Abey wants us over at the nets." He was very competitive and loved to win, whether it was basketball in the warm-ups or a table tennis competition. He had to control himself when he did lose. He was also a very funny man, with a very dry wit, although I still have trouble seeing him now as a dad.'

Key himself describes captaincy as a way of ensuring that the game remains as enjoyable as possible for him. 'I like to try stay pretty philosophical about the game and keep a perspective on it, which is one thing that I think helps me as a captain,' he explained. 'My approach is that I pretty much just try and enjoy myself; it is one of reasons I took the Kent job. I could have gone down the path of cricket not being very enjoyable with all the things people are cooking up off the field, with training and everything. I thought a lot of it didn't really have any value and was not going to improve people as players. I thought I was at that that stage where captaincy would be a fresh challenge and I could make sure I was going to enjoy my time as a cricketer because I wouldn't be doing anything I didn't want to do.'

Stressing that it didn't mean that Kent now took conditioning and preparation less seriously than other teams, he added, 'Our fitness test would be tougher than anyone else's; we just do it differently. Fitness is a big part of the game but I think you should be able to relate it to cricket. Is it going to help your cover drive or make you a better fielder? You try to ensure people can physically feel themselves improving the aspect of the game they want to.'

Fitness wasn't pre-eminent among Key's own attributes in early 1998. Bowler Jamie Grove recalled, 'The South Africans used to call him McDonalds when he came out to bat because he was so heavy. He never seemed to take anything too seriously, so to see what he has achieved at Kent is amazing because he never seemed like a captain, even though he was a strong character.'

His contribution to the Under-19s' success in South Africa was solid – that word again – without setting the tournament alight. Having passed 36 in three of his four innings in the Test series, his scores in the World Cup were 35, 27, 35, 57, 25 and 27, an impressively consistent run but lacking a major match-winning total. Teammate Giles Haywood said, 'I always thought Rob was a good bat, not the best in terms of talent but he kept it simple, didn't take too many risks and took his game forward. He expanded his game and his personality as he got older.' Wicketkeeper Nick Wilton added, 'Maybe Rob didn't score as many runs as he thought he should. I just remember him as a lovely down-to-earth guy who slept everywhere.'

Key's own assessment of his tournament is that 'I was OK'. He explained, 'We got off to decent starts. You realise now how important it is to go on and get a big score whereas I probably settled just for getting a good start. As pressurised as the cricket was, it was pleasing to get those good starts but looking back it was disappointing not to come away with more runs.'

Examining the stage his game had reached by the end of the tournament, he continued, 'My talent and my ability was probably close to as good as it could have been, whereas my experience was as low as it could have been. The best years are when those meet in the middle. I was always very aware that playing Under-19 cricket, as much as it was an honour, didn't mean much when it came to trying to get into the Kent first team or going on to play professional cricket for England. It is a sad thing to say because it was an unbelievable achievement to win the World Cup and no England team has got close to it since, but in the bigger picture of your career it doesn't mean a great deal. There wasn't any extra pressure on me after the tournament because I had always been aware of how tough it was going to be.'

With the benefit of hindsight, Key acknowledges that early success in the Kent first team – including a pair of centuries in 1998 and a place on the England A touring party to Zimbabwe – may have delayed his journey towards maturity. 'I was lucky that I got a hundred after four or five innings in county cricket and that was probably the biggest foot on the ladder I could have got as far as my own mind was concerned. But from then on it was almost the worst thing because maybe I started to think this was a little bit easier than it was. I'd get to a hundred and think, "Now I've got three or four games to relax and enjoy it without any pressure."'

The urging of arch-professional Alec Stewart to swap good times with his pals for a winter in Perth, working with renowned batting coach 'Noddy' Holder, set him on the path of self-improvement. 'I played six months of grade cricket and that was the start of it really for me. I'd got a decent reputation as an up and coming cricketer but I was still playing like an 18 year old. I didn't much care for professionalism. It wasn't until then that I worked out I had to go and do something about it.'

The unforgiving environment created by Rodney Marsh at England's Academy drove him even harder and Test selection for England was the reward; an honour that Key is eager to experience again. 'If I get to the end of my career and I've not got back in and done well at Test level I will be frustrated. I will feel unfulfilled as a cricketer because I believe I should be able to do it. My regret is that I only ever opened the batting for England twice. I didn't make the best of my opportunities but I am the player I am today because of the tough times, not the good times. I am a far better player now than when I played for England. I've become wiser; you get to know your game.'

Also, Key believes he would feel more at home in the current Test dressing room. 'A lot of those guys are people I have played with over the years. Graeme Swann I first played with when I was ten. It is easy to feel part of that team now because so many of those guys are friends. You can slip in quite easily, whereas when I first came in the team it was guys like Nasser Hussain and Alec Stewart, people I'd watched playing cricket as a kid, so it was tougher.'

Being a county captain with England aspirations can be a strange existence in the modern era of international cricket. A footballer, of course, can dream of winning the Premier League with his club and representing England – or, in the case of Arsenal players, France. And as recently as when Key and his peers entered county cricket it was possible to play a significant role in their team's bid for honours while holding down a place in the England line-up. Nowadays, prolonged status as international player means complete removal from domestic cricket, which could perhaps cloud the clarity of purpose for someone who is paid to guide the fortunes of his county side.

Key, however, is clearly comfortable with the co-existence of ambitions. 'I am pretty lucky at Kent in that I have Martin van Jaarsveld who can slide into the captaincy role pretty comfortably and I have got a decent team of senior players and wise heads. It is not going to be a disaster for them if I am not there.'

It means he can still actively pursue his England ambitions, including returning to Australia, family in tow, to work again with Holder. 'He is a coach I have put my faith in,' he explained. 'You can always improve. The game is evolving so much, with Twenty20 and the way people are hitting the ball. People are hitting it better than even three or four years ago. You have got to be a part of that somehow so that means looking into your own game, training in the gym or whatever it is. If someone is taking the game to another level you have got to try and catch up and get ahead of them.'

The demands of modern international cricket can, however, leave counties in the position of hoping that their players perform well enough to win games, but not quite well enough to earn higher recognition. 'If they get picked for England it means they must have been doing well for the county,' said Key, although adding, 'But if we lost four or five it would leave a big hole.'

Essex coach Paul Grayson had done his best to sound genuine when he said, 'If we have guys representing their country it shows as a club we are doing something right. As a coaching staff we want our lads to be playing international cricket. We are going to miss players of the quality of Alastair Cook, Ravi Bopara and maybe Graham Napier but that is why we have a squad of players. We are an attractive side to come and play for.'

Some counties tackle the problem of being left short-handed by shelling out for an overseas replacement. Middlesex, for example, signed Phil Hughes when Owais Shah's acceptance of a Delhi Daredevils contract, coupled with England one-day commitments, meant that a big bat needed to be replaced for the first few weeks of the season. The club's Director of Cricket, Angus Fraser, decided that the player most able, willing and affordable was the young Australian opener. Hughes would, therefore, get six weeks of preparation in England's unique cricketing conditions prior to the Ashes series. Confronted with accusations of aiding the enemy, Fraser rumbled, 'Let's be a little more mature. It's a slightly one-eyed, xenophobic view of life. I'm not having a go at Owais, but he wants to play in the IPL so we need a player.'

The murmurs of discontent around the English game over the signing of Hughes had risen to a scream when Key's Kent side announced the signing of Australian seamer Stuart Clark, looking to get some post-injury match practice. In the end, an early recall to the national team meant he never arrived at Canterbury, but in the meantime ECB Managing Director Hugh Morris had said, 'The decision of Kent to sign Stuart Clark so that he can continue his rehabilitation after injury to enable him to be fit for the Ashes series has been met with dismay throughout the game.'

Key had returned from New Zealand to find himself in the middle of that particular joust. 'I could not believe the fuss,' he said. 'To accuse Kent of disloyalty to England was simply ridiculous. It was not only a very blinkered and small-minded attitude but it also shows a lack of wider understanding of the game. Have not dozens of current English professionals bettered themselves over the years by playing in Australia? I've been on an Academy trip that was a backup squad to the last Ashes series in 2007. We were put up in Perth, given full permission to practise on the surface, given Western Australia's second team to play against and probably five of that squad went on to play in the successful one-day squad. So I'm not so sure that it's quite as simple as "they would never do it for us".'

At the heart of the issue was the conundrum that many counties are kept afloat by the annual handouts from the ECB – generated by the England team – yet the flow of responsibility goes in only one direction. Often it seems that there is no requirement for the counties to support the efforts of the England team to win as many games as possible. Meanwhile, the counties could claim to have been compromised by the ECB's allowance of its centrally contracted players to go to the IPL rather than spending time at their domestic sides early in the season.

When it comes to recognising the priorities of English cricket, the counties could also argue that they have been consistently confronted by ambiguity. After the signing of Hughes, Middlesex had reportedly received a questioning call from ECB chairman Giles Clarke. Yet earlier in the year, when announcing a new television deal with Sky, reportedly worth £300 million a year, Clarke had said, 'The single most important thing is the financial future of county cricket.' Middlesex and Kent could point to comments like that and feel justified in putting their own well-being – on the field and, by extension, financial – ahead of debatable concerns that they were sabotaging England's attempts at summer success.

BY LUNCHTIME of the third day against the West Indies at Derby, Key had seen his England Lions bowlers dismiss their opponents cheaply and had suffered a blow to his individual ambitions when trapped leg before by Jerome Taylor for a golden duck. His first-class tally for the season stood at a meagre 36 runs in five innings. But then came the announcement from Lord's of the 15-man England squad for the World Twenty20. Key had been overlooked for the captaincy in favour of Paul Collingwood, but was named as the apparent opening batting partner for Ravi Bopara. Alongside him in the squad were his old junior World Cup colleagues Shah, Swann and, earning his first England call-up, Napier. Key had never played a Twenty20 game for England and had scored only 54 runs in his five one-day internationals, but averaged just under 30 for Kent in the 20-over game.

'You work out how close you are I thought I had a chance of making the squad,' he said. 'Since I last played for England I have had some decent one-day years. The Twenty20 wasn't a game I was sure I was going to be any good at but I have thought about it quite a lot and my record at it has been pretty good.' By way of further endorsement, selector Geoff Miller confirmed that 'we did talk about Rob' in connection with the captaincy and named him as one of those who could 'offer a lot on the field and in the changing room'.

After bowling out the West Indies cheaply for a second time, Key's 33 off 29 balls helped the Lions advance rapidly to the 72 they needed for a 10-wicket victory at the end of the third day. The premature finish allowed him to join his Kent teammates the next day at Southgate, where he oversaw one of the more remarkable individual performances of the season. Off-spinner James Tredwell took an astonishing six wickets for four runs in his first four overs as Kent swept to victory in a low-scoring group game in the Friends Provident Trophy, prompting Key to comment dismissively on how little resemblance such contests bore to international one-day cricket.

The Trophy had been one of the two competitions in which Kent had been runners-up in 2008. Throw in their relegation from the top flight of the LV County Championship, and it left Key with a lot of unfinished business in the new season – quite apart from any England involvement. 'I think we have sufficient quality to mount a challenge in both four- and one-day cricket,' he asserted. 'The question is whether we can keep enough guys fit to sustain a challenge. We didn't step up to the big occasion last season and, if I'm honest, by the end of the summer we looked like a spent force. In tough financial times, players on development contracts and youngsters like [batsman] Sam Northeast are more likely to get thrown in at the deep end and may well end up getting a decent run. It is then a question of whether they are good enough and strong enough to take their chances.'

07

LOGAN'S RUN

'Warney was just an inspiration to be around. He changes your outlook on cricket and how to play the game' – **Richard Logan**

RICHARD LOGAN slumped down on the picnic bench and looked over to the opposite end of Henley's picturesque tree-line ground. 'Well at least you are seeing a lot of runs,' he sighed, the distant scoreboard displaying the 334 for 6 Wiltshire had just made in 50 overs. 'It's not a lot of fun for bowlers out there on days like this.' Sunshine, a flat pitch, belligerent batsmen and short boundaries were conspiring to make Logan's competitive debut for Berkshire in the Minor Counties Trophy a trying one.

Gathered beside the pavilion, four old coves sporting an eclectic mix of head-gear and walking aids had earlier been eager to learn more about their county's professional recruit. A green-blazered, cigar smoking official had greeted them with a cheery, 'Hello, lads,' and informed them that Richard Johnson, the former England, Middlesex and Somerset seamer, would be coaching this year, his place taken by Logan. 'He's been at Hampshire and Northants and they released him last season,' he explained. 'He's a bowler but he can bat as well.'

Duly informed, the quartet settled back to watch Logan running away from them with an economical, measured approach to the crease. As he completed his delivery stride with a fast whirl of the right arm, it was possible to detect the influence of Neil Foster, the former Essex and England opening bowler who had been his bowling coach as a young professional. 'Nice action,' was the verdict from the jury of four.

With the first ball of his second over, Logan beat his opponent for pace and trapped him in front of his stumps to win an lbw decision. In the next over, he generated enough lift to smack Wiltshire's former Somerset batsman Wes Durston in the side of the helmet, although when he tried it again a few deliveries later he was lifted over deep square leg. A couple more tight overs meant that, with 12 overs gone, Berkshire were exerting a certain amount of control at 42 for 2.

Yet by the time Logan returned briefly at the 35-over mark it was a very different picture. The wristy play of Durston, who would end the season playing in the Champions League for Somerset, and the bludgeoning of Zimbabwean Greg Lamb – a former Hampshire colleague of Logan's who in this setting resembled the village blacksmith enjoying his Sunday afternoon slog – had raised the run rate to almost six an over. Given the responsibility of the last two overs from his end, Logan eventually had Durston caught in the deep for 133 and saw another catch spilled at long-on, leaving him with the figures of 2 for 53 off his 10 overs. It was a respectable return in the circumstances, although not as rewarding as the 6 for 24 he'd taken a day earlier in his first Sussex League game for Chichester Priory Park.

Despite the score that now taunted him from across the ground, he explained, 'At the moment I am really enjoying my cricket. It's a lot different playing a couple of times a week to playing full throttle for six months. I am player-coach at Chichester, so that keeps me busy in the week and on Saturdays. They are good group of lads. At the end of last season I had to make a decision about whether I was going to play any cricket this summer. When I decided I was, then I wanted to play as much as possible. I am really good friends with Richard Morris, whose dad is the chairman here at Berkshire, and I know a lot of the lads, so I organised it to come here.'

Logan had spent the previous two summers back at his first professional club, Northamptonshire, having had stints at Nottinghamshire and Hampshire in between. Thoughts of full-time cricket were clearly still playing around his mind, if no longer at the forefront. 'I have just enough cricket to keep me going. If I have a really good year and someone asks me to go for a trial I definitely will because I think I have kept myself pretty fit and have not really had too many big injuries. But I am just going to enjoy this year and see what happens.'

Getting satisfaction from the sport, he explained, had been impossible during his final year at Northampton, when he played only one first-team game. 'It was hard work because it was irrelevant how well I was doing in the second team. I knew I wasn't going to get in because they had Lance Klusener, Andrew Hall, Johan van der Wath and Johann Louw, and Dave Lucas was also doing well. There was no room for anybody, however well the guys did in the second team. Generally I did OK and probably bowled better than I did the year before when I played half the season in the first team.

'It was frustrating to be let go without having the chance to play, but I didn't really grasp my chance the year before when I got in the team. Playing second-team cricket can be demoralising when you have played for 10 or 12 years. I didn't mind the year before because I did well enough to get in the first team. Last year I was not going to play, which made it tough mentally to get up for the games. You rely on personal pride and the hope that if you do well against a particular team they might pick you up. But at my age people generally know what I can do and if I take a five-for it is not really going to sway their opinion either way. I tried to get involved in helping the younger guys and doing more coaching. I didn't think I would enjoy it, but I really got into it.'

A first-class career that had produced 133 wickets in 54 matches, spread out across a decade, had its roots in club cricket in Cannock and representative games for Staffordshire. Bowling, Logan explained, had been a late addition to his skills. 'I was an opening bat. I played for the Midlands Under-14s in a regional festival and in three games I think I got a 70, a 30 and an 80 and just missed out on the England age group side. I needed to start doing something else so when I was 15 I began bowling and by the end of that season I was opening the bowling for England Under-15s. From then on my batting tailed off a bit.'

As Logan grew towards his eventual 6ft 1in., Northamptonshire saw enough potential to offer him a place on their winter coaching programme. 'I went there once every three weeks and spent the whole Saturday there. On a Tuesday I would go to Edgbaston and train with Warwickshire. Then Northants offered me a scholarship and at the end of that year, when I was 16, I signed a three-year contract.'

Having overcome back problems that turned out to be little more than the growing pains of a young bowler, Logan felt fortunate in having Foster, veteran of 29 Test matches, to take charge of his development. 'He was there at those schools of excellence in the winter and throughout the summer as well,' he said. And even though in later years he would make three visits to Dennis Lillee's bowling academy in Chennai, he insisted, 'Fozzie is still the best bowling coach I have ever worked with. He kept things very simple and he knew my action so well. Coming to bowling late probably helped a little because I had not got into bad habits.'

Despite progressing to play for England Under-17s, Logan had given little thought to being selected for the Under-19 tour of South Africa when the end of summer 1997 came around. While some candidates for the squad, many a year Logan's senior, had already become first-team regulars at their counties, he was still awaiting his chance in the Northants second eleven. 'I had not even thought about the tour until right at the end of the season when Fozzie mentioned that he thought I'd be going. I went to a few of the training camps and got picked. It all happened quite quickly and I was obviously chuffed to bits.'

Once on tour, Logan found himself in a battle with Essex's Jamie Grove for the role of partnering Paul Franks with the new ball. Each played in one Test match, while the World Cup group game against Namibia was the only international during the entire trip in which they both featured. 'I played the first Test and Jamie got in for the second,' Logan recalled, 'and in the World Cup we were back and forth. They gave me a go against Australia, which turned out to be a bit of a semi-final, and I bowled pretty well [1 for 17 off 8.2 overs]. That meant I was in the team for the final. Neither of us really took our chance until that game. It is a difficult situation because you are always trying to enjoy everybody's success and you always want the team to win, but you want to be in the team. You have to try to take it on your own shoulders and take your chance, rather than hoping others don't do very well.'

Physically, Logan didn't feel his bowling advanced in South Africa anywhere near as much as the following winter, when the Under-19s toured New Zealand, although he doesn't underestimate the education he received away from the action. It is an aspect he believes is often overlooked in the development of today's young players.

'We had some big characters in the team, like Swanny, who I lived with in Northampton, Keysy and Steve Peters. I sat back and tried to learn a lot, especially from Franksie, who was carrying the Notts attack at that time. We didn't have a bowling specialist on the tour, so he was a good guy to sit around with, chewing the fat. I believe in the old adage that you learn a lot in the bar. I picked up a lot in the early stages of my career, talking to guys like Nick Cook, who was second-eleven coach at Northants. He was good at teaching you how to play cricket, how to understand situations and be aware. It is something I have looked at with young lads these days, something they are very poor at sometimes. I don't think there is enough attention on that. They get great physical training, but there can be a bit too much focus on mechanics and not enough teaching of cricket awareness.'

Even armed with greater appreciation of his trade and having 'learned stuff about myself and my action' in New Zealand, Logan was still kept waiting for first-team opportunities at Northants. In 1999, he played against Cambridge University, the Sri Lankan tourists and in some one-day games and continued to take wickets for the England Under-19s. He then enjoyed a fruitful spell playing grade cricket at St George's in Sydney. Finally, in 2000, he was given a run in the county team, but a five-wicket haul against Middlesex was followed by a sequence of wicketless innings and a return to the second team.

David Capel, who ended up coaching Logan in his second spell at Northants, was among his senior teammates as he strove to force his way into the team. 'As a youngster there was quite a lot of ability there,' Capel recalled. 'He would run in and bowl as fast as anybody and he moved the ball away from the right-handed batsman. He was a smashing bloke and would be everybody's favourite teammate but he got a little bit lost cricket-wise. At the age of 19 his mother passed away and I believe that had quite an effect on his development and maturity. He had ability but it was frustrating that it never really matured in the way you would have liked. He had the pace and strength and there were times when he bowled well, but he never really nailed it.'

Logan's own recollection of that period was that 'it had been frustrating because I saw a lot of the England Under-19 lads playing regularly for their counties'. He added, 'Northants didn't think I was ready. But I came back from Sydney in good shape, had a good pre-season and started in the first team. I played six games, but then didn't play again all season. It's the story of my career really. I thought I should have been given more of a chance at that age because our three seamers, Devon Malcolm, Paul Taylor and Dave Follett, were all around 35 and were playing ahead of me and John Blain. Neither of us was getting an opportunity and it wasn't like we were 18 year olds. We were about 20 or 21. That was why, at the end of the season, I made the decision to leave. I spoke to Notts and that was it. It was the right move – I had two really good years to begin with.'

Arriving at Trent Bridge at the same time as Logan was a brash, young South African batsman intent on qualifying to play for England. 'Kevin Pietersen and I joined Notts at the same time, so we were the new boys and we hung out a lot of the time. We get on really well; he is a great bloke and a good friend.' Referring to the events of the previous winter, Logan added, 'I thought he would be a brilliant England captain. I think he would have been had he continued in the job. He was just so disappointed with the way it was all handled.'

While Pietersen set out single-mindedly on his path to rule the cricketing world, Logan thrived in new surroundings, recording 43 and 35 first-class wickets in his first two years. The next two, however, saw him used mainly as a Twenty20 bowler and an occasional stand-in when the Championship side was short of personnel. Logan traced his downturn in fortunes to the departure of team manager Clive Rice midway through the 2002 season. 'I got on really well with him, although he had some flaws as a coach, and he liked me as a player. Those two years when I was fit I played. It is a completely different feeling to go to the ground knowing you are going to play, as opposed to turning up and not knowing. When Mick Newell took over, Paul Franks came back in after his injury and it ended with me and Charlie Shreck going for one place and he got picked.'

It was becoming evident that Logan might not ever construct the kind of career expected of him after the World Cup. John Abrahams suggested, 'If he was ever going to play for England I felt that the timing would have to be just right – a Headingley pick if you like. As a county bowler day-in and day-out, bowling wicket to wicket at reasonable pace, I thought he would have had an established career, someone you would love to have in your side.'

A meeting with Australia and then-Hampshire batsman Michael Clarke, whom Logan had got to know during his winter of grade cricket, offered the opportunity to play under the captaincy of Shane Warne. 'I had got four wickets against Hampshire and Michael asked if I would think of moving because Warney liked me.' The move did not exactly result in bucketfuls of wickets. In 2005, Logan lost his place early in the county's victorious run in the Cheltenham and Gloucester Trophy after a poor outing against Ireland and then he missed the second half of 2006 with a stress fracture in his back. But he still cherishes the memories of life at the Rose Bowl.

'I loved it there and I still support Hampshire. I live in Southampton now and I met my fiancée when I was down there. Warney was just an inspiration to be around. He changes your outlook on cricket and how to play the game. He has an unforgiving drive and a belief that in any situation you can win. Obviously it helps when you are as good as he is, but he instilled that belief in everybody around him. He is so knowledgeable. I heard him do an interview a month ago on TV and when they went back to the studio everyone was in a trance listening to him talk. You just want to hear everything he has got to say. He was like that in team meetings and there was never a time when he wouldn't have everyone's attention. I often sat down talked about cricket with him.'

Knowing how easily Logan had been attracted to strong characters like Pietersen and Warne, Capel could not help wondering whether that had at times been detrimental to his career. 'Some of that consistency in his cricket could have come through a little bit more with an improved lifestyle,' he argued. 'Richard tended to latch on to people like Kevin Pietersen in his earlier days and Shane Warne. While he would have had a lovely time and his natural way was to live his life like that, I don't know whether that would have had an effect. Maybe he needed more of a hard-nosed approach, to look after himself and have that desire to be on the team sheet and perform at the highest level. Whether his sociability stood in the way of his own performance, I am not sure. You would like to have seen him at times in his career put in a more concerted effort and have a sharper focus. He got a bit frustrated with his own bowling at times, with one or two technical things. He seemed to wrestle a little bit with what he was doing with his bowling and never seemed to be 100 per cent really happy.'

Logan was disappointed, but not surprised, to be released by Hampshire, after which he went back to his professional roots by signing again for Northamptonshire. 'It was a natural move back,' he said. 'David Capel and David Ripley were in charge and I had played with them so it was easy to settle in again. They took a bit of a punt on me on the back of what I had done there before.'

Capel added, 'Richard came to me and said, "You know me. If anyone can get something out of me I would like to think you can." He had a regular girlfriend and I felt there was more maturity than there had been. It was not for any lack of effort that it didn't work out, but he picked up some untimely injuries, got a little frustrated and lost confidence. When one or two opportunities came along he didn't accept them in the way you would hope a more mature bowler would do. He was scarred a little bit by some experiences before he came to us. Maybe he didn't really let himself go, because of self- doubt. We tried to work at it and get through it. It was not through lack of endeavour but things didn't quite kick on as we hoped.'

Those who warn that 'you can never go back' might have foreseen the two years of disappointment that lay ahead of Logan. As well as his discontent at a lack of first-team action, he was underwhelmed by the atmosphere around the club. Critics of county cricket often accuse counties like Northamptonshire – those whose fate lies more in the hands of the ECB accountants than their own achievements – of settling for mediocrity. Logan stopped short of categorising his former team in such a way but he did point out, 'At Hampshire everyone is massively focused on winning things. With [chairman] Rod Bransgrove at the helm, he typifies the drive of the club and Warney reflected that. He has left a lot of good things behind in the senior players and everyone is pushing in the same direction. I know everyone wants to win things but there is difference in having that belief and drive to do it. I don't think that was there at Northampton in the last two years. Whether I was in the team or out of it, it was not an all-or-nothing, win-or-die-trying feeling.'

He also felt there was 'a bit of divide last year with so many South African guys'. Perhaps, though, that is merely something one senses more when several of those men are keeping you out of the team.

At that point in the conversation, it was time for Logan to depart and prepare for his innings, which he eventually began with Berkshire, the reigning Minor Counties champions and Trophy runners-up a year earlier, well behind the asking rate and running out of wickets. Having scored seven off his first three balls, he swung former teammate Lamb into the hands of long-off, although his team had clearly seen something promising in his brief stay at the crease. A week later he would be opening the batting and top-scoring with 64 off 59 balls as Berkshire again fell a long way short in a massive run chase. For now, though, there was still some work to be done before the end of the day, promoting to his opponents the business venture he and former Northants colleague Andy Crook had launched at the start of the season.

He explained, 'After we got released, Andy asked me what I was thinking of doing. One of my ideas was the League Cricketers' Association. We thought about it and felt it had good legs so we have focussed on that. We got it going, built a web site and launched in February.'

The concept of the LCA is that anyone playing, or connected with, league cricket can pay £9.95 a year to join the organisation and be eligible for, among other things, games against legends teams, the LCA Awards and discounted services from business partners. Logan continued, 'It is amazing how many contacts you build up in cricket. I didn't have to make a single cold call but we have 20 partners offering deals to members, like saving on mobile phone tariffs. Whoever wins our LCA Player of the Year will get a year's sponsorship from Gray-Nicolls – Nick Wilton has set that up. You'll also be able to go to the site and upload personal training programmes and nutritional stuff, details about how to get to matches, clothing deals and some fun and games.'

There are half a million club cricketers and Logan, he explained, had set himself a four-figure target for recruits by end of the season. 'The great thing about playing in these games is that most minor county teams will cover several club teams. Club cricket is very incestuous; everyone talks to each other. We are getting bat stickers made up to send to members and I am going to try to get one of the Hampshire lads using them.' And with that, he was off to complete his final delivery of a long day, heading to the bar with a stack of promotional fliers.

08

TOO MUCH TOO YOUNG

'I turned up at Lord's to make my Test debut and I don't think they had actually seen me bowl at all' – **Chris Schofield**

ENGLAND'S LAST home Test match had been played in a different age; those faraway, innocent days when Allen Stanford was thought of as 'a good thing' and Kevin Pietersen and Peter Moores were the leadership team to recapture the Ashes. So much had happened since victory over South Africa eight months earlier that it was easy to forget how recently Graeme Swann had emerged as his country's premier spinner.

Even the man himself had to be reminded that the first of two Tests against the West Indies, the *hors d'oeuvres* to the main courses of the summer's international cricket, would hold a special significance. 'I hadn't even realised until Alastair Cook said the day before Lord's, "This will be your home debut." During the winter there were bombs going off, flights home, petulance here, captains going there and different coaches, it was like being in a pantomime. I thought I must have played 50-60 Tests by now.'

Swann had shared the spinner's duties with Monty Panesar in three of his five Tests, but it was clear that only one would play in the earliest-starting home

Test in England's history. No one was surprised when Panesar was sent back to Northampton on the morning of the match. 'Sometimes I still find it hard to believe I'm playing for England,' Swann admitted. 'I wake up every day with a little smile on my face, a bit of a cheeky grin, because I still feel like a bit of a charlatan, sneaking a living.'

Swann's full recovery from the elbow operation he'd had in Colorado enabled the England selectors to make their selection based on form rather than fitness and justified his early departure from the West Indies. Simon Timson, the ECB's Head of Science and Medicine, believes it also highlighted the strong working relationship between county and country. 'It is a classic example of how effectively the ECB and the counties work,' he said. 'There was ongoing discussion of when was the right time for Nottinghamshire and England and what Graeme himself wanted. We found the right time and the best surgeon in the world. In working with Notts, Graeme was rehabbed really effectively.'

Having seen his team lose the toss and bat, it was not until a few minutes before the close of the first day that Swann got to walk the gauntlet of MCC members in the Long Room and emerge as a Test player in front of a home crowd. And he did so with unlikely batting advice ringing in his ears from England spin bowling coach Mushtaq Ahmed, whose average in 52 Tests for Pakistan was 11. 'Mushy said, "Go out and really enjoy yourself. Let yourself flow and hit the ball if it is there."'

Seven not out at close of play, Swann played the next day as though the spirit of Graham Gooch rather than Mushtaq Ahmed was with him at the crease. Sharing something of the former England captain's distinctive posture – bat raised high as the bowler approaches – Swann drove successive off-side boundaries off Fidel Edwards; caressed Jerome Taylor through the covers; forced the next ball on the up for another four and completed a 50 partnership with centurion Ravi Bopara by squeezing a half-volley square for four more. Lionel Baker was slashed to the boundary and pulled in front of square for six as Swann reached his half-century in 73 deliveries.

It was the kind of batting that had been a bigger part of his game as a youngster, when his ability had hinted at more than the four first-class centuries to have so far come his way. Northamptonshire coach David Capel, a former Wantage Road teammate, recalled the young Swann as having 'no shortage of confidence with his batting' and being 'a very natural, uncomplicated striker of the ball'. As one of a group of players in the late '80s burdened with being seen as potential successors to Ian Botham, Capel highlighted the problems in maintaining the highest professional level in both disciplines of the all-rounder's game. 'Graeme showed through the age groups that he could do some pretty useful things with the bat, even when he started playing second-eleven cricket when he was 16. Inevitably, when you come into first-class cricket, there is a main focus on one string and you take care of that. The other one merely supports it. It has worked for Graeme in that he has taken his off-spin seriously and become a very good performer. But he still has that natural ability with the bat and I think it has improved again. He used to annoy himself with some of the ways he would get himself out and feel he could have done better.'

Having ended unbeaten on 63 out of England's 377, Swann was unexpectedly at the thick of things when the West Indies batted, given the opening two overs from the Pavilion End. It was assumed that his mastery over opener Devon Smith had prompted the experiment but, bowling to Chris Gayle with a long-on and long-off, he managed to turn one down the slope past the visiting skipper's outside edge. 'I was probably the first spinner to open the bowling at Lord's in May on a green top,' he admitted. 'We got a little bit funky with it and tried to see what would happen. All praise to Andy Flower and Andrew Strauss for having the *cojones* to actually do it. It was a nice surprise.' In the press box, however, opinion was divided. Jonathan Agnew hailed Strauss's 'great ingenuity', while former England captain Michael Atherton called it 'a crass, smart-arse, look-at-me piece of captaincy'. Whatever one's view of the tactic, it was easier to imagine it being brazened out by Swann, a man with the in-your-face mentality of an opening bowler, than the diffident Panesar.

'I only get nervous in games I can't affect; if I have batted or bowled already,' Swann explained later. 'I don't get performance anxiety. As a kid, knowing I was better than everyone else, it gets ingrained in you. Obviously, the opposition gets better but if you start off with that approach it becomes a natural thing.'

The validity of Strauss's thinking was strengthened when, with the West Indies on 99 for 2, Swann returned and bowled Smith with his first ball. In came Shivnarine Chanderpaul, the world's top-rated batsman, and out he went, caught first ball by Paul Collingwood at slip, with Swann leaping and punching the air like a Cup final goalscorer. He was still fighting to keep the smile off his face as he delivered his hat-trick ball to Brendan Nash, who knocked it safely into the ground, only to fall to the Collingwood-Swann combination a little later. At 117 for 5, Swann took a back seat as Durham's wiry seamer Graham Onions picked up the final five wickets, although Swann did pull off a diving catch to dismiss Suleiman Benn, who had dashed to the crease in a state of comical undress during the clatter of wickets.

Following on, the West Indies were hastened to a third-day defeat, with Swann taking three more wickets. He had now taken at least three in all seven innings in which he'd bowled in 2009 and his total of 25 was the best of anyone in the world. His first Man of the Match award in Test cricket was handed to him, appropriately, by one of the greatest of England's slow bowlers, Derek Underwood.

Any remaining questions about the identity of England's first-choice spinner for the Ashes series had been answered emphatically. Swann's success against a West Indies line-up heavy with left-handers boded well for a confrontation with an Australian team that could have five southpaws in its top eight. 'I wish the world could be left-handed to be honest,' Swann mused. 'It is purely the fact that the ball moves away, although you also get more rough to play with. Lefties always have big pot holes in front of them so it always plays on their mind. Growing up, because you don't bowl at many left-handers it seems strange to have so many playing in world cricket. I don't think I bowl any better at the left-handers – it is just that you have more methods of getting them out. Lbw comes in to play.'

Swann's success and self-assurance had increased his captain's belief in a man who was fast becoming one of his spearheads. 'I like to be in the thick of it and when you keep getting thrown the ball it is a nice feeling,' he admitted. 'You don't want to bowl five overs and go and stand at third man because the captain thinks you are a bit of a tosser.'

A consequence of Swann's arrival as a bona fide Test player was that the English cricket community had for now put aside its obsession with the search for a 'mystery spinner'; someone who could conjure up the variations of Shane Warne, contort his limbs like Muralitharan, or replicate Saqlain Mushtaq's doosra. For the first time since John Emburey began his 64-match England career three decades earlier, an old-fashioned right-arm finger spinner seemed like enough.

Ironically, the Under-19 team that returned from South Africa with the World Cup in 1998 was thought, for a while, to contain the answer to England's slow bowling problems. Not in Swann, but in a Rochdale-born leg spinner. By that time, England had already suffered greatly at the hands of Warne, who had taken 85 wickets in the three full Ashes series in which he'd participated. Now, was this the answer stepping off the plane? He certainly looked the part, down to the blond highlights.

THE STREAKED hair was hidden under a helmet as Chris Schofield set about the task of batting Surrey to safety at The Oval the day after the conclusion of Swann's latest heroics. Without a Test match on television and with local rivals Middlesex in opposition, a decent Saturday crowd was watching the home side attempt to eke out enough runs to make themselves safe from an opposition chase. Schofield's arrival at number seven shortly after lunch, with his team only 102 runs ahead, had apparently been much anticipated by the bowling side. Earlier, after the fall of the third wicket, Tim Murtagh had yelled from third man, 'Come on boys. Two more for Schoey,' indicating a belief that he represented the beginning of a long tail.

Schofield, though, was no mug with the bat. After all, he'd been one of the last England slow bowlers before Swann to score a Test fifty – the high point of that brief and ill-fated period when he represented England's spinning solution. He had also begun the season with a career average above 28 and had made 47 in the first innings of this game. However, the first four balls he faced offered an indication of an erratic streak in his batting that had been spotted by his England Under-19 colleagues all those years ago: survival of an lbw appeal, a swept boundary, a play and miss, and an on-driven four.

'He always had a funky way of batting,' wicketkeeper Nick Wilton recalled. 'He was a bit unorthodox, reverse sweeping everywhere.' According to Giles Haywood, 'He was a funny guy really, a little bit aloof and shy. He did his own thing, like going out and playing the reverse sweep. When you can pull that off it is great, but sometimes county coaches don't understand why you've done it.' Even the way Schofield looks at the crease is somewhat individual, the side padding in his helmet discarded so that you can see that his ears have been shoved down and folded over. If he'd been old enough to recall him, Schofield might have looked in the mirror and been reminded of bowler-hatted comedian Freddie 'Parrot Face' Davies.

Having slapped a full toss for four and executed a clinical cover drive, Schofield had reached 20 when he became one of Shaun Udal's six victims by edging an attempted sweep to slip. Middlesex ended up needing 186 to win in 25 overs and, within two balls, there was no doubting the intent of Aussie Phil Hughes, scorer of big centuries in each of his three Championship games. Advancing down the track, he forced fast bowler Andre Nel into the indignity of having eight fielders on the boundary in his first over. By the time Nel stomped back to the safety of the changing room, replaced by Schofield at the Pavilion End, Middlesex had scored 71 without loss in only nine overs. As Surrey's director of cricket, Chris Adams, commented, 'Ten years ago when a captain was faced with 186 in 25 overs you would shake hands and say, "See you next time." That is what Twenty20 cricket has done.'

Ironically, for a style of cricket based so much on big hitting, the shortest form of the game had also played an important part in the rehabilitation of Schofield, who'd found himself in England's first World Twenty20 team in 2007 only two years after being out of the professional game and embroiled in a court case against his former employers at Lancashire. Yet it had been Schofield's earlier, premature elevation to the England team that marked the moment when it all started to go wrong; the point when a career that had been fast-tracked to the heights of Test cricket at Lord's began a miserable slide into lawyers' offices and Minor Counties cricket.

'I felt when I was very young that I wanted to play cricket for a living,' Schofield reflected during a break in the hectic schedule of the season. 'At school they said, "Make sure you do your homework," but I had that drive to play cricket.'

His love of football curtailed by a hip injury, it was Schofield's early experience of indoor cricket that propelled him down the path of bowling wrist-spin. 'On the surface in the indoor centres the ball bounced and turned quite a lot so I was able to spin it. I used to bowl seamers as well but as a 13 year old playing against seniors you are just not fast enough to beat them with seam, so I found out that spin was the way to go. I was aware that there weren't a great deal of leg-spinners around. I played a lot of cricket at that time with the sons of John Holder, the umpire, and he taught me how to bowl a googly and a flipper. It was really difficult to bowl consistently but I kept trying and my batting and fielding helped me out a lot.'

Progressing from Littleborough Cricket Club into Lancashire's second team, where he was able to work with former Australian leg-spinner Peter Sleep, Schofield felt he was the junior slow bowler in the party when selected for the England Under-19s' trip to South Africa in the winter of 1997-98. 'I had just been given a contract by Lancashire, had a half decent season in the second team and did quite well for England in the youth tournament in Bermuda. But Jonny Powell and Graeme Swann had played a lot more cricket than me at the time; Swanny had played a lot of youth internationals and Powelly had been in the England development system since very young.'

Schofield, who had taken four wickets in his Under-19 Test debut against Zimbabwe, struggled as much as any other bowler in the four-day games against South Africa, failing to take a wicket in two matches. But he recalled, 'I learned a lot from that. I hadn't played a lot of cricket with the team before and I didn't know the majority of the lads. But we got to learn a lot about each other and the conditions. All of a sudden we were competing and playing very well. It seemed like we were a team that fought and wanted to do well for each other.'

The pattern of his own World Cup performances was to bowl economically at between three and four runs per over and chip in with the occasional wicket; six in total in the tournament. 'There was still a lot of inconsistency in my bowling. I knew when I put it in the right areas there was a great opportunity for me. Most of my games were OK and I bowled pretty well.' With the bat he contributed useful knocks of 34 and 25 against Bangladesh and Pakistan respectively, with coach John Abrahams recalling, 'He gave us a bit of invention down the order.'

Schofield's first-class debut came at Glamorgan the following summer, but it was in his second game, against Gloucestershire, where he made an impact with four wickets in each innings. In 1999, he played 10 Championship matches, taking 29 wickets at less than 33 and helping Lancashire to second place in the table. It earned him selection for England A's winter tour to Bangladesh and New Zealand. Enjoying the dusty Asian wickets, he took a career-best 6 for 120 against the full Bangladesh team, before continuing his good form on the greener tracks in New Zealand, where he also contributed three first-class fifties. 'The wickets in Bangladesh had taken spin lovely and then I had bowled well every game in New Zealand, taking three or four wickets an innings,' he remembered. But even after his 35 wickets on tour, few observers were expecting the developments of the early summer of 2000.

The need for the England team to have greater control over the amount and nature of cricket played by its key players had been one of the recurring themes as the dismal performances of the 1990s were dissected. To have those men centrally contracted to the ECB rather than their counties, in the manner of several other Test nations, was considered the solution. When the first 12 such men were announced few expected established names such as Nasser Hussain, Michael Atherton and Alec Stewart to be joined by that of Schofield. Clearly, the new procedures were not going to rule out some of the eccentricities of selection that had for so long characterised the England set-up.

'It came as a surprise,' Schofield confessed. 'I just felt I would go back to Lancashire, play a full season and carry on with what I was doing. Hopefully there might be a call-up for international cricket somewhere down the line. But suddenly I was being talked about and the day before they announced it I got a call from David Graveney to tell me I was getting a central contract. I think Mike Gatting had a big say. He toured with us in the winter and must have said I was worth a look. At the time I had never met Nasser Hussain or played against him. I don't think he'd ever seen me play. The same with Duncan Fletcher.'

Plenty of players have been unexpectedly selected for England over the years, but this was not just for a one-off Test. This was for a full year's contract, which raised the stakes considerably. It looked even more curious when Schofield was dumped after the two early-season Tests against Zimbabwe. In the first, he'd picked up a third-ball duck and not bowled, while the second game saw him hit a useful 57 and send down 18 wicketless overs. In that spell he had gone from being England's answer to Warne to someone who would never again darken the door of the Test dressing room.

'I turned up at Lord's to make my debut and I don't think they had actually seen me bowl at all. After that first Test they had an opinion on me and thought, "He is not quite good enough." I got another game and bowled on a very flat wicket at Trent Bridge against the best batter in the world at the time, Andy Flower. Playing Test cricket in May means the wickets are not really conducive to spin. Had I come in at Old Trafford in August it might have suited me.'

Admitting that the 'Shane Warne factor' played a significant part in his selection, Schofield's regret is that he was not held back for the tours to Pakistan later in the year, when left-armer Ashley Giles and leggie Ian Salisbury were chosen as the spinners. 'Over the three years before then, all the cricket where I had done really well was touring with England abroad. I had not been that outstanding in England. I look back and think they missed a trick when they went to Pakistan, where the wickets would have been brilliant for me. Instead I got two Tests – on a good batting track at Trent Bridge and a green seamer at Lord's.'

Under-19 teammate Graeme Swann had to wait more than eight years longer than Schofield to play in a Test match, a delay for which he remains grateful when comparing his fate. 'Schoey was a good leg-spinner but to think of him as a senior England player at the age of 20, well he wasn't good enough,' he suggested. 'He was still trying to play consistent county cricket yet he was given that central contract. It wasn't fair on him and I felt sorry for him. He didn't ask for that attention yet people in the country, like guys he was playing against, were absolutely slating him for the next two or three years. I heard things like, "You Under-19s, you won the World Cup and you think you've been kissed on the cock. He is not good enough for a contract." I'd say, "Go easy on the lad. He is not good enough but it's not his fault he got the contract." I was glad I was not in that situation. I would have hated to have got abused because people thought I had been handed silver jugs for the future. The abuse I got as a youngster was justified because people saw me strutting about and I needed knocking down a peg or two. You can deal with that when you are 19 or 20, but I don't think I could have dealt with people not thinking I was good enough. That would have killed me.'

Returning to Lancashire, Schofield not only had the opinions of the public and his profession to combat, but the feeling that he was a forgotten man, despite the central contract in his pocket. 'I pretty much never heard from England. But that happens with most cricketers; if you are not in the fold you don't get a call. If they see you at the ground they might have a chat with you, but you just hope your name is in the hat when they are picking the team.'

He managed to finish the season with 39 wickets, good enough for another England A tour to the West Indies to participate in the region's domestic tournament, the Busta Cup. He took 22 wickets in five first-class matches but already he feared that his career had begun moving in the wrong direction. 'At Lancashire, I didn't get the opportunity to bowl a great deal because we had Muttiah Muralitharan, and Gary Keedy was coming through. There is nothing better than playing every game and getting the ball thrown to you and told you are going to bowl 30 overs. But to get the ball out of their hands was pretty difficult.' So much so that in 2001 he took only 14 wickets at an average of 57.

'Peter Sleep left around that time so it was pretty difficult,' Schofield continued, his voice betraying the regret of that loss. 'Peter was fantastic over four years of my career. It started to go downhill when he left because I didn't have that guidance. I tried to keep a mental picture of what he had been telling me for years but it felt like I actually needed someone there to help me along. It was difficult to turn to somebody. You get ideas in the dressing room but really they don't know much about leg-spin bowling. You try and listen but unfortunately some things you are told are not going to work for you. The thing with me was that I actually said to people, "That is not what I want to do. That is not how I want to bowl. My action doesn't work like that."'

During a televised game early in 2009, Schofield's former England and Lancashire colleague Michael Atherton had accused him of having 'not developed one iota' since his England selection. Pointing out that his left arm remained largely redundant in his bowling action, Atherton added, 'He was like that when he came to Lancashire as a kid and he is like that now.'

Schofield confessed, 'My action is a bit indifferent and I was not prepared to change.' Asked if that stubborn approach was held against him, he responded. 'Yes, I think it was. I was trying to bowl well, but I had a lot of people trying to tell me to do something that wasn't natural to me. Under the likes of Wasim Akram a few years earlier it would have been so different. The first year I turned up he threw me the ball and said, "I just want you to bowl overs." Unfortunately Warren Hegg took over and he was a little bit of a negative captain. He didn't want runs to be given away very easily and didn't understand that leg-spinners do bowl bad balls.'

Schofield did head his team's National League one-day averages in 2001 and spent another winter away with the England Academy squad in Australia, but from 2002 onwards his contribution to the Lancashire team diminished annually. In 2004, he played only three first-class games, scoring fifties in each, and the county announced his release at the end of an unsuccessful season.

John Abrahams ventured, 'There are probably two people who, when they first came on the scene, I thought could really make it. Alex Tudor was one and then Schoey because of what he does; a leg-spinner who can also bat. I thought he would go far because back then leg-spinners were the ones winning Test matches. He had all the attributes at that age to go on and potentially succeed at highest level so it's a little bit disappointing. Did he get too much too early? Possibly. And whether that quick transition from Under-19s to central contract was handled properly from the boy's point of view I don't know. I know Schoey well and I'm glad he has made a comeback. I know he was gutted to be released by Lancashire.'

Schofield's feelings ran deeper than mere disappointment. He claimed unfair dismissal, arguing that he had been released without a full appraisal and without notice, undermining his hopes of finding another club. Two years earlier Leicestershire had settled out of court after similar claims by Neil Burns and Carl Crowe, but this time there was no such deal.

Recalling the unfolding of the story, Schofield said, 'I had been told by the club that if I was going to play it would be predominantly as a batter, so I made sure I scored a lot of runs in the second team so they would have to pick me in the first team. I averaged into the 40s in the Championship my last two years and bowled a few overs here and there. That was my role. I wasn't getting a great deal of overs but I was doing well with the bat. I got released with [reserve keeper] Jamie Haynes at the end of 2004, but during the summer we'd both got told we were going to get a contract. I didn't know at the time, but Jamie turned to the club and said, "Legally you cannot do that."'

Haynes explained to his colleague that the club had agreed to pay him the equivalent of a full year's salary, but Lancashire preferred to let Schofield's case go to court rather than make the same arrangement. 'The PCA lawyer said, "How can you do one thing for one man and not another?" All I was asking for was the same,' Schofield continued.

While he got busy writing to every other county advising them of his availability – a fruitless exercise – his legal team prepared for a three-man employment tribunal in Manchester in April 2005. Lancashire argued that a procedure of verbal and written warnings would have harmed Schofield's confidence and ability to perform at the highest standard. They said that the decision to release him had been ratified by the cricket committee and then given to the player on September 23.

When the tribunal delivered its verdict the umpire's finger of guilt was lifted in the direction of the county, who it was ruled had not followed employment law procedures. Schofield was subsequently awarded his year's salary, reported to be close to £60,000. 'We won the battle and now the players are getting full appraisals and being told if they are in job or not, so it has worked out better,' he reflected. 'My case is the one that made it that way.'

The legal victory could not alter the fact that he was a player without a professional team. Instead, he played for his old club, Littleborough, and, like the hopeful actor traipsing across the country in rep, hawked his services around the Minor Counties and second-eleven circuits. 'It was a hard slog. I was up and down the country and used a lot of my own savings to keep me going. I did a bit of painting and decorating to help out. I felt pretty down at times.'

During 2005 he played for Cheshire, for whom he scored a century against Herefordshire, and the reserve teams of Durham, Sussex and Derbyshire. The following summer, he began taking wickets regularly for Suffolk, the result of a calculated move to attract greater attention. 'I'd had a great season in Minor Counties cricket and played really good second-team cricket and still no county came in for me. I thought as one last try I would go down south, where there was better media reporting. Suffolk are a good club who go about their cricket very professionally and I thought there would be a lot of clubs around in that area who might be able to pick me up.'

The turning point was a game early in July against Hertfordshire at Long Marston, where his 13 wickets included the double dismissal of former Surrey batsman David Ward. 'I had a beer with Wardy afterwards and he said, "What are you doing playing here? You have got so much to offer. Give me your number." A week later I got a call off [Surrey second eleven coach] Nadeem Shaheed.'

Late in August, almost two years since his last major match, Schofield forced his way into the full Surrey side for four Pro40 games and a couple of County Championship contests. A full contract for 2007 followed and the feat of taking 17 wickets in the Twenty20 Cup, including 10 in a three-game run, saw him named in England's party for the inaugural World Twenty20 in South Africa. 'It just shows how things can change with a bit of faith and hard work,' he said. With four wickets in four matches, Schofield hardly set the tournament alight, but neither did England.

David Graveney, then chairman of England selectors, had announced the decision to recall Schofield by stating, 'He is one of the great stories to be told.' In 2009, looking back at his role in the earlier chapters of the spinner's career, Graveney confessed, 'Selection is never a precise science and at the time [in 2000] there was a bit of a feeling that we needed to have wrist spinners involved. In hindsight, that was probably too quick a leap for Chris. That is no knock on his ability, but if we had our time again we'd say that leg-spin is the most difficult of cricket skills to perform, not least when you are trying to do it against world-class performers.'

Schofield believes he is still learning that craft but says there is no comparison between the boy of 2000 and the man who, particularly in limited overs cricket, has come much closer to achieving the dependability he began striving for all those years ago. 'I think I have matured a lot, learned a lot and my bowling is a lot more consistent,' he said. 'In those two years out of the professional game I had to go away and find my bowling again. I have been given an opportunity in a side where I have had a captain in Mark Butcher who has looked after spin bowlers for a long time. He understands there are going to be bad balls and knows what kind of fields you need.'

BACK IN the Middlesex game, Phil Hughes greeted Schofield with disdain, as he had most English bowlers during his time in county cricket. He drove his first ball along the ground for four and sent the second climbing into the pavilion. Nineteen off his first over. This was a different Schofield, however, to the fragile figure of a few years earlier. This was a player on the way to being the country's leading wicket taker in the group stages of the Friends Provident Trophy; 20 victims in eight games and at least two every time he bowled. A few days after this game he would run through Sussex's order, taking 5 for 32 through thoughtful placement of his deliveries rather than an attempt at extravagant variations of turn.

Explaining his success in the shorter game, which always used to be a killing field for the slow men, Schofield suggested, 'In the Championship, batsmen can just tick over, rotate the strike and wait for the bad ball. In the one-day stuff I have always found it easier to tie somebody down, to try and make them hit big shots out of the ground. Hopefully, if you have got the field in the right place you can take wickets. I think I have a lot of variation in my action anyway and I have dropped the ball short a couple of times. I get a lot of variation in that way, not always putting it exactly where I want to, and I also have the variation of a googly and a flipper.'

Retained in the attack in the face of Hughes's assault, Schofield's right arm uncoiled again, a brisk motion from which he achieves effective changes of flight and pace. Hughes misjudged the length and edged his sweep to the keeper. Dawid Malan was bowled attempting the same shot. Middlesex, however, advanced to 169 for 3 with three overs remaining, 17 short of victory. After the dangerous Eoin Morgan was caught in the deep, Schofield returned for the penultimate over to have Billy Godleman stumped and to bowl Neil Dexter.

Three more wickets went in the frantic final over, leaving Middlesex one run behind Surrey in the most thrilling of draws. Relieved but relaxed, Chris Schofield left the field with the air of a man who had seen enough ups and downs in his career not to have his equanimity upset too much by the small matter of a last-ball finish.

09

ONLY A GAME

'You get other kids who just want to play cricket, while I preferred to keep my options open' – **Giles Haywood**

LONDON WAS offering the kind of weather that allowed West End workers to take their cigarette break in shirtsleeves. In a bright, sun-filled meeting room in the offices of a property investment company, Giles Haywood was pouring tea and discussing life after cricket. While many of his junior World Cup teammates had spent recent months in far flung corners of the world, wearing various England jerseys or accompanying county teams to warm-weather training in Portugal or Dubai, Haywood had been facing up to the challenges posed to his company by the global economic recession. It was still a welcome change, he admitted, from the many years of fretting over his batting average.

The end of his playing career had arrived less than three years after his part-time medium-pace bowling had proved such an important part of England's success in the final of 1998, when he had taken 3 for 18 off 10 overs to put the brakes on New Zealand's batsmen in Johannesburg. Most of his cricket beyond that had revolved around the often fruitless search of runs in county second elevens. He had played only one game of first-class cricket.

'It was a relief in the end,' he said of his departure from Nottinghamshire, his second county, after the summer of 2000. 'In business, essentially what you put in you should get out, given a bit of luck. With cricket, sometimes it just doesn't happen and you can beat yourself up thinking about why you are not scoring runs. At the time I stopped playing, I think if I had asked most players in the second team, "Are you enjoying it? Is this what you thought your life was going to be about?" – I don't think many would have said so.'

By the time Haywood left Trent Bridge, he was still only 20, but it had already been five years since he'd broken into the second team at Sussex. 'There was just so much cricket from when I was 17 or 18. I remember most of my mates planning to go to university and talking about taking the summer off. I was playing cricket every day of the week. There was just too much. If there had been one or two games less, then you could really prepare for it and really want it.'

The older generation commentators often scoff at the idea of more time off, especially for batsmen, claiming that no one ever improved their craft by not playing. In various crickets diaries written over the past two or three decades – by the likes of Bob Willis, Brian Brain, Jonathan Agnew and Justin Langer – the amount of cricket played has been a recurring theme. It is no surprise to hear such comments from seasoned, often world-weary professionals, but it says a lot when an 18 year old believes he is being forced to play too much. It probably reveals as much about Haywood as it does about the structure of cricket.

John Abrahams, his England Under-19 coach, offered, 'Giles would probably never have played for England, but he was capable of being a good bread and butter county player, a little bit in the Mark Ealham mould. Whether his heart was genuinely in it, I don't know. He had other skills and abilities and was an intelligent lad. Cricket was not the be all and end all for him.'

During the course of interviews with teammates, it was Haywood's whereabouts that most frequently prompted questions, his success in the world of business and commerce surprising no one. Still lean and athletic, he delivered the assessment of his career without regret or bitterness, acknowledging that he probably lacked the necessary single-mindedness. 'You could put it down to mental toughness at a young age and how much you really want it,' he suggested. 'I wanted it, but also I was at university and had other options. I knew that even if you finish cricket at 35, unless you are a fantastic cricketer or coach or commentator there is not a lot you can do in the game, so that was in the back of my mind. I'd always had other interests.'

Former colleague Stephen Peters remembered thinking, 'Giles always seemed destined to become something in the City. Some guys were really determined and others were just loving it at the time and have drifted off since – Giles and Jonathan Powell are a couple who spring to mind. You wondered if it was what they really wanted.'

Cricket had been the dominant part of Haywood's life from an early age, ever since his father, Ron, took him and older brother Marcus out into the cricket net he had erected in their back garden. 'I went to Lancing College from the age of 12 and during the summer it was just play, play, play. I had been pushed through to the Sussex youth set-up from about 11 and the coaching there was very good, very structured. Peter Moores was the first-team keeper when I was young and he was still playing when I was offered a contract at 16. I would play four or five games a week and my parents still say to me, "Do you remember those times when we used to drive you around the country?" You needed to be quite privileged to have parents who could do that. Dad was a property developer, self-employed, so he could take the time to do it.'

Haywood, a left-handed batsman whose professional heroes included Brian Lara and Hove's resident Australian, Michael Bevan, offered enough promise for Sussex to play him in three second-eleven games in 1995, before his 16th birthday. 'It was quite daunting,' he confessed. 'At that age you have not developed as an individual and I was quite shy. You go into a dressing room where there are established county cricketers and the captain and coach at that time was David Smith, a former England player, who was about 38 and coming to the end of his career. But the majority of my experience was very positive.'

Exposure to the realities of professional competition was offered a year later when he made his first-team debut in the Axa and Equity Law League against Derbyshire, scoring three after going in at number four. 'Dean Jones, the Australian batsman, was their captain and first ball he was fielding almost in my popping crease. That had never happened before; he was right in my face. It made you realise you were in with the big boys. They gave me a good working over but we won the game and it was a really good atmosphere. In youth cricket it was kind of "win one, lose one" but this win mattered. It was fantastic.'

The next milestone was reached in 1997, with a first call-up for the England Under-17 and Under-19 teams. In the latter he found himself batting just ahead of Andrew Flintoff, who would be making his Test debut within another year. 'Everyone knew what a fantastic cricketer he was from very young, and I think he thought he should be playing for Lancashire rather than in Under-19 cricket. In those days it was usual for counties to take their guys out of age group cricket and into first-class matches because they thought their time was better served there. I effectively replaced guys like Ben Hollioake and David Sales because they went to play for their counties. First-class cricket was the higher standard, especially if we were up against someone like Zimbabwe. It was a backward step for someone like Flintoff. These days, it seems that the important thing is playing for England at whatever level.'

Selection for the England Under-19s' winter programme in South Africa, including the World Cup, gave Haywood a chance to experience the feeling of being within a professional national set-up. 'It was around that time that there was a transition to become Team England,' he said, recalling the training camps at the Lilleshall sports centre. It was on those car journeys to the Shropshire countryside that he got to know teammate Robert Key. 'My parents would drive to Beckenham to pick him up. We roomed together at the beginning of the tour and became good mates. He was a great laugh, but so serious when he got the bat in his hand.'

The preparation left England's hopefuls under no illusion about the importance attached to their winter's endeavours. 'When I first started playing cricket some of the pre-season tours we went on with Sussex were pretty relaxed; a few drinks, get everyone together, enjoy a bit of sunshine. As the years went on it was getting more professional, especially with England with all the sponsorship that was coming in and the advisers, nutritionists, physios and the various support staffs. It was very well organised. We even had a journalist, John Stern, following us around. It made everyone very proud to be there. We were only young men, but we were professional cricketers. If someone stepped out of line we knew they would be dealt with, but John Abrahams was a great guy, very supportive and very determined to make sure we succeeded.

'It was a long trip and different people felt that differently – just as you see with the top guys these days. I remember the first few weeks as being very hard. We were young kids getting to know each other. A lot of us had not been abroad playing cricket and you have to learn about preparation, about when you can relax and go out for a drink. It took about six weeks before we really gelled and started enjoying each other's company. Then we didn't want it to stop. Having that time helped us in terms of the World Cup because if we had gone straight into it like some other countries we might have been having that difficult period during the tournament.'

Having played in one Test, Haywood was left on the sidelines for the opening World Cup game but became a fixture for the remainder of the tournament, batting in the lower middle order and bowling his economical medium pacers. 'I remember being really happy about being in the squad because it was a 50-50 decision,' he said. 'I had been on the fringes of the team and had played some Under-19 cricket in 1997, but I had not done particularly well. I was told that I was picked partly because I could bowl a bit. They saw me a bit more as an all-rounder, especially in the one-day games. I got on well with Ian Flanagan, even though we were probably competing for the same place. He was seen more as a four-day player.'

Never was Haywood's value to the team more evident than in the final at the Wanderers Stadium. Having bowled steadily, if unspectacularly, throughout the tournament, his nagging accuracy incapacitated the New Zealand batsmen after their fast start. His three victims included future internationals Hamish Marshall and Lou Vincent and he was the only England bowler to be given his full complement of 10 overs.

'That's the nature of one-day cricket,' he explained, eager to downplay his abilities as a match-winning bowler. 'Often your quicker guys tend to go the boundary quicker so you consolidate with a medium pacer who bowls straight, like a Dimi Mascarenhas, who can set the field back and keep it quiet. I could bowl straight and vary the pace a little bit, with the keeper standing up. I thought if I could get away with four or five an over it would be fantastic. But I was lucky enough to get a couple of early wickets and suddenly the Kiwis were under pressure. They were a couple of wickets down and they were thinking, "I have got to come to the wicket and smash it over the top." I think those guys were pretty nervous about the whole situation and the overs got away from them.'

Haywood's overriding memory of the triumph is 'relief that we had not let anyone down after all the preparation and investment' – a sentiment that seems somewhat lacking in the *joie de vivre* you might expect from a celebrating teenager. Or maybe he was being coy and the statement that 'we had a couple of days off in Johannesburg and the atmosphere was just brilliant' contains untold stories of Flintoff-like celebrations.

In any case, Haywood returned home with a realistic enough view of his contribution in South Africa not to misjudge his place in the cricketing universe. 'I didn't have a particularly good tour,' he admitted. 'I had a couple of good games and managed to play well in the final.' The course of his career over the next two years would ensure that his feet remained grounded. There were a couple of five-wicket hauls in the Sussex second team during the following summer and a place on the England Under-19 tour to New Zealand, but for someone who still saw himself primarily as a batsman, the runs never came in sufficient quantities. The 1999 season saw him play seven games as Sussex won Division Two of the 45-

over National League, while the highlight of a third summer in the England Under-19s was a one-day fifty against Australia. And there was his one and only appearance in first-class cricket, which produced scores of 14 and 1 and bowling figures of 0 for 66 against Leicestershire.

'I thought 1998 was when I was going to break into the first team but it was a quiet year for me,' he said ruefully. 'I should have really got stuck into second-eleven cricket and scored a lot of runs, but it didn't happen.' Without looking to lay the blame elsewhere, he did voice a view shared by fellow-batsman Flanagan that varied advice from different sources didn't help his game. 'In some respects you are getting too much attention at that age. You are in the England set-up and getting people like John Abrahams telling you something. Then your county coaches would tell you something different. And then you have got your dad, and other people and players, and then you have got your own mind. I think it comes back to maturity and having confidence in your own game.'

Haywood also recalled realising too late that the game was mostly hard work. 'Part of the problem with me was that at a young level I realised I could play quite a few shots and I was really pampered. That is not what it is all about. I remember Chris Adams telling me in a net session that early in his career he had been getting 20s and 30s and the Derbyshire members were slating him, but then something clicked. He started playing for himself. Four-day cricket is more about mental toughness than hitting the ball out of the ground.'

Without the runs in the longer game to force him up the Sussex pecking order, Haywood had to content himself with being seen as a bits-and-pieces one-day player. 'That is where you can get away with bowling a few tight overs and batting a bit, but in a lot of those games I wasn't really given the chance. You come in at number seven or eight after Chris Adams has hit a hundred, you are given three or four overs at the end and people look at your average at the end of the season and think, "You have not done that well, have you?" What you should be doing is getting those hundreds in second team cricket, being selfish and doing the best you can. But in my last game for Sussex seconds I batted at eight. They sat down at end of season and said, "You haven't come on as you should have as a batsman." They felt I had not progressed in terms of the scores I was getting.'

Haywood was 'gutted and upset' when told of his release by Sussex and believes he should have concentrated solely on his studies at Sussex University after that 1999 season. Instead, he quickly accepted when Nottinghamshire second-eleven coach Mick Newell called and asked, 'Do you fancy coming up for a couple of trial games?'

He explained, 'I didn't think about quitting but I should have done. I got a great offer from a fantastic club but I should have left it two or three years, finished my degree and gone back to club cricket. Then, at 22 or 23, if I thought it was right, I could have gone back to Sussex and asked for a few second-eleven games. Peter Moores said at the time said that the door was not shut completely. I didn't have any problem with that, but I wanted to prove people wrong.'

In Nottingham, Haywood lived with another World Cup teammate, Paul Franks. But while his friend was establishing himself as one of the county's leading bowlers and earning England selection, Haywood was having to content himself with the odd game in the one-day team. His performances in the second eleven failed to match the early promise of an April century against Surrey. 'Towards the end of the season I am thinking, "Is this it? What am I doing playing second-team cricket at Worksop and Middlesbrough?" I spoke to Mick Newell and said I was going to finish. I was rushing back and forth from Sussex University doing exams and it was like a breath of fresh air to stop playing. I think they might have released me anyway.'

For a while, Haywood played club cricket for Steyning 'because they were paying a bit of money on Saturdays and it was only once a week so I enjoyed it'. But having completed his geography degree and then qualified as a chartered surveyor, the business world was more than enough to satisfy any remaining competitive urges. 'We take money from investors and put it mainly into commercial properties,' he explained. 'It is tough times at the moment. Among our investors are some of the big names who are struggling. But we have got money to spend this year and we are just waiting for the right opportunity to come along. If we can get two or three fantastic deals in the next couple of years rather than five or six average ones we will be very happy.'

As far as cricket is concerned, Haywood's ambitions lie away from the field. 'My dad and I have started to sponsor a team in Hastings, supporting their youth cricket,' he said as he ventured out of his office into the tree-lined London square, sidestepping workers on their way to grab an early lunch. 'I'd like to get to know more people and get into cricket administration. Maybe fund-raising or owning a cricket club. But not as a career. Cricket could never be my sole thing.'

10

THE SEASON AFTER THE NIGHT BEFORE

'Sometimes if you take an opportunity it can be the difference between having a career or not' – **Graham Napier**

RIGHT PLACE, right time. It was becoming the hallmark of a career that was brought blinking into the sunlight on a mid-summer evening in Chelmsford in 2008 after a decade hidden away in rarely-inspected corners of county changing rooms.

That Graham Napier chose an occasion when the cameras of Sky Sports were in attendance to crash 152 off 58 balls in a Twenty20 Cup game against Sussex – including 16 sixes, a world record for that format of the game – had proved as fortuitous as the BBC Wales decision 40 years earlier to send a camera crew to Swansea on the day Garry Sobers became the first man to hit six sixes in an over. Sobers, of course, was already a superstar but his feat needed the elixir of the camera to give it immortality. In the same way, the repeats of Napier's shots flying to all corners of Essex made him a living, breathing celebrity in his sport rather than a footnote in the next day's newspapers.

Almost a year later, his name inked into the England squad for the World Twenty20, Napier explained, 'In the past 12 months I have gone from looking at careers outside cricket to potentially having a few more years and being successful with it. I had a year to run on my contract with Essex but I was starting to get application forms together for training or jobs so that I had something behind me. If this year didn't work out, I would have had something to fall back on.'

Suddenly, at the age of 28, Napier's life had gone from that of a journeyman county player to a media darling; his story of overnight success after a decade in the game captivating a public eager to get behind the underdog. Speaking after a post-training shower and before dashing to yet another television engagement, he recalled receiving a congratulatory phone call from Sir Elton John, although at first he thought it was a practical joke by his teammates.

'There has been lots of that – not calls from Elton John, but other strange stuff. I have gone from obscurity to rushing off and having to do things with the media. Managing your time becomes quite a priority, achieving the balance between your cricket, which is what has got you there in the first place, and getting enough time to do stuff with the media that helps to promote you. There is no experience that could ever have prepared me for this, but if it had happened when I was a bit younger it would have been easy to let it all get blown out of proportion. I have been able to maintain a realistic approach towards it all. I can deal with things better than I would have done as a naïve young player. But even now there are times when it gets on top of you and you need some time away from it.'

He continued, however, 'I am trying to do as much media stuff as I can and to be involved in reporting on cricket at some stage would be great. You get the lifestyle without having to actually play! The media is a very fickle world, especially TV, but it is an area I would like to use and look into – although I know there will only ever be four or five who make it out of every hundred who want to do it.' He had also revived his personal internet site, saying, 'It is a way to capitalise. If people are interested in you it is a good opportunity to show them what you are about. Sportsmen's careers are very short. You are a long time retired so you need other means to survive in the real world.'

Napier's elevation to his first full England squad, and his progress further towards the centre of the cricketing spotlight, had received additional assistance by once again being in the right location. As the spring of 2009 approached and the England Lions party in New Zealand began losing its players to cover for injuries in the full England squad in the Caribbean, Napier was the obvious choice to fill the gap. Not only had his performances on the field been elevated to new levels since his heroics of the previous summer, he just happened to be planning a few days fishing on Lake Taupo after finishing a stint with Wellington during New Zealand's first-class season.

Yet his summons to join the Lions for their one-day engagements against New Zealand was down to more than lucky geography. His name had been bandied about as a possible England candidate ever since his eye-popping hitting at Chelmsford. Partly, his case owed something to new-car syndrome; that experience of buying a make you'd previously been unfamiliar with and then spending the next few weeks seeing them on every street corner. Once he had a name, people began noticing his performances, which had included thumping six sixes in an innings of 61 in the Friends Provident Trophy semi-final against Yorkshire not along after his Twenty20 century.

'What I can do is try to be consistent in my performances and win as many games for Essex as possible,' he explained. 'How many games I can contribute to is a mark of where I am and how I am playing. On the batting front, I have put together some innings where I might previously have got out for 15. Now if I get 40 and up the run rate and get us across the line then it becomes a bit of a headline for Sky or the papers, so it does help in being recognised.'

Essex coach Paul Grayson said that 'we have probably seen the real Graham Napier in last 18 months'. He continued, 'He has found his game and taken a bit more responsibility upon himself. I sat him down last season and we tried to focus on the things that he is good at. In the past people had perhaps focused on what he couldn't do. So what can he do? Well, he can bowl the white ball in the mid-80s, touching 90, and he can hit the ball out of the ground. A lot of people in county cricket can't do that. I think he has felt quite confident in the environment we have created and obviously he expressed himself last year.'

Despite his eye-catching batting, it was his performances with the ball in New Zealand that had made him a valid option when Kent's Amjad Khan flew off to the England tour of the West Indies. As well as being joint leading wicket-taker in the State Twenty20 group games, he had the second-highest number of victims in both the 50-over State Shield and the four-day State Championship prior to his departure at the half-way stage of the competition. 'People still forget that I actually bowl,' he laughed. 'But it was my form with the ball that contributed most to the call-up.'

England had been held to draws in both four-day 'Test' matches against their New Zealand counterparts, the bowlers being unable to get the necessary wickets after their batsmen had posted big totals – echoes of their senior counterparts. When the two 50-over games arrived, Napier was straight into the line-up, with national selector Geoff Miller commenting, 'We've been monitoring Graham's progress for some time.'

Anyone in Palmerston North would have liked what they saw from Napier, if not from an England team that failed by 35 runs to match New Zealand's 373. He muscled 74 off only 41 balls, having earlier taken three wickets in his 10 overs, albeit at the cost of 74 runs. 'I was pleased with the way I started with the new ball,' he said. 'My first two bowling spells went to plan but then my last couple of overs spoiled my figures. I was able to free myself up with the bat and got away quickly.' More modest performances with both bat and ball followed in the second one-day international and the only Twenty20 contest, both comfortable New Zealand victories, but proof that Napier had established himself in the selectors' thoughts came in the announcement of England's squad for the summer tournament back home.

No one was more delighted at Napier's belated recognition than his former England Under-19 coach, John Abrahams. 'There are some people who you would really like to be successful,' he said. 'I am glad to see that what Graham has always done is now showing benefits. He has a very simple approach to the game and loves playing cricket. He knows he can hit the ball hard and straight and can bowl quickly wicket to wicket. Twenty20 is his game. For a while he put himself under pressure and would let people's perception of what he could do affect the way he was playing. For example, he would go out and start playing risky shots too early. He has worked his socks off, is a fine physical specimen – maybe a bit muscle-bound if anything – but I am glad to see him succeed.'

Napier's previous sniff of international recognition had been a place in England's provisional squad of 30 for the Champions Trophy in 2004, preceded by selection for the England A tour of Malaysia and India earlier in the year. Before that, of course, had been his contribution to the Under-19 World Cup victory. 'I remember beginning the summer after that being full of confidence as an 18 year old. I was just starting to break into the side when I broke down with injury a month into the season. It was a major injury, a stress fracture in my back, and took me out of bowling for two years. I ended up having a screw put in my back that is there for life. I began bowling again in 2001 and it took me a season or two to gradually build up. Then I was named in the 30-man squad for the Champions Trophy and was just starting to think I would be pushing again when I got another injury. They haven't struck at the right time.' And with an England shirt finally within his grasp, he added quickly, 'I am going to be wrapped in cotton wool for the next few weeks!'

The Popeye-like upper body strength, accentuated by the tight-fitting modern one-day uniforms, was well disguised by the smart jacket Napier was wearing for his TV appearance as he recalled the Under-19 tour to South Africa. It had been there that he had developed his passion for the gymnasium, several years before Twenty20 cricket had given him the perfect opportunity to put his muscles to good use. 'A few of us went to a youth tournament in Bermuda with the Under-17 side earlier in the year and saw it as an opportunity to get picked for the Under-19 World Cup team,' he said. 'We won the tournament and I scored a few runs in most of the games. I played in the Under-19 Tests against Zimbabwe in the summer and was named the squad for South Africa to cap it all off.

'My role was first-change bowler and to have a bit of a dash down the order, although I probably wasn't as sure about what I was good at then as I am now. The coaches made us realise that if you want to play at the top level there is a lot of hard work. I did a lot of training on that tour and discovered what an advantage going to the gym could be to me. During the season these days I don't spend as much time in the gym as I would like but in the off-season I am there for three or four quality sessions a week. I work on my strength. I am not a great runner, although I have to do it because it is part of the job. But strength work helps my all-round game and I have always enjoyed it.'

The only one of three brothers to pursue sport to any serious degree, Napier had progressed through the Essex age-group teams to earn England recognition and was one of the youngest players on the South African tour. Giles Haywood said, 'I love Napes. He was the guy everyone took the piss out of in the changing room but he took it well and made jokes about himself. My clearest memory of him is that he could never understand why, when people got out, they smashed their kit up. Keysy used to smash his coffin and Napes said to him, "If you respect your kit, your kit will respect you." We all went, "What? What does that mean?"'

Like all the other bowlers, Napier had little success in the Test matches, but was able to chip with regular wickets during the World Cup, his figures becoming more economical as the tournament progressed. 'We were a bit dejected about our performances going into it, but in a way it loosened us up. The shackles came off.' It was Napier's dismissal of the New Zealand openers and his bowling partnership with Haywood that turned the final in England's favour. 'We made a terrible start and we had to drag it back. When Giles and I came on there were about five or six maidens in a row and suddenly the rate was back down to about four an over and we were able to pin them down. It was a good deck with a bit of pace in it. We knew we had managed to keep them to reasonable score, but we never expected to see Steve Peters play the innings he did.'

The back injury Napier suffered after returning from South Africa led to a complete re-shaping of his bowling technique. 'I used to have a more traditional side-on action and now it has changed to more front-on,' he explained. 'While I couldn't bowl for two years it was at least an opportunity to concentrate on my batting, which was a good thing for me. I gained some better technique and I am seeing the benefit now.'

In 2001, Napier achieved a maiden first-class century against Cambridge University and earned a run in the first eleven late in the season on the back of an innings of 73 and six wickets in a Norwich Union League game against Worcestershire. An appearance on the losing team in the Benson and Hedges Cup final against Warwickshire was one of the big moments of 2002 – run out for 17 batting at number three – but it was 2003 when his new bowling technique brought its most significant rewards. His 33 wickets in the National League at a little over 16 was a season record for his county and helped earn him a place in the England Academy squad to go to Malaysia and India. The following summer he followed up with another 25 National League wickets and averaged more than 35 with the bat in first-class cricket.

For the next three years, however, injuries and inconsistency found him bouncing between Essex's first and second teams. In the winter of 2007-08 he got away from it all by walking to the Everest Base Camp to support the Professional Cricketers' Association Benevolent Fund and then travelled on to New Zealand. Although he'd arrived to play club cricket, he ended up replacing England Lions recruit Charlie Shreck in the Wellington side. 'It's a good standard,' he explained. 'There's only a limited number of teams so the talent is concentrated. There's a bit of a break in the games so you get to practise, recover and get to the gym.'

Despite that positive experience, he arrived at the 2008 English season aware of his mortality as a professional cricketer and wondering if skills such as his interest in photography could perhaps be translated into a career away from the sport. Then, late in June, came the evening when Essex sent him in at number three and watched him change the course of his career. 'It is very much a blur,' he said. 'I wasn't consciously trying to remember it at the time, although I have watched it a few times since. I have tried to take all the best bits out of the innings and use them in mental preparation, visualisation and cementing techniques, knowing what works for me.'

In the wake of his historic knock, he achieved enough consistency to finish the season with a bowling average of 26 in all competitions, including 16 wickets as Essex reached the last four of the Twenty20 Cup. His important contributions to the team's further success in the Friends Provident Trophy and Division Two of the NatWest Pro40 led to a two-year contract extension at Essex through to the end of 2011. County coach Grayson said, 'We didn't play him in the first few matches in four-day cricket last year but he scored consistent runs and took wickets in the shorter games and eventually forced us to get him into the Championship side as well. He can change the game when he bats; people come out of the marquees to watch him. Hopefully we are going to get even more consistency from him over the next few years. He has matured as person and as a cricketer and the next three or four years should be best of his career. He had that big knock on TV, he is happy and confident and his skill levels have improved.'

That was also clearly the view of Indian Premier League team Mumbai Indians, who provided Napier with another exciting spin-off from his new-found status in his profession. Having not yet played full international cricket, he was free to cut his own IPL deal outside the regulations of the league's auction – which, incidentally, he did without the services of an agent. Although a few had offered their services, he explained, 'I can manage without it. Agents are not interested in you; they are just looking to make money.'

So it was that Napier had arrived home from Lions duties in New Zealand preparing to join the likes of Sachin Tendulkar, Sanath Jayasuriya and Dwayne Bravo in Mumbai. Yet barely had he started browsing his Berlitz guide book than Shashank Manohar, head of the Board of Control for Cricket in India, was announcing, 'Due to the attitude of the government that it cannot provide security for the tournament we are forced to move the IPL out of India.'

After the terrorist attacks on the Sri Lanka team in the Pakistani city of Lahore a few weeks earlier, security had become the main issue of concern for the league as it planned its second season. Despite offering the Indian government several alternative schedules, the IPL had to concede defeat. There was simply no way for local security forces to cope with the increased demands of the tournament at a time when they were stretched to handle the drawn-out voting process of the Indian general election.

The IPL needed a new home and, for a dizzying 24 hours, England and Wales emerged ahead of South Africa as the leading contender, being the apparent preference of the eight team owners. Then, on the day that the IPL's official website quoted a BCCI official saying 'it is 99 per cent England', the spring sunshine gave way to eye-watering winds and swirling rain, and someone remembered that this was Britain they were talking about. In April and May. When it rains. A lot. And even if it didn't, a game starting at 11.30 a.m. – as many would have to in order to suit the Indian TV schedule – offered the prospect of batsmen in two sweaters collapsing against a wildly swinging ball on a green pitch. A wet Wednesday morning in Derby was definitely not the showbiz setting the organisers had in mind when they launched their competition.

South Africa it was and, having got over the disappointment of missing out on the full Bollywood experience that was the IPL's first season, Napier joined his fellow-Englishmen in expressing regret at not being able to sleep in their own beds during the tournament. 'It would have been a great experience in front of the Indian fans, but South Africa will also be a very exciting experience. There is always the chance of April showers back here and there is a massive difference in the pitches and conditions between South Africa and England at the moment.'

Napier's involvement with the IPL was to be minimal but rewarding nevertheless. Limited to a two-week stint by the need to play some part in Essex's Friends Provident Trophy campaign, he sat out the first few IPL games behind his team's more illustrious recruits. Finally, he was named to bat at number six against the Kolkata Knight Riders and was caught for 15 when he hit a Chris Gayle full toss to deep square leg. Given the new ball, he took 1 for 27 in his four overs in a 10-run victory for the Indians.

He flew home with not a moment's regret about his adventure. 'It was a great experience. Out of everything that has happened since last summer, that topped it all,' he insisted. 'It was great working with coaches like Shaun Pollock and Jonty Rhodes and to play with Tendulkar is something to bore the grandchildren with. The franchises there are very shrewd in how they pick their sides. They have owners with a lot of money who want to win the tournament. To be one of only seven English players involved certainly would have helped progress me into the England Twenty20 side.'

Any further advancement in his career would, Napier knew, depend on continuing to deliver the performances of the previous 12 months. A place in the England one-day international squad remained a tantalising possibility, although he described such ambition as 'not a goal as such because you don't want to be disappointed if it doesn't happen, but it is something you can aim for'.

Self-improvement, though, remained a very realistic, attainable objective. He concluded, 'If you stop trying to improve you are not going anywhere. You should always be trying to iron out flaws.' And, of course, there was the new experience of being one of the players the opposition were targeting. 'There is pressure when I walk on to the pitch now because people regard me as a dangerous player rather than someone who could be dangerous. With that comes confidence of knowing I am a problem to them. That has helped me. I am a much more relaxed player than I was a year ago because I have had some success out of it.'

Discussing his technique at the crease, Napier explained that the key against bowlers trying to deliver run-saving yorkers was to 'set yourself deep in the crease so if he doesn't quite get the length you have a good distance to get underneath the ball and hit it straight'. He added, 'If [the bowler] tries to chuck in some variations you can look to drag a bit and hit towards the mid-wicket area. Another get-out could be walking across the crease and just turning it to short fine leg. Someone like Eoin Morgan can get down and reverse sweep the fast bowler, but that is not really my cup of tea. I want to be hitting the ball straight back down the ground. There are no fielders behind the bowler and most grounds are not a long hit straight.'

He also has the lessons of his unforgettable night in June 2008 with him every time he bats. 'There was a time towards the end of that innings when it was a case of not having to worry about anything,' he said, smiling at the memory. 'It became a question of pushing myself to see what I could do, where could I hit the ball. Could I manipulate the field and manipulate the bowlers into bowling the ball where I wanted to hit it? I have been able to take that out of the innings and use it in to my advantage in other games.'

ENGLAND EXPECTS

'It really hurts me. Certain people get six, seven, eight months in the Test side not performing and then I have two bad Test matches and I am out. That is just bizarre'
– **Owais Shah**

NOTHING IN the cricketing career of Owais Shah, it seemed, was straightforward. He'd ended his comeback Test in Antigua feeling he had advanced his cause to be his country's long-term number three and looking forward to a productive stint in the Indian Premier League. Yet as he sat chatting on a sun-drenched bench in the Harris Memorial Garden behind the Lord's pavilion a few months later, someone else had been scoring consecutive centuries in his position in the England team and his IPL experience had amounted to three weeks sitting in the Delhi Daredevils' dug-out in South Africa.

By the time England lost the series in the West Indies by virtue of their defeat in Jamaica, Shah had stumbled backwards in the queue of candidates to face Australia in the summer's Ashes series. Temperament, more than technique, was the issue in question – the one aspect of a batsman's game that can't be worked on in the nets. In only one of his Tests in the Caribbean had he unequivocally failed; but in two others he had run himself out when a big first-innings score was there for the taking, before falling cheaply in search of quick second-innings runs. Throw in an attack of the cramps, his habitually skittish behaviour at the crease and the emergence of a new middle-order rival, and one wondered how quickly his failure to confirm his suitability for the highest level of international cricket would become an assumption by the selectors that he never would.

There was still that nagging feeling that he didn't quite fit in, even in the post-Duncan Fletcher era, and that he would not be granted the patience afforded others in the previous year or two. It was perhaps why he had seemed so subdued on the first day of the fourth Test in Barbados, where, having watched Andrew Strauss and Alastair Cook pass 200 for the first wicket, he'd laboured for an hour over seven runs before cutting Sulieman Benn to slip. One writer described his efforts as 'inept'. Once the same bowler had trapped him leg before for 21 on a meaningless final day, his newly-won place appeared under threat. Replacing the injured Andrew Flintoff, the precocious Essex batsman Ravi Bopara had ridden his luck all the way to a bright and carefree 103, although he would sit out the final Test in Trinidad to allow England to play five bowlers in search of the win required to level the series.

The importance of Shah's innings on the first day at Port of Spain appeared not to be lost on him and it was 40 minutes before he got off the mark with a quick single – always a panic-inducing event in his case. He had already edged short of the slips and twice been struck dangerously on the pads.

Regrettably, his natural manner at the crease does give the impression of an attack of nerves but, to be honest, he looks no less twitchy when he has three figures to his name. 'I am just fidgety,' he said. 'It might come across as nervy, but that's life.' Jeremy Snape, off-spinner turned sports psychologist to the South African team explained to author Lawrence Booth in *Cricket, Lovely Cricket?* that players' mannerisms are not so much indicators of panic than they are the pathway by which the batsman takes himself from conscious analysis of the task in hand to instinctive execution. They can also help to block out external influences such as the taunts of the fielders and the bloodlust of a fired-up crowd.

This is not to say that Shah refutes entirely the accusations of tension at the crease. 'I believe everyone gets nervous. I get nervous when I am batting whether I am on one or 150 because I don't want to get out,' he admitted. 'I want to play well and I want to get more and more runs. But I have found a way of being consistent. What what works for me day-in and day-out at county level, I am going to apply that for England. I believe the game is the same; it is just the environment that is different.' And, of course, in the same way that David Gower's relaxed air did not mean he didn't care, so Shah's twitchiness doesn't mean he is dreading every delivery. Even so, when he drove two consecutive deliveries to the boundary in Trinidad, first straight and then through the covers, everyone calmed a little.

But then an old enemy was to arrive unbidden on the scene. The heat and humidity were proving more challenging than the West Indian attack, reduced by selection to only three regular bowlers and relying heavily on Brendan Nash bowling his left-arm dobbers to a tightly-packed off-side field. In mid-afternoon, with only 29 against his name off 115 balls, Shah experienced the familiar grip of cramp in his left arm. With fingers curled involuntarily into his palms like an arthritic, he winced as England physiotherapist Kirk Russell attempted to massage some life back into his hand. It quickly became clear that he needed to retire, just as he had during his debut Test innings in India. Among the critical members of the media, the episode was seen as a sign of hyper-tension or lack of fitness, either of which, it was said, rendered Shah unsuitable for the role of a Test match number three.

Yet Simon Timson, the ECB's Head of Science and Medicine, is quick to defend both the player and his preparation. 'Cramps are like injuries,' he explained later. 'It is not an exact science knowing when it is going to happen. With Owais we took him off and got the right electrolytes in him. It is a case of making sure he drinks in morning, drinks in the run-up to play and during it. He was unlucky. He is fit, does the right things and doesn't drink [alcohol]. The players are educated to do the right things. Unfortunately it happened to Owais in a goldfish bowl, but I don't think it fair to judge him on that. Judge him on the runs he scores and way he performs.'

In the evening session, instead of punishing the bowling of Ryan Hinds and Chris Gayle, Shah sat in his pads watching Paul Collingwood starting to compile his second century of the series. The Durham man's low back-lift and flat-footed appearance at the crease make him only a fraction as pleasing on the eye as Shah in full flow, but how England's number three must have wished for the same effectiveness. He was becoming a difficult man for people to love; a drama queen some felt. This time 'a bizarre cameo' was the description his innings had attracted.

The following morning, after Strauss's third consecutive first-innings hundred had been curtailed, Shah was back in the middle. He drove his second delivery handsomely past the bowler for four, but then set off on a risky single to mid-wicket, a position being filled by all-rounder Dwayne Bravo, aiding his recovery from injury with a stint as twelfth man. He swiftly picked up and, with a flick of the wrist, scored a direct hit on the stumps. The leaden-footed Shah had appeared mesmerised by Bravo's dexterity. Against an attack that clearly had no great ambition, Shah had given himself up.

Late on day four, he was batting again. This time, no sooner had the thought been delivered that the pursuit of quick runs might be just what he needed to give him the freedom play a more attacking innings, he bottom-edged a wide delivery from Lionel Baker and was gone for a single. When Kevin Pietersen replaced him at the crease and duly reached three figures, it was England's eighth century in three Tests, none of them from the pivotal position of first wicket down. While five English batsmen averaged more than 50 in the series, not including Bopara's century in his only knock, Shah had struggled to get above 20.

The road to redemption proved not to lay along the course of a cumbersome five-game series of one-day internationals. While his critics looked for him to play the match-defining innings that had been lacking in the longer game, Shah, publicly at least, turned away suggestions that he was once again auditioning for his Test place. 'It is a one-day series as far as I am concerned. I have played enough cricket to not get too far ahead of myself. I know I can play the game and it is just a matter of scoring my runs.'

Having entered the series as England's most in-form batsman in the 50-over game, Shah's return in the 3-2 series win was somewhat disappointing. Since the beginning of the 2008 English season, he'd averaged 46 and his consistently inventive scoring had been one of the few bright spots of a 5-0 series defeat in India. Yet after scoring 62 in the opening game in Guyana, he made only 22 and 17 in the next two contests, was not needed in a rain-reduced victory in game four and holed out tamely for six in the decider. He'd stuck around just long enough to create the impression that his game had lost its edge at the end of a long and often frustrating tour.

'I WAS told I didn't play very well in the last two Test matches; that was the reason I was given by the selectors for being dropped.' That was how Shah, continuing his conversation in the shadow of English cricket's most iconic building, explained the end of his brief tenure as his country's Test match number three. Instead, Bopara had been the player coming down those famous Lord's pavilion steps when England began their home series against the West Indies.

'They gave me a little run and I got 50 in my first innings back. Then I had an average Test match and a not very good one.' Shah shrugged and continued. 'So you can go from playing really well, to not playing well in two Test matches and find yourself out of the team. That doesn't tell me much apart from the fact that, literally, as soon as you didn't perform you were out of there. I admit I didn't play very well in those other two games, but I played very well in that Test in Antigua. To me it is very surprising that if you have two bad matches you are out. It hurts me a little bit. I have been playing consistently in the one-day internationals and people know what I can do. If I have two bad one-day games I don't get dropped, but it happened in Test matches.'

When reminded of the long runs of ill-form that more established England players have been able to indulge in during recent times, Shah threw open his arms and said, 'Exactly. It really hurts me. Certain people get six, seven, eight months in the Test side not performing and then I have two bad Test matches and I am out. That is just bizarre. But it is the way English cricket is and you can't worry about anything except putting yourself in position to be the next cab off the rank and saying, "Look, I am still here performing so you have got to create a space for me because I am a good enough player."

'I have performed very well for England over the last two or three years in the one-dayers. And I certainly believe I can take that form into Test matches because although I have had two bad Tests I have had some bloody good Test matches as well. People don't ever say that. It is always, "You had two bad matches. See you later, you are out." And, to me, that is not a very good environment, not just for me but youngsters coming through. If a youngster comes in and has two bad Test matches, does that mean he is out and sitting back playing for his county? That is not the right way to go about things. But that has happened and you have got to move on quickly and say, "I accept that. I am going to be the next man in line." I always bring it back to what I control. I need to go and perform and if I am performing well, then I am the next man in.'

Shah's vacillation between anger and philosophical acceptance suggested a man being careful to emphasise professional ambition rather than burn bridges. 'I definitely do believe in fate,' he added. 'I work out what I have to do to get to a place and, after that, if you don't control it you don't worry about it. I don't pick the England team'

It was interesting, a few days later, to hear the sympathetic views of a man who did pick the team for a long time. David Graveney, chairman of England selectors throughout Shah's years of pressing for his Test debut, said, 'Owais is very talented and I suppose, on reflection, when judging batsmen you do need to be able to give them decent run because it is probably harder to be able to assess a batsmen than it is a bowler. When you make a mistake as a batsman or other people make errors, like the umpire, it becomes difficult. Owais has been on the fringes and people who have been involved in selection may reflect that for his development it might have been better if he'd had a decent run in the team, but you can't pick everybody. He is still involved and has progressed, but has not had as many opportunities as he would have liked to play in the senior team.'

Shah's eventual elevation at the expense of Ian Bell had been endorsed by most experts, some of whom felt it was an overdue move, yet Shah appeared to have few supporters left by the start of the English season. As had been the case ever since he burst on the scene as a precocious teenager – maybe because of that – he remains a player about whom the media have strong opinions and pet theories. Angus Fraser, who has been Shah's teammate and manager, as well as a former newspaper correspondent, once said that 'few modern players in England have been misunderstood more'. It is a view with which Shah agrees.

'With the media, mate, I believe there is always something they want to talk about,' he sighed. 'They talk about my grip; they are constantly going on about me being nervous or tense, bla bla bla. But that is one person's view and I can respect that because generally the guys commentating have played a lot of cricket and captained England and are great players, legends in the game. But it doesn't necessarily make them great commentators or coaches.'

Yet there is always the fear that, in a media-driven age, if enough people say the same things often enough, they become difficult for the selectors to ignore. 'I think it probably does [have an effect]. It is the way English cricket is and the way English media is. It does get into their minds, but what can I do about it? What can I do about not looking nervous? I am not going to worry about not looking nervous; the only thing I am going to worry about is being consistent.'

More eyebrows had been raised in Shah's direction when he joined the Delhi Daredevil for three weeks instead of, as some saw it, staying in England to fight for his Test place. When he, along with Delhi teammate Paul Collingwood, was left to deliver drinks to the likes of A.B. de Villiers and Tillekaratne Dilshan, the tut-tutting grew even louder. His decision to sit out his county's game against the touring South Africans when he had been vying for a Test place the previous summer was dredged up as further evidence against either his commitment or his smart-thinking.

John Abrahams, defending the player he'd seen average more than 58 in Under-19 Tests, suggested, 'Enigma is the right word for him. Owais would be totally honest with himself and, although there would be an element of wondering if he has always been treated fairly, he would also ask if he had done enough. He is naturally talented and has worked out a method for himself that has been successful at county level and occasionally at international level. He has not changed over the years and is still a lovely lad. He has always behaved with dignity and for people to say he doesn't care is wrong. He cares a hell of a lot.'

Yet former England fast bowler Darren Gough had fumed, 'What are Collingwood and Shah doing there? Not playing cricket, that's for sure. They are just sitting on their backsides. It's disgraceful and embarrassing that they are not playing. They went to the IPL for the money. This has cost Shah his England place.' This perhaps seemed a bit rich coming from someone who had once asked not to be selected for an England trip to Pakistan and instead ended up prancing around on *Strictly Come Dancing*. Others felt it was hard to dispute the logic on offer and that each day Shah spent as a Delhi cheerleader resulted in his Test place disappearing further into the distance. Having signed up for the IPL at a time when he was out of the Test team, maybe he could have reassessed his priorities after his experiences in the West Indies. Even his pre-tournament claim that the England players 'can get valuable experience under our belts with the World Twenty20 being held just two months away' had lost its previous legitimacy.

'I don't know if people held that against me, but I hope not,' he said. 'For me to get runs in two four-day games; does that really determine whether I am good enough to play Test cricket? I have done it for the last seven or eight years and I was good enough to go on the last few Test tours. If you are putting it down to two four-day games that is just petty. They either think you are good enough or they think, "Get him out of here because we want someone else." That is fine and I can accept that but don't tell me the reason you are not being picked is because you didn't play those two four-day games.'

AT THE time when Shah and his international colleagues had arrived in the West Indies in January, Robert Key was still the only Under-19 World Cup winner to have been given a run in the England Test team, while Shah, Graeme Swann and Chris Schofield had played two Tests each for a combined total among the group of 21 games. In the same 11-year time frame following the first youth World Cup in 1988, the England players from that tournament had racked up almost 300 Test appearances. Michael Atherton had captained England a record 54 times and had played most of his 115 Tests, while Nasser Hussain had become established in the middle order and would soon be leading the team.

Mark Ramprakash, although never fulfilling his potential at the top level, had played the bulk of his 52 Tests. Chris Lewis had played 32, Warren Hegg had been behind the stumps in two and Martin Bicknell had also been capped. Whereas Shah and Swann were still considered promising but unproven at the age of 30, Atherton, Hussain and Ramprakash had achieved the status of experienced veterans by the same age.

Perhaps the success of the 1988 group was just a quirk of nature. Having emerged in a period when national selection was renowned for its inconsistency and the England set-up less embracing of the age-group players, you would expect the return to be less than that of a squad that achieved greater success in the Under-19 arena. Yet of the seven members of the 1998 side still playing first-class cricket in 2009, only one now appeared likely to see any Test match action during the summer – although four had been named in the World Twenty20 squad.

Swann had begun the season well enough to be the favourite to own the spinner's berth in all forms of the game, while Shah's Caribbean struggles made it probable that he would be restricted to one-day duty. Key's poor start to the season had ended discussion of him being an Ashes outsider, but, along with Graham Napier, he was booked in for the 20-over festival. Paul Franks had long been absent from selection discussions, while Chris Schofield, a Test player briefly in 2000, had returned in the first World Twenty20 as recently as two years earlier. He believed his injury-hit 2008 season, during which he had freakishly broken both thumbs, had cost him any hope of the England recall for which his wickets in the Friends Provident Trophy might have made a sound case. 'I felt there was still an opportunity to play Twenty20 and one-day internationals for England but because of injury last year my name got overlooked,' he said.

At Northamptonshire, Stephen Peters was the personification of the phrase 'honest county pro', the only one of the class of '98 still in first-class cricket who had never played for England, despite the expectations of observers and his teammates. Shah recalled him as the man most likely to go on to a successful Test career, 'The guy gets a hundred in the final and was one of our main batsmen, but after the Under-19s he didn't really kick on. It is disappointing because I have known Stephen since he was 15 and he always looked a good player.'

Peters had fought to come to terms with never having measured up to the optimistic projections about his career. 'Being realistic, unless I get six hundreds in my first six innings and there are a couple of injuries, I won't get a game,' he'd admitted as he began the season with a career batting average of 32.60. 'My time has probably gone.'

He had, though, come within a few inches of a place on the open-top bus tour that celebrated England's Ashes victory of 2005. Durham's Gary Pratt ended up waving to the crowds along with the hung-over Andrew Flintoff thanks to his famous run out of Aussie captain Ricky Ponting as twelfth man at Trent Bridge. In the previous game at Old Trafford, Ponting had helped his team hold out for a draw on the last day after Peters, the substitute fielder, just missed out a moment of Pratt-like immortality with eight wickets down. 'I couldn't believe they set off,' said Peters of Ponting's push into the covers off Steve Harmison. 'My immediate thought was to throw the stumps down.' A toss to Michael Vaughan might have done the job instead and, before long, the England skipper was summoning him to the close of play huddle and saying, 'Pedro, get in here. Look at them celebrating a draw.'

And that remains the extent of his involvement with the senior England team. 'It's a disappointment, obviously, after I came back from the World Cup tipped for this and that,' he conceded. 'But I didn't deal with the expectation very well. I think people thought I didn't want it enough, but I would still love to play for England. I have got a little upset when I have read certain things in the past.'

One incident vividly demonstrates, he believes, how far the nurturing of young talent at England level still had to progress a decade ago compared to the time, attention and scientific study invested in it these days. The winter after the World Cup, the England A team toured South Africa and Zimbabwe. Peters, then still an Essex player, recalled, 'There was a lot of talk that several of the Under-19 team were going to go. I didn't get picked and I took a real confidence knock. I had played a full part for Essex that season and helped us win the Benson and Hedges Cup. What devastated me was that no one told me why. I didn't have any feedback from anybody about why I had not gone on tour, while others – who I had done as well as – did go. If they'd said I was not good enough I could have worked to prove them wrong. If they'd said "your attitude stinks" I could have asked them why. Anything would have been good. It knocked me back a lot. That wouldn't happen to a young player now. If you get in that [England] loop, you are there for four or five years no matter how you are playing. I felt I had been cast aside.'

These days, a joint venture between the ECB and the Professional Cricketers' Association has created a team of people assigned to assist the welfare of players at all levels, from county academy members to seasoned pros. 'If Pedro was in that position again he would have someone to talk to,' said former Glamorgan player Ian Thomas, whose role as one of those regional Performance Lifestyle Advisers takes in Peters's county of Northamptonshire. 'We now have people in place to cover those elements of an athlete's life that need support. You are looking to improve performance but ultimately you are trying to support the individual as well, whereas a coach is interested mainly in performance. Sports psychology is slightly different from what we do because, again, it is purely performance based; making players more mentally adept to deal with cricket. Our focus is more external to the performance, but those factors – whether it is relationship problems or whatever – can have a big influence on what happens on the field.'

John Abrahams, still responsible for the nurturing of young England talent, admitted, 'I don't know if we helped Steve manage his situation as well as we could have done. These days, [Under-19s coach] Andy Pick sits with the player and his county coach to have a chat about what they are working on. After a tour, he will go again and discuss, "Have we met these goals? Why haven't we? What sort of things came up that you might work on?"' But even with that circle of care being more fully rounded, Abrahams added, 'Ultimately we want to push the message that it is the player's responsibility. We want him to realise what is going to hold him back and work on it.'

Experiences like that of Peters were not, it emerged, confined entirely to the past. A few days after the Northants batsman spoke about that period of his life, an established England veteran, Matthew Hoggard, accused the England management of a 'staggering lack of interest' after discarding him from the Test team in New Zealand early in 2008. He claimed they'd had no contact with him after the tour until informing him several months later that his central contract was not being renewed. Then Worcestershire keeper Steve Davies said he'd learned of being dropped from the latest England one-day squad via a phone call from a friend who had seen news reports of the announcement.

Peters, remembering his decision to spend the winter of his greatest disappointment working rather than finding some cricket to play overseas, explained that 'the painting and decorating thing' is still used by some people as an example of him lacking the ambition required to become an England player. 'I wanted it as badly as anyone,' he insisted. 'I look at it now and say maybe I just wasn't good enough. Perhaps if I had been kept in the set-up like others are today I would have had a chance because I really thrived with the Under-19s and I might have kept kicking on. I thought I would have been involved and had people to talk to about the pressure and the expectation. That still grates a little but, that aside, I am not going to sit awake every night worrying. I have moments of seeing guys and thinking that it could have been me and I would have liked to have worn the shirt for my parents. But you can't beat yourself up. For every Alastair Cook, who has gone straight in and kicked on, there is a Stephen Peters.'

Meanwhile, eight years on from his one day in an England shirt, Paul Franks recalled the feelings of disillusionment he had taken back to Nottinghamshire. The extent to which newcomers to the England team were made to feel at home had remained a hot topic of conversation, right up to the arrival on the scene of Franks's Nottinghamshire teammate Darren Pattinson after his surprise selection for a single Test against South Africa in the summer of 2008.

'What I wasn't prepared for,' Franks explained, 'was how much you get left to your own devices to drive your own game. Someone like Alec Stewart could do that but I felt quite isolated. I think in international cricket you have to be quite self-prepared. Not selfish, but self-prepared. A lot of guys in that team had been there a long time and were experienced. I didn't know what happened at international level. It was a wonderful experience but when you are not in the team you feel a million miles away. Some players were coming and going and returning to county cricket for form. It was a three-week tournament and I didn't play for three weeks leading up to my game. It would have suited me to go and play at Hove the week before.'

Even though no longer an automatic choice for Nottinghamshire, Franks explained that his mental make-up as a cricketer wouldn't allow him to ever completely discount the thought of adding to that solitary one-day appearance. 'I would be lying if I said didn't still have England ambitions, even if I wouldn't openly admit it in any other conversation. I don't think there are many players who don't. Personally, I need to have that, even though I can't control it. All I can control is what I do.

'In the early period of my career, the first five years, I was constantly thinking about England; every morning, every ball, every session. I was looking at the players I was competing with – Gavin Hamilton, Andrew Flintoff, Steve Harmison, Ben Hollioake – and wondering, "Am I getting more wickets? More runs? Am I in a better position?" It preoccupied my mind and ultimately it wore me down. There is only so much thinking about other people you can do. Since I missed a year with injury I am more focused on what I can do, not worrying about everybody else. I can only control how I bowl and bat.'

Franks's hopes might have seemed a bit more far-fetched, even to himself, after a qualifying group campaign in the Friends Provident Trophy in which his batting average of nearly 42 was not matched by his bowling: six games without a wicket. But at least the new England management, under team director Andy Flower, had displayed an open-minded selection policy, with the likes of Graham Onions and Tim Bresnan winning first caps against the West Indies. According to Graham Napier, 'I think that says to every cricketer that they are looking for guys who perform well. They are not looking at the same faces. Anyone doing well in the county circuit has a chance of being looked at.'

12

SHORT AND SWEET

'I'm disappointed we are not going with the franchises as we proposed. I think it is the best model for English cricket and we are missing a massive opportunity' – MCC Chief Executive **Keith Bradshaw**

FEW CITIES in England have managed to blend tradition and modernity, both physically and culturally, more than Brighton and Hove. An iconic seaside resort by day, it becomes a vibrant night spot for a diverse community. Housed among the Regency architecture is the hub of much of the nation's new media industry. It is appropriate, then, that a healthy stroll along the seafront, beyond Brighton's West Pier, sits the County Ground at Hove, the embodiment of the fusion between cricket's 21st century pragmatism and the time-honoured gentility of the county game.

An arena renowned for its quaint provision of deckchairs for many of its patrons was the first in England to fully embrace the concept of games under floodlights, installing a permanent system in 1998. That was five years before the advent of the Twenty20 Cup, which has led most other grounds – even Lord's – to erect their own illuminations. It had also been Sussex who took most quickly to one-day cricket by winning the first two Gillette Cups in the 1960s, when the introduction of the new-fangled form of cricket had made the same impact on an ailing domestic game as Twenty20 four decades later.

The lights were on as fans made their way in for Sussex's first home game in the 2009 tournament, even though the clear blue sky that framed the pylons and the flats at the Sea End ensured it would be some time into the match against Essex before they came into their own. As young children made their way briskly to the front of the family section – all the better to be able to mug for the Sky Sports camera – much of the buzz around the ground was about English cricket's first Twenty20-produced star, Graham Napier. *The Times* had previewed the competition by printing a big colour picture of him and asking who would emulate his feats this year. As the Sussex fans wondered whether he would punish their bowling in the manner of 11 months earlier, they could see him being interviewed at the wicket by Nasser Hussain.

With every Essex wicket that fell, eyes were cast expectantly towards the visitors' dug-out, where Napier sat padded up from the start of the innings. Yet coach Paul Grayson and skipper Mark Pettini chose on this occasion to keep their big gun holstered. By the time Napier made it to the middle in the number eight position, the evening shadows were stretching across the ground and only six overs of the innings remained. Still enough time for an entertaining cameo if the muse was with Napier, who nudged his score to four off his first three balls.

'There is a lot of expectation,' he'd explained earlier. 'Every time I walk to the crease now people expect something, but realistically things like that don't happen very often.' At least, not on this night. He was called for a quick single by Ryan ten Doeschate and his sliding bat was still well short of the crease as keeper Ben Brown broke the stumps. Angrily, he ripped off his helmet, while the home fans wondered whether to be relieved or disappointed. His mood improved little when Sussex, chasing 149 to win, took ten off his opening over.

Back for a second over midway through the innings, by which time sawdust was being thrown on to the bowlers' run-ups to soak up the evening dew, he was clipped for four by the dangerous West Indian Dwayne Smith. His response showcased the best of his bowling: the ball held back to a slightly shorter length and his low delivery action helping it skid through to trap the batsman leg before. By the time Napier was given a third over, Sussex's target was 27 off 18 balls. Ed Joyce slapped a full toss straight to mid-wicket and Napier's next delivery, the first of a final over from which the home team needed 18, beat Brown's heave and ended the innings.

In the space of a couple of overs Napier had gone from scowling frustration to joyful celebration, which is both the strength and weakness of

Twenty20; the reason it is perfect for those who are new to the sport and why, for those with a more mature and deep-rooted love of the sport, it remains their least favourite form. Of course, it offers moments of high excitement, but little of the drama that gives sport its rich contextual layers. The argument in favour of the longer game is that which is offered, justifiably, by fans of basketball – or those American motor races that consist of driving in circles for 500 laps – when people ask them why they don't just watch the final few minutes. Without experiencing the journey the protagonists have been on to arrive at those brief, climactic moments, how can you really care about and appreciate the outcome? In Twenty20 cricket, the teams take the field, finish the game with a bish, bash, bosh and that's it. The personality of the protagonists, the 'storyline' as the journalists would have it, has little opportunity to develop in the way it does during the slow, unfolding theatre of a Test match, or even a one-day international. Meanwhile, even a one-sided game – of which even such a brief format offers plenty – have no significant individual achievements to sustain interest and prompt debate in the pub in the manner of even a dead first-class match.

The more Twenty20 that is played, the greater the fear that part of what brought mass numbers to it in the first place – the lack of a need to understand all the nuances of the game, or to know all the sport's characters and narratives – will be the thing that undermines it. If the authorities around the world allow too much of the sport to become a mere swirl of faceless six-hitting, with confusion over the importance and context of the various 20-over competitions, they risk failing to capitalize on all the good that the format can bring to the sport. All that will be left is the same confusing mass that 50-over cricket has threatened to become. Perhaps one of the benefits of Twenty20 might be, not the death of the longer one-day international, but a contracted, coherent and more meaningful schedule of those games.

It is interesting to look back on some comments about the effect of Kerry Packer's World Series Cricket and the effect it had in creating the dominant era of the Australians from the mid-90s onwards. 'It's because of what happened then that cricket is so strong now,' said Richie Benaud, while Ian Chappell argued, 'It's not the sole factor, but because WSC paved the way in opening up the game to a wider audience, I have no doubt that this contributed to Australia being well ahead of England all these years.'

Whether Twenty20 will attract the same endorsement in England, the country of its origin, in years to come will depend on how it is managed over the next few years. As the ECB worked on its plans for the proposed 2010 introduction of a new Pro20 league format, to sit alongside the existing competition, the established Twenty20 Cup was experiencing a significant reduction in attendances during its early games. The tournament-opening match between holders Middlesex and arch-rivals Surrey on a sunny Bank Holiday Monday afternoon at Lord's pulled in only 10,000, down by 50 per cent on the previous year.

Sussex's loss to Essex was attended by 3,800 – 700 down on their lowest crowd of 2008. It left club chief executive Dave Brooks warning, 'I think there is a risk of overkill. I expect it is too late to stop the P20 next year. Sponsorship packages are probably being tied up as we speak.' In 2003, the first year of Twenty20, counties had been guaranteed to play only five games. In 2010, the minimum number would be 18. 'Most of the counties have got reservations about a second Twenty20 tournament, including ourselves,' Brooks continued. 'The counties will have to market the two competitions very differently.'

After only 4,000 advance tickets were sold for the first game under the new Lord's lights, installed at a reported cost of £2.7 million, MCC Chief Executive Keith Bradshaw was even more baffled about why English cricket was poised to introduce another county competition rather than the IPL-style event he and Surrey chairman David Stewart had proposed. 'Looking to the future, I'm disappointed we are not going with the franchises as we proposed. I think it is the best model for English cricket and we are missing a massive opportunity, as we can see by the success of the IPL.' Reporting interest from investors in the English game, he added, 'The fact is, though, they are not interested in getting involved in an 18-team P20.'

One reason offered by some for the empty seats was the tournament's earlier start, even though it coincided with a fabulous hot spell. Another was that some people had saved their money for the World Twenty20, an argument only really relevant to London and Nottingham, where those games would be played. If nothing else, the missing fans had raised the stakes for the international event, with the ECB hoping that a successful tournament would rekindle the apparent declining domestic interest.

Who was to say that an England triumph would not do what India's success in the first World Twenty20 in 2007 had done for the short game in that country, where the last-ball win in the final against Pakistan in South Africa caused an explosion of interest in a format in which the nation had previously been disinterested.[2] Such notions seemed wildly unrealistic, however, when England faced the possibility of being eliminated within 48 hours of the first ball of the event.

WITH FOUR Under-19 World Cup winners in England's squad, the World Twenty20 offered the possibility of three appearing together in a senior national side for the first time. It was not that fanciful to suggest they might have been joined by a fifth member of the group after Andrew Flintoff pulled out unfit. Yet the selectors called up Adil Rashid, even though the young leg-spinner was unable to get into Yorkshire's one-day line-up, while another wrist spinner, Chris Schofield, was ignored despite being the country's leading wicket taker in one-day cricket.

'It was strange how that worked,' Schofield said later. 'You think, "Hang on a minute the lad isn't actually playing for his county while I have had two months of cricket where I have performed at the highest level, taken a load of wickets and gone at four an over in one-day cricket." I thought there was an opportunity for my name to be put in there, but fair play to Adil; in the end he bowled exceptionally well.'

As you would expect, Rashid's career has been watched closely by Schofield, who added, 'I have spoken to him about what happened to me and said, "There are going to be a lot of people giving you information. You have got to just take on the information that is going to be good for your cricket."'

Schofield accepted that England had decided not to venture outside their original 30-man squad for Flintoff's replacement. While that may have helped justify Rashid's elevation, few could understand when Rashid, the late stand-in, was picked ahead of Graeme Swann, England's new number one spinner, for the opening World Twenty20 game.

Many of those attending the matches would have been ill-equipped to argue the case one way or another. Throughout the tournament it was possible to gauge the nature of the crowd by snatches of conversation in the stands. Established cricket lovers were spending much of their time educating less knowledgeable companions on subjects ranging from the Lord's slope and The Oval's gasometer to Chris Gayle's ambivalence towards Test cricket and why Lasith Malinga's

[2] A similar phenomenon had been witnessed when India won the 1983 World Cup, causing one-day internationals to become the most popular and lucrative version of the game. In turn, this led to the vast television interest in the country that has led to India becoming the dominant economic force in world cricket.

bowling action made it hard for batsmen to locate the ball. What remained pretty well inexplicable, however, was how England managed to lose to the mostly amateur cricketers of Holland.

England's form in 50-over cricket had been decent enough prior to the shorter game. Against the West Indies, they had comfortably won both the internationals allowed by the weather. Swann had grabbed centre stage once more in the first game at Bristol when brought on to bowl to the destructive Chris Gayle inside the first ten overs. After seeing his first ball disappear over his head for six, he beat the West Indies captain's hack at the next one and bowled him. 'It is brilliant to know your captain backs you like that,' Swann said. 'But I didn't like him so much when he threw me the ball at Bristol when Gayle was smashing everyone. In the noise that followed after he smacked the first ball for six I just whispered to Straussy, so no one could hear, "I think you are a cunt for doing this." He just giggled and I giggled, and then I bowled him next ball so I loved him to pieces. He has got a great sense of humour and he thinks I am a buffoon.'

Owais Shah, meanwhile, found some form again in an England shirt with a stylish 75 in the second match in support of top scorer Matt Prior. With the exception of Paul Collingwood leading instead of Andrew Strauss, plus a couple of wild-card selections, it was the same core unit that was entrusted with England's Twenty20 hopes.

A decent score hung in the balance after they were put in by Holland; time, then, for a big-hitter like Graham Napier or Dimitri Mascarenhas to come in at number six in the late overs. Appearing at the crease instead was Rob Key, horribly out of form and overlooked for his team's two pre-tournament practice matches. A late replacement because of Kevin Pietersen's aching Achilles tendon, Key had been pacing around in his pads and helmet since the first ball, an opening batsman unused to having to wait his turn. Had an early wicket fallen, his experience against the new ball would have been used at number three but with England reaching beyond halfway without loss, thanks to a century stand between Ravi Bopara and Luke Wright, his late appearance was horribly incongruous, a surgeon asked to do the job of the lumberjack.

Up in the dining area atop the Mound Stand, England cricket's managing director Hugh Morris had said he was looking for between 160 and 180. 'Hugh's got his 160,' said one of his guests as the innings ended, but within a few overs some fearless Dutch batting suggested that England, who had made 162 for 5, needed to be at the upper end of that projection. By the time Holland ran a joyous overthrow to win the game on the last ball – with Lord's erupting in a mix of shock, horror and, for those wearing orange, ecstasy – only a win two days later against Pakistan could save the hosts from being knocked out before some teams even played their first match.

'People were writing us off as a laughing stock; the biggest low in the history of cricket,' Swann remarked. 'People are very fickle.' He was speaking after a much-changed team, in which he had returned as part of a two-spinner attack, had salvaged its tournament by thumping the always unpredictable Pakistanis. Key had given way to the prodigal Pietersen, whose half-century – supported by 30s from Wright and Shah – lifted England to 185 for 5. It was far too much for their opponents in a match played in a crackling, yet good-natured, atmosphere; a World Cup football match without the unpleasantness, and a reminder of the vibrancy Pakistan and its supporters can bring to the game. No wonder the ECB would soon be announcing an agreement to host Pakistan Test matches and limited-overs games in 2010.

The crowd quickly became part of the story when England faced South Africa in their first match of the Super Eight stage at Trent Bridge. This time it was boos rather than cheers that drifted out into the middle; intended for the ears of Shah. Having seen England lose their top three batsmen for 25, Shah found himself in that no-man's land of uncertainty, torn between consolidation and counter-attack. When his dead bat approach brought him only 10 runs off 18 deliveries, the crowd decided he had erred in favour of the former and – this being far from a genteel MCC gathering – were not afraid to let him know it. One contributor to the BBC's website later described him an 'an oaf'.

'I am not going to take on the spinner if wickets are falling around me,' Shah explained later. 'You have got to play the situation, build a partnership and go on from there. That is the way it was. If you get a partnership going you can take the game away from the opposition.' Whether or not in response to the barracking, he did finally unleash a barrage of sixes and fours against the South African spinners to climb to 38 before Jacques Kallis found the edge of his defensive bat. There was no other resistance and a total of 111 all out was never going to be sufficient.

Against India at Lord's, England found themselves in the strange situation of walking out to warm up and being booed by the Indian fans, who made up more than half the crowd. According to Graeme Swann, 'That was when I thought, "Right, we can win this competition now," just to stick it up the so-called English citizens who were booing us. I have never been so riled. I was thinking, "Anyone in this ground with a British passport who has booed us should be put in the fucking army." I was livid. That was the sweetest win I have ever had for England.'

It appeared that England's score of 153 for 7 was again at the low end of competitive. But India, who had slipped from pre-tournament favouritism to the brink of elimination, were making a poor fist of dealing with England's short-pitched seam bowling by the time Swann took the 14th over. Preferred this time to junior partner Rashid when England picked an extra quick bowler, his two overs had cost only nine runs. But now the threatening Yuvraj Singh, inexplicably held back in the batting order, slammed his first ball over the ropes. A quicker full toss produced only a single and then the inexperienced Ravindra Jadeja was caught by a leaping Stuart Broad at long-on. Looking for a big finish to the over, Yuvraj missed a drive and lifted his back foot for the split-second it took James Foster to break the stumps. Swann punched the air as the third umpire's decision rolled up on the big-screen fruit machine. In the end, India scored only 15 of the 19 they needed off a final over delivered by Ryan Sidebottom. They were out, while victory the next day against the West Indies would put England into the final four.

And then it rained. Just as the Indian Premier League organisers had warned it would. Just as it always does at some point in an English summer. Just as England were preparing to defend 161 for 6 at The Oval. By the time it stopped, the West Indies were told that the Duckworth-Lewis calculations left them needing 80 off nine overs; a far easier-looking target.

It might have been bad luck on England, but for the fourth time in the tournament they had fallen short in their batting. A day earlier, they had gone boundary-less between the 10th and 16th overs. This time their failure to find the ropes between Shah's lofted leg-side six off the second ball of the 11th over and Stuart Broad's 10 runs off the final two balls of the innings probably left them 20 runs adrift of a winning total. They had been indebted to a half-century by Bopara, while Shah had fallen for 18 to an athletic catch by Andre Fletcher off a flat pull shot that was bound for the stands.

Once again, he had missed out on delivering a game-changing innings. And once again he was the England batsman who caused most debate. In Sky's studio, Nick Knight questioned his continued place in England's limited overs line-up and lumped him together with Paul Collingwood as having had a poor tournament, even though Shah had at least played two innings of substance and scored almost twice as many runs as his struggling skipper. Knight's colleague, Ian Ward, had questioned in mid-tournament whether Eoin Morgan should be selected instead of his Middlesex teammate, at which point an exasperated Nasser Hussain groaned, 'Why are we always picking on Owais Shah?' Even two weeks later, after Shah's unbeaten 61 off 41 balls had won a game for Middlesex against Surrey, Knight managed to turn the Man of the Match presentation into an interrogation over why he had not been as punishing in England colours. Shah's tournament had been one of useful contributions and memorable shots without proving himself a regular match-winner. He was still being described as a 'nearly man' eight years after his England debut

Meanwhile, having reduced the West Indies to 45 for 5, it looked as though England's bowlers might pull them through once more. Swann and Foster had combined again to get rid of the threatening Dwayne Bravo, a mirror image of the dismissal of the left-handed Yuvraj. Swann's reputation continued to rise every time he pulled on an England shirt. Yet a target of 29 off the final three overs proved well within the capabilities of old hands Ramnaresh Sarwan and Shivnarine Chanderpaul and the World Twenty20 would reach its climax without England. And, it would transpire, without the West Indies, who would be beaten in the semi-finals by Sri Lanka. They in turn lost the final by seven wickets to a Pakistan team transformed from the disjointed unit beaten so easily by England.

While most observers lauded the event, Shah felt it had relied too heavily on England going all the way in order for its potential to be fully realised. 'Personally I was a bit disappointed by it,' he said, perhaps influenced by the frustration of his and his team's tournament. 'I think the ICC could have run it a bit better, perhaps taken a leaf out of the IPL book with all the razzmatazz. With a lot of the games in London it could have created more hype and really got into the schools to get awareness of the tournament. Twenty20 is a wonderful product and a great way to promote the game and we should be promoting it everywhere.'

Yet Swann argued that 'the World Twenty20 has got the whole country in the mood for cricket again'. Once again, the newest version of the game was dividing opinion.

13

THE UMPIRE STRIDES BACK

'I needed to be able to say to someone, "This is where I am in my life. What you do you think?" But there was always that connotation of being weak' – **Michael Gough**

FOR A man who had walked away from cricket because he'd lost his love of the game, Michael Gough was engagingly excited about the prospect of the final day of an LV County Championship match that had a good chance of going nowhere. 'I have always had a real genuine love of watching the game,' he said, seated before play beneath photographs of David Gower and Ray Illingworth in one of the restaurants at Leicestershire's Grace Road ground. 'I am a traditionalist. I could sit down and watch a five-day Test match no problem.'

Typically for a low-key game county game played while most people were at work, there would not be too many people at the ground to share Gough's fervour. The vast majority of the few hundred spectators were into retirement, with the occasional middle-aged man armed with scorebook and coloured pens among the more youthful element. Even in the treasure trove that is the Leicestershire Supporters' Club shop and café, the daily special of tea and cake for £1.25 was hardly flying off the Formica-topped table. None of that, however, could dampen the professional enthusiasm of a man enjoying his debut season on the full list of first-class umpires. 'Leicestershire have made a made a bit of a fist of it in their second innings, so unless Surrey take a few early wickets we should be here for the duration,' he said with no hint of hoping for an early finish so that he could hit the road back home to Hartlepool. 'It's still in the balance. If they knock over a few early and bowl them out it could be a tight finish.'

As one of the youngest full-time umpires in the sport's history, Gough's appearance on grounds in white coat and Panama hat – adding a few more imposing inches to his slender 6ft 5in. frame – still provokes conversation among the players he played alongside. Today, he would find himself umpiring one of his former England Under-19 colleagues in South Africa, Chris Schofield. 'Players will obviously have a laugh and a joke about the times we played together and ask why I gave up,' he revealed. 'But as soon as you are on the field everyone has a job to do and that is left behind.'

Gough was only ever an accidental cricketer; his exit from the professional game seemingly a mere matter of time. As the teams went through their warm-up rituals – Surrey's happy-go-lucky football and Leicester's regimented physical jerks reflecting their relative comfort within the game situation – he explained that his progress through English youth cricket into a contract with Durham had been anything but a cunning career plan.

The son of a Durham Minor Counties player and professional in league cricket, Michael senior, Gough had been the traditional cricketing offspring, carrying his bat and boots to his dad's games in the hope of a late drop-out or a stint fielding at third man. 'I started taking it seriously at about 14 or 15 and got in the first team at Hartlepool. That's when it really kicked off,' he said. But even then football could have claimed him.

'I had trials as a centre-half at Arsenal and Sheffield United and was with the Middlesbrough academy for a couple of years. I was asked for two trials at Arsenal but unfortunately I got an Achilles injury after the first one, when they had already offered me YTS terms to go down and live there. Michael Owen was in the same trial and so was Neil Clement, who played for West Brom. I had the injury in the winter, and in the summer the cricket season came along and I had the chance to go Lilleshall with the England Under-15s. I got asked to go back for another trial at Arsenal but the cricket season was taking off so I stuck with that.'

Gough admitted that his style as a batsman was not far removed from the mentality of the stopper centre-half he had been on the football field. 'My strength was probably my mental approach to the game. I was never the most talented but I had a good work ethic. I learned my strengths and probably only had three or four scoring areas, but I was dedicated, worked hard and made use of my ability.'

Having been a member of the successful England Under-17 team in Bermuda early in the summer of 1997, he was offered further opportunities to advance his career when the Zimbabwe Under-19s arrived in England. Picked to play against them for an England Under-18 team at Sleaford, he scored a century. 'I remember batting a lot with Swanny and off the back of that I got some second-team games for Durham. Then in September the letter dropped saying I had been selected for the Under-19s to go to South Africa. I was at college doing A-levels so I went in and told them I wouldn't be coming back. My mind was made up. Two months in South Africa playing cricket? It wasn't the hardest decision to make.'

Only 17 when the tour began, Gough was one of the younger players on tour. 'For a lot of the guys who were 19 it was important for them to do well as a way of getting into their county sides. For guys like me it was about development and experience, but it was made clear we were expected to do well.'

The two drawn Tests marked Gough's first experience of international cricket at Under-19 level. Batting at number five, he acquitted himself well with an unbeaten 32 in the second innings of the first game and a half-century in the second match. 'Cape Town was my debut and I batted about 200 balls for 30-odd,' he recalled. 'We ended up hanging on for a draw. It suited me. I liked that mental challenge of just being able to bat for the duration. My strength was spending time at the crease.'

Colleague Giles Haywood revealed, 'I loved Goughie. He was so serious. He was a very dogged batsman and would never give his wicket away. He had fantastic technique and in terms of mental toughness and how he prepared he was probably miles ahead of everyone else in that squad.'

Gough recalled how much the poor results against South Africa in the two one-day matches lowered expectation about the World Cup. 'We had such a bad series that it took the pressure off us. We went in with no fear and that is probably why we did so well.' In fact, Gough had been one of the few bright spots, scoring 22 and 56 not out in the middle order. 'John [Abrahams] and Phil [Neale] asked me if I fancied the challenge of opening. Unfortunately I then had a bad patch of form at the wrong time. I had three low scores [18, 2 and 0] and the loss to Bangladesh was a real low. It was my last game.'

He wasn't, however, going to let that spoil the trip of a lifetime. 'I wasn't too disappointed because I was having a great time with the lads. Probably the best day I ever had in cricket was winning the World Cup and I wasn't even in the team. Being part of that trip was brilliant. We all went out together and did things together on our days off. We were young kids still learning the game and learning about life. I went away a boy and, pardon the cliché, came back a man. I had hardly ever been out Hartlepool; never been on a foreign holiday. You go away and you learn about your cricket and life in general. Phil and John's role was to understand us as young men. There were times when we did cross the line and when we didn't quite achieve the standards that were expected and they had to come down on us hard, but we deserved it. I felt a more rounded person in general when I came back.'

The summer of 1998 went, according to Gough, 'in a blur; I just turned up for whatever team picked me'. His first-class debut against Essex brought him a score of 62 in his first innings and his next match, against Cambridge University, a maiden first-class hundred. 'On the morning of my debut, I remember that about quarter past ten John Morris pulled out of the game. Norman Gifford and Graham Gooch, who was our batting coach, came up and said, "You are playing. You are going to open." I had to call my mum and dad, so I put 10 pence into the payphone and said, "Get yourselves down to the Riverside." It took me about two and half sessions to get to 50. I just wanted to stay out there and soak it all up.'

A solid series for England Under-19s against Pakistan and a prolific winter for the side in New Zealand saw him captaining the team against Australia in the summer of 1999. It should have been a happy time, yet it left him with doubts about his future in the game. And during a period when he most needed someone to talk to, he found himself trying to find his own path through his uncertainty.

'Even when I got picked for the Under-19s I didn't know what I wanted to do long term. I just knew it beat going back for my A-levels. Durham offered me a three-year contract and it was better than getting a job. It wasn't that I chose cricket over everything else I just fell into it. I enjoyed my first season with Durham but even then I was wondering if it was right for me. I felt as though there was maybe something else I wanted to do. I took each day as it came and didn't think much about the future. I never felt I had a full career ahead of me.

'I did OK for England against the Aussies, but being captain was difficult. It meant I had my own room and that was tough. I liked being with the lads and it was quite lonely in your room at night. I couldn't really say, "I am not enjoying it," because people expect you to be loving it because you are doing well. I started thinking, "Is cricket really for me?" I wasn't doing that well, but I kept doing well enough for them to come back with better contracts and decent money. The problem was that I kept everything to myself. I needed to be able to go and speak to someone at that age, when you are still learning about yourself and moulding your own character. It was a weird time.'

Having heard Gough's story, Graeme Swann was able to sympathise. 'I always assumed as a 19 year old that if I am doing this and loving it then surely everyone else in the team feels exactly the same. In reality, it is not like that and Goughie didn't enjoy it that much. If you are into something by accident and happen to be good at it, then it is not a surprise that you get to that point. My equivalent is as a kid playing rugby. I ended up playing for the county and I hated it. I would come home every week and my shoulder was hurting and I would see people getting the shit kicked out of them and I didn't want to mess up my cricket. Had I carried on with rugby and got Young England honours I would have been the same as Goughie. I wouldn't have enjoyed it and I would have felt like a charlatan.'

John Abrahams described Gough as 'a great technician', adding. 'He was very keen, very brave and a role model professional. I think he suffered from it because he put too much pressure on himself. He was the one would go back to his room and write why he had got out in his diary. He didn't quite fulfil his potential at county level and needed a bit of a release perhaps.'

That release could have come simply from having a mentor to whom he could turn. Had he been born a decade later, Gough would have found more support available to him. 'The way the Professional Cricketers' Association has developed in the last ten years is fantastic,' Gough said. 'Now there are so many people you can talk to. I needed to be able to say to someone, "This is where I am in my life. What you do you think?" But then there was always that connotation of being weak if you had to go and speak to someone.'

Despite being selected for the England A tour to Bangladesh and New Zealand in 1999-2000, Gough reached the 2002 season without having added to that solitary first-class hundred. But then a century in the Cheltenham and Gloucester Trophy against the Welsh Minor Counties was followed by two big hundreds for the second team and finally a three-figure score in the County Championship against Essex. Playing in the final half dozen games, he finished the season with a first-class average of 51.33. Yet that mark dived to little more than 23 in the 13 matches he played in 2003, at the end of which he finally decided to lay down his bat.

'I had a really good year in 2002,' he recalled. 'I didn't do well at the start and I'd decided it would be my last season. I'd had enough and I wanted to do something else. I didn't tell anyone, but I just knew it in my heart. By the end of the season I averaged over 50, played without any worries and the runs had come. Durham offered improved terms again and I didn't fancy working in my dad's trophy engraving business full-time so I carried on. I had winter the in Australia but didn't play much because of injury and had time to think about what I wanted to do. I got to the end of the next season and thought, "Enough is enough." I had a year left on my contract but Durham agreed to a sabbatical. I knew I would never go back.'

BUT HERE he was. Back. Albeit in a different uniform as he took his place at the Turner End of the ground on a bright morning that had the Union Jack next to the George Geary Stand blowing horizontally, although not always in the same direction. For most of the day there was little more arduous for him to perform than to balance the various bowlers' sweaters and signal a relentless sequence of boundaries – the latter act achieved with none of the affectations that curiously afflict so many of his colleagues. The Surrey seamer, Chris Jordan, did have one loud lbw appeal turned down early in the day with an authoritative 'not out' that was clearly audible at the boundary's edge. But then the South African batsmen Hylton Ackerman and Boeta Dippenaar both marched into three figures on their way to a partnership of 314 that made the game safe. Schofield appealed in vain to Gough at square leg for a stumping but the day meandered to its logical conclusion.

For the umpire, of course, there is no let-up. A meaningless dismissal in the context of the match can be threatening to a batsman's average and his mental well-being. Gough explained that his brief walks between balls were to preserve his concentration for such key moments. 'The players expect us to get the majority of the big decisions right and to have a nice manner on the field. You have got to learn to switch off between balls otherwise it is impossible. It is like being a batsman. If you are going to bat all day you can't concentrate the whole time. The bowler runs in and then you try and home in on the ball.'

Even the frenzied activity of a Twenty20 game is no guarantee of having a crucial decision to make on virtually every ball. 'I have had about five Twenty20 games so far and had two decisions. The wickets are good and the ball doesn't swing, so you tend to find yourself out of the game; just shouting "over" and getting in position for the next one.'

A momentary lapse, though, a hairline decision that is called in favour of the wrong player, can undo hours of good work. 'We are only human beings and unfortunately we do make mistakes and don't get every decision right. It takes a big man to walk off the field and say, "I mucked up there." You know yourself if you have had a good day or not. You are your own biggest critic and I am tougher on myself now than I was as a player. The public tends to think that umpires give a decision and they don't care. Nothing could be further from the truth. On the motorway home it is only thing going through your mind.'

Gough, like most of his profession – including the administrators – is unsure of the merits of the referral system being introduced in Tests after a series of trials. 'The ICC looks at every decision and about 95 per cent of them are right, so why do we need referral? Is it for the armchair viewer, or is it so that players don't think they are getting on the wrong end of a decision? Only the ICC can tell us the reason behind it. When we used the referral system here in the Friends Provident Trophy the players were just as miffed as umpires. They felt they were undermining the umpires and they didn't like that. We were all taught to respect the umpires. Anyway, we love the game because it gives us talking points. Everyone loves that aspect of sport. Then again, until we give the technology a full try we don't know what the benefits might be.'

If it all appears to be creating scrutiny around the umpires, then Gough is not unduly concerned. He found that he revelled in that kind of pressure as soon as he put on his white coat. 'I'd thought of getting into coaching, but umpiring was something that always appealed to me. When I was playing I used to talk to the guys about what it entailed. After 2003, I had a year working with my dad and playing club cricket for Hartlepool and then I thought, "Why not give umpiring a go?" From the moment I did a third-team game at Bishop Auckland, my first-ever game on a Sunday afternoon, I loved it. I did one full summer in 2005 and tried to fit in as much as I could so I could apply to get on the reserve list. I applied at the back end of the season. I was lucky that it was the final year in which you could apply; now you have to be asked. I got asked for an interview at Lord's in December and had a call a couple of days later inviting me onto the reserve list. Funnily enough, my first first-class game was at Cambridge, where I got my first first-class hundred, and my first Championship match was at Colchester, where I got my first Championship hundred.'

It was remarkable progress for a 26 year old with only a year's amateur experience, and a bold move by the ECB to put such faith in him. But Gough insisted he has never been worried by the challenge of umpiring, nor experienced the ambivalence he felt about playing. 'I have never ever been nervous going out to umpire. I cherish it. Even my first TV game at Headingley in front of a 12,000 crowd didn't worry me.'

Gough acknowledges that the life of an umpire could be hard on his wife, Charlotte, and any future children. 'It is already tough travelling all the time. I enjoy it out on the field but you have to deal with all the stuff that comes with it, the travelling and packing. That has been the hardest thing and my wife is very understanding. We are contracted to do about 80 or 90 days and living in Hartlepool makes it difficult for me to get home for the days off. If I am umpiring somewhere I will often stay there on my day off instead of travelling all the way back home and all the way back again. A home game for me would be Durham but I have been kept off them with it being my first year. Headingley is the closest for me but that is still a 90-minute or two-hour drive so it is an overnight stay. But I am not going to slag it off because we only do four or five months and then get the rest of the winter off!'

Now, unlike his days as a batsman, he has a clear career path he intends to pursue. 'My goal is to establish myself on the first-class panel with a good reputation and ultimately get on the ICC panel then their elite panel. As a player, I never really had any ambitions because I didn't know what I wanted to do. It is different as an umpire. I really love it and want to try to move up the ladder.'

14

MIDSUMMER DREAMS

'It comes down to not being concerned with the shit around the edges, just concentrating on what you have got to concentrate on' – Northants coach **David Capel**

FAR FROM the madding crowd of the World Twenty20, Stephen Peters was taking an important step in the quieter surroundings of Wantage Road. Tucked pleasantly between rows of terraced housing in the manner that distinguishes the traditional English sports stadium, Northamptonshire's County Ground had soaked up enough of the overnight rain to allow a prompt start against Surrey. This was one of a batch of LV County Championship matches that the schedulers had crammed into the diary during the international tournament, almost in the hope, it seemed, that no one would notice. A scattering of sharp-eyed spectators, choosing between the banks of blue or white seating, were taking their places as Peters returned to cricket after almost two months' absence with a broken right thumb.

'My fingers have never been good,' he said, recalling the injury he suffered in the field in a Friends Provident Trophy game. 'It was the third time I have broken my thumb and I have broken a few fingers too. It usually happens in the field. I tend to field at backward point in the one-day games and the ball is hit at you pretty hard. I was unfit to play for about five weeks and then the Twenty20 Cup started. I haven't ever really featured very heavily in that anyway. It meant I got about ten good days of practice before playing again.'

Even after his work in the nets, what he wanted as he restarted his season was to be facing a bowler who didn't know him well enough to ensure that he didn't give him any width. Enter Ryan Harris, an Australian all-rounder who had recently been playing in the IPL and had once played very briefly for Sussex. Peters duly got his gentle reintroduction to first-team action with a series of balls well outside off stump, enabling him to cut happily down to the vacant third man position. From the other end, however, Andre Nel was intent on making life a little more difficult.

Nel, who earlier in the year had exchanged the hope of a recall to the South African team for a Kolpak contract at The Oval, is one of cricket's cartoon characters, the Merv Hughes of his day. Two decades earlier, the popular Australian had managed to hide that he was a rather ordinary fast-medium bowler behind a heck of a moustache and an aggressive, engaging personality. Where Hughes had facial hair, Nel has his self-created alter-ego, Gunther, a snarling pantomime act who tries to look hard even if his bowling is going round the park. Both Hughes and Nel have been big-hearted triers without breaking into the elite of their profession.

'Andre is a good guy, very in-your-face and competitive, with good pace and aggression,' Peters explained. 'I enjoy facing him. I try to fly under the radar with guys like that and not get involved in a slanging match. There is only going to be one winner in that and it is not going to be the batter.'

On this day, Nel was proving what a handful he could be at county level. Bowling at pace and testing Peters's technique around his off stump, he slowed the batsman's progress and, on 28, got him to edge to Chris Schofield at slip, where his former England youth colleague juggled and dropped the ball. With wickets falling regularly around him, Peters went for 15 balls without a run as Nel pounded into the second hour of play, but after 75 minutes he drove Jade Dernbach down the ground for his first boundary in front of square. Having seen off Nel – who would finish with six wickets – the hard work appeared to have been completed, only for another drive off Dernbach after lunch to settle in the hands of Mark Ramprakash at mid-off. Dismissed for 59, Peters threw back his head in frustration.

By the time he batted again on the third day, Northants were facing a first-innings deficit of more than 300. Again, his was a lonely resistance, with six wickets being taken during his four hours at the crease. Following the pattern of his truncated season, he'd gone quickly into the 20s, then consolidated and dug in as the pace went off the ball. The team's only hope was to make it to the end of the day and hope for rain, but five minutes before stumps he played back to Schofield, bowling round the wicket, and edged to slip. Another solid knock, 78, would not be enough to save Northants but at least his second start to the season had gone well.

Schofield, meanwhile, continued to take wickets as steadily as he had done all season. Unused in Northants' brief first innings he struck quickly, if fortuitously, in the second when Nicky Boje clipped the ball into the shins of short leg Michael Brown, who took the catch on the rebound. After pinning David Willey in front of the stumps he got the wicket of Peters. And on the final morning, the home team's prayers for rain having gone unanswered, he won another lbw appeal against David Lucas and had the big-hitting Johan van der Wath caught in the deep as he returned figures of 5 for 40, his best in the County Championship. It helped Surrey to their first win in the competition since late in 2007.

'Our batsmen gave us a good chance to bowl well,' said Schofield, on the boundary edge as cricket bags were being hurriedly packed in order to take advantage of what was now virtually a day off. '[Brown] took a great chance to set it up and things like that show that it could be your day. To walk away with five wickets is a great achievement. To perform well in all forms of cricket this year is good for me and the team.'

Peters's good form was to continue, first of all with an unbeaten 61 in his first Twenty20 Cup appearance of the season, a low-scoring game against Worcestershire that saw Northamptonshire clinch first place in their group. 'Twenty20 doesn't particularly suit my style and we have plenty of batsmen in the side who can clear the ropes,' he said. 'But Ian Harvey was ill [with swine flu] and it was great to be involved because we needed to win to reach the quarter-final. If we had been chasing 180 I might not have opened, but I was able to go out and play my way. There is going to be more Twenty20 cricket played going forward so it will be nice to be more involved.'

After an undistinguished match against Glamorgan, Peters played his most productive innings for three years. Having seen his team lose early wickets again after batting first in their home game against Derbyshire, Peters made brisk progress once more into the 30s before settling back to allow Rikki Wessels, Nicky Boje and Andrew Hall to set the pace. All perished before building an innings of substance, leaving their opener to drive, cut and nudge his way into three figures and on towards one of the highest scores of his life. Having scored

175 off 284 balls, three short of a career best, he was caught off the bowling of South African Nantie Hayward. For good measure, with the game dead on the final afternoon, he rattled off an unbeaten 64, leaving him with a first-class average for the season of just under 70, more than twice his career mark.

A few days later, Northants coach and former England all-rounder David Capel, a fixture at the club in various capacities for three decades, considered the greater returns being achieved by his player and suggested, 'He was not feeling wanted at Worcester and he has battled away here and found his feet. He has really warmed to the task and become very much a Northamptonshire cricketer, and coming from someone like me that is meant as a big accolade. He is a gutsy player and really gets stuck in. He puts a lot time into good preparation, puts a lot of thought into it and has worked his game out technically.'

Most significantly, Capel ventured, Peters was more at ease with himself than at any time during a career which even the player himself admitted had been affected by outside influences – the politics of the professional game. 'I think for the first time he has made sure he is clear in his mind. He has shown maturity in being open-minded and taking that route. I think he was carrying a bit of baggage around, performing but maybe not to his full capability. He has turned a few stones over in the pursuit of maximising what he has got and I admire that.'

Pushed for further explanation, Capel added, 'It comes down to not being concerned with the shit around the edges, just concentrating on what you have got to concentrate on. In the past he might have got involved in tittle-tattle and the bollocks that goes on and being concerned with other people's business. Now he is just focused on what he is doing. I think that has been a sea change and a step forward. He is a very valuable member of the team. I have seen greater maturity in the past 12 to 18 months and he is very stable in his life with his partner. The same kind of thing has happened with Graeme Swann. As a batsman, I think Stephen is one of those cricketers who can go on getting better and better. We have seen it with someone like Mark Ramprakash. Providing he can stay fit and keep his hunger for what he is doing and keeps coming at it in the same way, there is no reason why he shouldn't go on and have even more success in his career.'

A LITTLE more than 12 hours after England's Twenty20 exit, Graham Napier had been back on the cricket field after two weeks on the sidelines. His non-appearance in the ICC tournament was a mystery to many, especially given England's chronic inability to find the boundary in the late overs, although coach

Andy Flower pointed out that his inclusion would have meant the omission of one of the front-line bowlers.

He would never have described it as such, but there was a certain 'up yours' element to Napier's performance in Essex's Championship game against Kent at Tunbridge Wells. Coming in on the first day at 173 for 6, he took brutal advantage of anything slightly wayward in racing to an unbeaten 64 off 68 balls – not far off Twenty20 pace. As well as seven fours, he twice hit the ball out of the ground, never to be found. Before the close, there was just enough time for him to bowl one over, trapping poor old Rob Key lbw for a golden duck with his first ball. The next morning he took his tally to four wickets and then thumped 48 not out off only 45 deliveries, with another two balls disappearing out of the arena. His only second innings wicket was the one that completed an easy Essex win.

Key, meanwhile, followed his unsatisfactory England return and his first innings duck with a painful 105-minute stay at the crease before being bowled for 21, a continuation of the form that he admitted had cost him the England opener's place that appeared to have been his when the Twenty20 squad was announced. 'I wasn't in great form at the time,' he said later in the year. 'I think I would have done all right in that competition but they didn't want to take the gamble. It's a game that can really kick start your season. I will always back myself to do well on the big occasions but Luke Wright took his chance, got runs early on and there was no point in me going in at five or six. In hindsight I probably shouldn't have played [against Holland] because it left us short of bowling.'

As midsummer came and went, the country was agonising over the Wimbledon fortunes of Andy Murray; the House of Commons had a new Speaker, expected to restore confidence after the MPs' expenses scandal; and the music world was mourning Michael Jackson. For cricket followers, the real story of the summer, the Ashes, was about to begin, while the sport's participants still had three months in which their seasons could head off in varying directions.

The half-term report on those boys of '98 still in the professional game offered predictably mixed findings. Napier had spent longer than he would have liked watching from the dug-outs of the Mumbai Indians and England but was now finding his best form of the season, including a quick-fire 47 in an important, but unsuccessful, Twenty20 Cup game against Hampshire. Paul Franks had been banging out plenty of runs for his beloved club side Farnsfield but had been out of senior action for a month – again a victim of Nottinghamshire's strong squad and a side injury. He'd proved his fitness to bowl by facing the Sri Lanka team in the nets and returned to captain his county against Oxford University before being recalled to the 20-over team. Meanwhile, the two spinners, Swann and Schofield, were each performing well in their respective arenas, although Schofield came in for heavy fire at the end of Surrey's disappointing campaign in the short game.

Owais Shah had made a half-century after returning to first-class cricket for the first time since Trinidad almost four months earlier and then scored consistently in Middlesex's remaining Twenty20 matches. But there had not even been a place for him in the England Lions team named to face Australia in the final warm-up game prior to the Ashes battle. The day before the Lions took the field at Worcester, he went out to bat against Surrey at Lord's with the air of a man on a mission.

On a slow wicket in only his second Championship game of the season, he marked his arrival by sending former England paceman Alex Tudor to the boundary with an off-drive and a flick off his hips. Having seen Shah caught near the leg-side rope several times during the World Twenty20, Surrey appeared to think they had stumbled on a weakness, but the efforts of Tudor and Chris Jordan to lure him into the trap floundered when the batsman had time to pull them off the front foot through mid-wicket. When debutant off-spinner Simon King, playing because of Schofield's injured finger, entered the attack, his first ball disappeared square for four. There was a minor delay when Shah received treatment for an attack of cramp as the temperature beat him into the 90s, but then he raced into three figures. Middlesex had barely 150 on the board at the time and the clenched fist with which he greeted his century demonstrated the importance he attached to his innings.

'I don't want to get hundreds; I don't want to get fifties; I don't want to get 300s,' he'd said when discussing a possible path back to the England Test team. 'I want to consistently perform. It's all I ever want to do.' But nothing speaks to that quality better than a few eye-catching centuries. By the time he was caught low at slip off the bowling of Nel late in the day, he had hit 23 fours, scored 159 of his team's 259 runs and batted for almost six hours. On the final day, his second innings got off to a tentative start, including a top edge over the keeper and a leading edge that almost carried to mid-off. Then he tore into the bowling, swinging Nel over mid-on and down the ground before going down on his knee to drive Murtaza Hussain through extra cover. As Middlesex pushed for an afternoon declaration, he hit three successive fours before being caught for 61. His team fell short of forcing victory but a personal point had been forcefully made.

NONE OF the survivors of the junior World Cup had struggled for form as much as Rob Key. Those in the surprisingly long queues forming outside the Hobbs Gates at The Oval on the first morning of Kent's LV County Championship game against Surrey were not, it could be safely assumed, standing in line specifically to enjoy the sight of the visiting captain at the crease. Indeed, it turned out that the delay in the entry process was caused by lightning having struck the pavilion three days earlier and thrown out the electronics, including the machines that read the members' admission cards.

By the time those members had made their way grumpily into an impressively packed pavilion, Key was standing in shin guards and helmet at short leg as Surrey's opening pair of Michael Brown and Jonathan Batty set off briskly towards a 100 partnership. He spent most of the day either jumping for safety from under the batsmen's noses or passing the time at mid-on, where Mark Butcher managed to present him with a catch. Key saw his bowlers exert some control after a wayward start, but Mark Ramprakash spent a serene afternoon compiling an effortless 86 before five wickets fell in the final session. Chris Schofield's creative batting against new ball brought the day to a fast-paced finish and he completed a half-century the following morning before being the last man out.

It was time for Key to begin his 12th first-class innings of the season, none of which had seen him advance past 33. In helping Kent secure a quarter-final place in the Twenty20 Cup he had at least discovered some green shoots of form with knocks of 58 not out and 44 in consecutive games, his best scores in any cricket since the England Lions tour in the winter. Even his status as leader of the Lions had fallen victim to his lack of runs. 'There is no worst feeling in the game than not knowing where your next run is coming from,' he admitted. 'I spent countless hours in the nets with coaches desperately trying to find out what had thrown me off course. I tried standing more open in my stance and kept nicking to the slips. I tried closing my stance and kept getting out lbw. Nothing was working.'

Yet after spending some time with former Kent batsman Neil Taylor, now a teacher and coach at St Dunstan's College in South London, he sensed a corner about to be turned. 'Sometimes little flaws do creep into your game. Neil worked with me a lot when I was younger and I had a chat with him up at Beckenham during the Gloucestershire game. He'd spotted a few things about how I was standing at the crease. He felt my hands were a little too far away from my body too, so I made a few alterations.'

The first proof of Key's progress was when he forced Chris Jordan through point off the back foot to complete a solid start to his innings and, at last, record a first-class fifty. He survived an appeal for caught behind and then almost took Jordan off his feet by driving past him for four. He and Joe Denly had taken the score to 152 for 0 by the time rain during the tea break ended the day prematurely, but the third morning began with no shift in momentum. Denly went to his century, before Key top-edged a hook off Alex Tudor over the ropes and swung Murtaza Hussain over long-on for another six. He swept the next delivery for four to reach 99 and then, having waited on the ball, drove to the cover boundary for two runs. A century that must have seemed a long way off during the previous weeks had taken 155 balls and was only halted when, after two wickets had fallen, Martin van Jaarsveld leathered the ball down the wicket and saw it ricochet off Murtaza's right hand on to the stumps. Caught out of his ground, Key departed miserably for 123, the bad luck of his season clearly not completely behind him.

News of his innings travelled quickly to the first Ashes Test at Cardiff, where two England fans had taken marker pens to the sponsors' boundary cards in order to instruct the selectors to 'Bring Back Rob Key'. Even though he would have acknowledged the premature nature of such a message, he admitted, 'It was nice to get the three figures. I feel like I'm hitting the ball well. It's not been easy for me, captaining the side when I didn't feel I was performing, but I'm feeling good again now.'

His well-being increased further when Kent's busy schedule took them to Cardiff to take on Glamorgan after only one day of rest. Rain meant that the first two days allowed only enough time for the home team to post a modest total of 317, but the weather perked up enough to permit the third to become one of the most productive of Key's career. He survived a confident appeal for a catch to the keeper in Garnett Kruger's opening over and then edged James Harris short of first slip. Further chances off the same two bowlers went begging, growing evidence that it was Key's turn in fortune's good books. Not that he needed much further assistance as his innings became a more assured piece of batting. He shared a three-figure stand with Geraint Jones and then brought up another with van Jaarsveld with a quick single that also took him to his own century. There was no stopping him now. As Justin Kemp launched into attack at the other end, Key was relentless – a different player to the walking wicket he'd been only days earlier. In the final over of the day he passed 200 for the first time in County Championship cricket, closing on 202 not out.

On the final morning, there was still work to be done. The personal milestone of passing his career-best 221 for England against the West Indies was quickly behind him. By the time Kemp was out to end a 215-run partnership, Key was unbeaten on a monstrous 270 and he declared with a lead of 240. Explaining his decision not to go for the personal milestone of a triple hundred, he said, 'We wanted to get them in and attack them. We wanted to bowl them out because we knew the wicket was deteriorating.'

As they had been unable to do against Surrey, Key's bowlers proceeded to tear through the Glamorgan batting with 17 overs in hand and Kent found themselves 13 points clear of Derbyshire at the top of the Division Two table. Key's season was certainly looking up.

15

DR COMFORT'S ASHES REVELATIONS

'Graeme's a spinner with a huge drift. I've never seen any off-spinner, including Saqlain and Murali, who can drift the ball and spin it that way' – England spin coach **Mushtaq Ahmed**

GRAEME SWANN sipped on his orange juice and lemonade and admitted that the forthcoming Ashes series would not be as he had always visualised. 'When I was a kid thinking about playing Australia, I could always see myself taking five wickets in Sydney to win the Ashes, so it feels a bit strange that I am going to be playing the Ashes at home,' he said, 'especially starting at Cardiff.'

With his own county stadium a ten-minute walk away from the sports bar in which he was sat on a rare day off, he continued, 'For me, the disappointing thing is that Trent Bridge hasn't got a game because I would love to play a Test match here. It's the best ground in the country outside Lord's. It has everything.'

Cardiff's SWALEC Stadium had instead been awarded its first Test match thanks to promises of £3.2 million to the ECB in revenue, partly courtesy of a grant by the Welsh Assembly Government. 'It's a shame that money has dictated where the games are rather than the grounds England have traditionally won on,' said Swann. 'I think it is a bit one-eyed. But we have to play wherever we are told.

Cardiff might be magnificent and could work out well for me, but it could be a shambles. I would rather the first Test was at Lord's.'

Swann's appetite for Ashes cricket had been further whetted by the smallest morsel of offered to him four years earlier when asked to fulfil twelfth man duties during the second Test at Edgbaston. 'After Flintoff got Ponting out I remember running on with the drinks and it was the most incredible noise I have ever heard at a cricket ground. It was phenomenal.'

The very fact that he was able to talk this time round with the assurance of someone expecting to play a full part was evidence of the remarkable change his life had undergone in the previous six months. 'Being involved with the Test team makes a massive difference,' he said. 'I have been involved with the one-dayers for a couple of years, but there is nowhere near the prestige or recognition. Since getting back from the West Indies I have really noticed it, especially after the World Twenty20 as well. It is strange the places you get recognised. Around Trent Bridge and West Bridgford, where I live, there has always been recognition. Now, suddenly you have schoolkids recognising you, whereas before it was mostly middle-aged blokes. When you are a kid you want to be famous and you want people to pretend to be you. It is nice now when you turn up for events and people know who you are, instead of being disappointed when you are not Kevin Pietersen or Andrew Flintoff.

'It feels like I am not playing as much cricket as normal but I am busy non-stop. I have always seen the media stuff as part and parcel of the job; it is the travelling and the hotels more than anything. Even though we are back in England, people probably don't realise how little time we spend at home. I have had five days at home since the series started against the West Indies. You are forever in hotel rooms. I don't complain about that because I quite enjoy it, but sometimes you stop yourself and say, "Christ, this is a whirlwind."'

Swann's heightened profile meant that, not only had he been signed as a columnist by *The Sun*, even members of his family were in demand from the media. While he was taking wickets in the West Indies, his grandmother Mina was being pictured and interviewed by her local newspaper in Blyth, recounting how she fielded for her grandchildren in the back garden 'That was quite sweet,' Swann smiled. 'A guy who used to play cricket with my dad in Northumberland was working for the paper up there and knew my grandma still lived there. She was dead chuffed. Then a local rag in Northampton, where my mum and dad live, went round to do what I can only call a cringe-worthy photo of them stood in the dining room holding a framed picture of me. It was like I had been killed in the war or something; the grieving parents with a proud picture. They were not used to that sort of thing and didn't know what to do. It makes me laugh.'

The biggest downside of his cricketing elevation was, he explained, the lack of time he was able to devote to singing in his band, Dr Comfort and the Lurid Revelations, who also include former Notts player Andy Afford and Jim Hemmings, son of ex-England spinner Eddie. His commitments to the England cause meant that he had been able to play only one gig in 2009, following his return from the Caribbean. 'I feel like a charlatan because I don't do anything. They say they are going to do these songs and I say, "Brilliant, I will learn them," and then I turn up and do one rehearsal the day before we do a gig. They have written some brilliant stuff of their own. I do play the guitar but we have enough guitars already and I don't want to add to the noise, so I just sing. I absolutely love doing it and I have a whale of a time. It is probably the best hour you can have. It is a better feeling than anything, apart from taking a wicket for England.'

On the subject of why those wickets had come in such numbers so far in his short Test career, Swann was unable to offer a scientific explanation. In part, he felt it was a virtuous circle; the better he played, the more relaxed he felt, and the more his performance improved. 'Maybe my way of dealing with pressure is to laugh it off and say to myself, "You could be doing lot worse things than this." Now many more long-term options have opened up to me, like working in the media, so there is not so much pressure on me to do well in that respect. That is a big difference. Technically, I have not made a conscious effort to change anything over the years, but as a spin bowler you do improve with age because it is a tough skill. You never have the yorker or the bouncer to revert to so you have to work on your variations and it takes years.'

Maturity and knowledge of his craft were also the key elements identified by two men who had been part of Swann's story, both slow bowlers. David Graveney, chairman of selectors when the young Swann first toured for England in 1999 said, 'You have to factor in the development of an individual. Suddenly he sees the light or a switch is hit and he realises the dedication and sacrifice you need to make the top level. That seems to have happened with Graeme and he has become our major spinner.'

Mushtaq Ahmed, England's spin bowling coach, offered, 'He is a very experienced cricketer now and has shown that he's got a proper temperament and courage. He's improving and he's trying to bowl a couple of different deliveries – a quicker one, the straight one. Hopefully he can develop that and then he can be a threat for anybody. I believe that spinners become more effective after 30. I'm happy for him.'

Swann had shown that he was clearly not going to be intimidated in the most intense of cricketing battles. In just a handful of Tests, he had identified himself as one of those cricketers who simply don't know how to take a backward step – whether it was in responding to an attacking batsman by becoming even more aggressive himself or in challenging his own captain to ensure that he got exactly the field he wanted.

Ironically those traits might have made people nervous about offering him a place in the international set-up. His Under-19 coach, John Abrahams, explained, 'He always had that touch of cockiness; arrogant but not in a negative sense. People's perception of him not being serious is wrong. He works really hard at his game and wants to play at the highest level. Because someone plays with a smile it doesn't necessarily mean they don't care as much as someone dour and serious. Why shouldn't you enjoy yourself? He has always used humour to hide his nerves a bit. He is a very funny guy who is very direct, loves to take the piss and won't worry about upsetting you.'

England Under-19 teammate Giles Haywood said, 'Swanny has not changed at all. You see him now on Sky and he is exactly the same. You see him taking the piss out of Nasser and he would have done exactly that ten years ago.' Another junior England colleague, Jonathan Powell, added, 'I remember playing against Swanny from the age of 11. He was always the captain and always the gobby one. He never held back and you always knew what he was thinking.'

Former Northamptonshire colleague and current coach David Capel explained, 'He is a delightful character, a smashing lad with an awful lot to offer. In those early days it is easy to see how he may have offended one or two people with a lack of awareness of others and the situation. It is all about maturity and knowing the appropriate timing of things. When you are young and exuberant you don't realise that there is right time to do things. The people at Notts seem to have helped him a lot and he has grown into a smashing bloke. His game has improved all-round – tactically, technically and in the general way he goes about his business – and he is putting in some valuable performances.'

Nottinghamshire teammate Paul Franks recalled having got to know Swann at the age of 12 and said, 'I have seen him develop into a fantastic bowler. I knew he was good. He got a bad rap after first his first go in the England team and now he has come back and has developed the confidence to help him perform at international level.'

Swann agrees that he has managed to become a little more discriminating in his approach to the game without losing the essence of his vibrant personality. 'You learn when you can laugh and joke and when you can take the piss out of someone in the opposition to undermine them rather than just abusing them,' he explained. 'You learn to channel your exuberance. I fall out with a lot less people than I used to. I used to have an in-your-face attitude and strut and arrogance that wasn't justified. I always come across as confident on TV because people see me laughing and joking at slip. There, you can talk to other people and my nature is not to be serious so I laugh and joke wherever I can. I do enjoy my cricket but I have my times when I am pissed off. That is the time when the cameras are not on you. I hope I would be known as a happy-go-lucky bloke on the circuit, but I am glad there are a couple of people who absolutely hate me because I have got no love for them whatsoever.' Pushed for identities, he gave a secretive smile and said, 'A couple of the older generation and one or two of the younger ones. That's as far as I'll go.'

According to England mentor Mushtaq Ahmed, Swann 'still has lots of years left in him' but on that point Swann himself was being cautious. Maybe it was seeing the advances during the World Twenty20 of young leg-spinner Adil Rashid, named in England's pre-Ashes training camp. Or maybe it was pragmatism born of seeing England search for a 'mystery spinner' for so long before turning to his orthodox off-spin. 'Cricket is one of those things where I truly believe there is a big wheel and it turns at different speeds,' Swann said. 'I reckon in five years' time we will be looking for a mystery leg-spinner again, so if it's my time over the next two or three years then so be it. I am going to enjoy every minute of it. I'll be really hyped up in the dressing room when the Ashes starts. This is a massive series for all us players and someone at some stage will have to do something special. It can be one spell of bowling that changes things. I'd love it if I can be that man.'

One of Swann's earliest memories of watching cricket, and the genesis of his particular Ashes daydream, was seeing England triumph in Australia in 1986-87 with an off-spinner and slow left-armer working in unison. 'I grew up watching John Emburey and Phil Edmonds and I'd love it if we go into each game with two spinners,' he said. He doesn't, however, recall a conscious decision to follow the path of that Middlesex duo. 'I can only assume that as a kid I was so small that to get the ball down the other end it had to have a lot of flight on it. I assume it would have been my dad who said, "If you are doing that, you might as well twist it when you let it go and see what happens." I actually grew up desperately wanting to be a wicketkeeper because my brother was. You were always in the game and I used to get bored stupid fielding. Alec gave it up at 14 because he said it hurt his back too much and that made me look at it and think, "Yes, it is hard work."'

It meant that when Paul Collingwood took the gloves in place of the injured Matt Prior in the second West Indian Test at the Riverside, he had to fight off Swann's attempts to get there first. 'I was gutted. I really wanted to have a go. Still, deep down, if anyone asked me what I wanted to be I would say a keeper. I have done it a few times at different levels. It is great on cold days when everyone's hands are falling off and they have got big gloves on.'

THE FANTASIES that had placed Swann in the role of wicket-taking hero in Sydney had presumably not allowed for the possibility of him completing his first Ashes match without a single victim, yet boasting a batting average of 78. It is also doubtful that he would have foreseen a pre-match ceremony that, with its various national anthems, hymns and collection of opera singers, was closer to the Last Night of the Proms than any first morning of the Ashes that anyone could remember. Both, however, were among the experiences he would take away from Cardiff.

There had been two days of practice and familiarisation with new surroundings. In the case of Swann, that entailed getting used to the outfield one day, fine tuning his bowling and slogging Mushtaq's throw-downs around the ground the next. Then came the pomp and circumstance, in the midst of which England won the toss before proceeding to bat through the first day. Swann arrived at the crease when Stuart Broad was the first man out on the second morning. England's hopes of pushing on to a score of 400, considered the minimum on a slow, low wicket, were delicately balanced. But with a freedom that helped whip the 16,000 crowd into the kind of fervour normally associated with the late-afternoon beer intake, Swann set about the Australian bowling. Three times in as many balls he hit the off-spin of Nathan Hauritz to the boundary, twice dancing down the track and hitting over mid-on before executing a reverse sweep. Looking as excited as if he was on stage he then deposited a short-arm jab over the head of seamer Brad Hilfenhaus. Within the first hour of the day, England had added another 90 and it was only the dismissals of Jimmy Anderson and Monty Panesar that brought his breathless assault to a halt at 47 not out. 'I was having the time of my life,' he reflected later. 'Ever since I was a kid I have enjoyed playing in big matches. I think my game improves when I am under pressure and performing in front of big crowds and millions on TV. It really helps me, especially when I bat. I want to go out and show off and entertain people.'

His morning's work was not quite finished. As Australia set about hunting down England's total of 435, he was into the attack in the sixth over, a few minutes before lunch. Ominously, he saw little of the turn that the unconsidered Hauritz had been extracting late in England's innings. The momentum of the morning's happy hitting had gone, and would not be glimpsed over the next two days. 'I was happy for the most part with how I bowled in the series, but I didn't start particularly well,' he would admit. 'Inevitably over seven weeks your form is going to ebb and flow. Very few players can maintain consistency throughout, and that has a lot to do with the size and scope of the games.'

As Swann and others toiled, a procession of Australian batsmen marched into three figures: Simon Katich, Ricky Ponting, Marcus North and, with the final flourish of the innings, wicketkeeper Brad Haddin. Suddenly, Test cricket looked a rather more demanding game than when Swann had faced the West Indies. His first over of the fourth day was probably his most threatening, but it was one of the 38 wicketless overs he sent down. England's five frontline bowlers all conceded more than 100 runs. Ponting was able to declare at 674 for 6 and whip out the first two English batsmen before rain halted the fourth day at tea.

Twenty-four hours later, Swann's batting was called upon once more, with England struggling at 159 for 7 after Hauritz picked up his sixth wicket of the match. They were still 80 runs adrift with more than 38 overs left in the match. Only Collingwood was resisting, reaching his second half-century of the match by combining immovable defence with the look of someone who had barely picked up a bat before in his life.

When Peter Siddle gave Swann a quick bouncer, it was a sign of what was to come. Miffed a few balls later at seeing the batsman credited with runs when the ball clearly went to the ropes via the pads, Siddle banged in another short straight ball. Swann jerked back his head and felt the jab of the ball biting into his left hand. After trainer Steve McCaig had administered a pain-numbing spray, Swann took guard again and two balls later another lifting delivery hit him on the left elbow. Out came the spray again. The next ball smacked into his right hand; a manful effort from Siddle on a dead, Indian-style pitch.

Ponting made a very public show of instructing Siddle to bowl round the wicket at Swann's ribs. When he tried, by way of variation, to pitch the ball up, Swann drove him expertly through mid-off. Siddle responded by rattling Swann's helmet, but the assault had been survived. Steering Hauritz to third man and edging Hilfenhaus to the same boundary, Swann's share of a 50 partnership was 27. But after adding four more with a crisp cover drive, he tried to pull a Hilfenhaus delivery that failed to bounce and was trapped leg before. Swann's had been a valuable contribution to the cause of survival, but when Collingwood played a rare, ill-advised swish at a short ball from Siddle and was caught in the gully for 74 after almost six hours, England appeared condemned at 233 for 9.

Back in the changing room, Swann couldn't watch as James Anderson and Monty Panesar set about tackling the remaining 11 overs. Instead, he switched the television to a re-run of the German Grand Prix, undaunted by the apparent omen of an Australian, Mark Webber, racing to victory. 'It was my way of dealing with it. I thought I would pretend it wasn't going on. Even then I got annoyed because Brawn messed up their tactics and I wanted Jenson Button to win.'

The cheers of every block and leave by the final two batsmen reached Swann's ears, dispelling any fears about how whole-heartedly the Welsh public would get behind the England team. By now, of course, superstition precluded Swann from going to take a look. Everyone was pinned to their 'lucky' positions. 'Most players are superstitious,' Swann added. 'Straussy had sunburn on his legs because he didn't move all day from his seat on the balcony.'

At last, 69 balls had been seen off and England had got the draw that might have been undeserved but was a thrillingly nail-biting way in which to begin the series. The only blemish was England's clumsy attempt at time-wasting by sending the twelfth man to the crease with new gloves twice in the space of little more than five minutes.

In the cold light of day, however, the home team's optimism, particularly about the superiority of their attack, had been shaken. 'We worked really hard to get either reverse swing or traditional swing and it did nothing,' Swann recalled. 'We did not bowl really well as a unit, part from a few balls. The disappointing thing for me was that I bowled a few full tosses. The the ball didn't come out of my hand how I wanted; I didn't have the rhythm I wanted.'

Lord's offered a no happier prospect for the second Test. The home team had not won an Ashes match there since 1934.

Once again, Swann spent the first day as a spectator as England, who included Graham Onion's seam for Panesar's spin, batted throughout. This time, though, his contribution with the bat on the second morning was restricted to a leg-side boundary and a catch to the slip cordon. He was scarcely more involved when England took the field and dismissed Australia for 215 prior to Saturday lunchtime, 210 behind a total built around captain Andrew Strauss's 161. The swing of Anderson and Onions under cloudy skies was enough to keep Australia's batsmen marching regularly up and down the pavilion steps and Swann bowled only one token over. A quick dash for runs allowed Strauss to declare at the start of the fourth day with a lead of 521. Unless Australia showed an uncharacteristic lack of mettle for two innings in a row, Swann was likely to be much busier for the remainder of the match.

Prior to the game Andrew Flintoff had either set himself up for a fall or prepared the stage for the most dramatic of episodes by announcing his intention to retire from Test cricket at the end of the series. Injury-prone throughout his career, his body parts had begun wearing out with even greater frequency since the 2005 Ashes, the undoubted apogee of his career. England's selectors must at times have felt like claiming their £2,000 under the government's scrappage allowance scheme. Flintoff had saved them the bother by deciding to limit his exertions to one-day cricket, for his country, for Lancashire and anyone else who could afford his wages.

With only 34 on the board, Flintoff had removed openers Simon Katich and Phillip Hughes, whose contribution to the series had hardly been the frightening one predicted by the grumps who took offence to his early-season burst for Middlesex. With three wickets down and the reliable Michael Clarke and Michael Hussey affecting a recovery, Swann came on to bowl in mid-afternoon. Shirt buttoned to the neck and long sleeves rolled down, he looked all business. His presence at the Nursery End indicated his intent to turn the ball up the slope, the untraditional approach for a Lord's off-spinner but one that brought the footmarks of left-armer Mitchell Johnson into play. He began his second over by presenting Clarke with a full toss that he drove to the ropes.

Never short on self-belief, Swann had managed to massage the disappointment of Cardiff into a positive attitude going into to this match, convincing himself that his bowling had been getting better as the first Test had worn on. 'I was feeling confident going into the game,' he explained. The turning point, literally, came when the left-handed Hussey drove hard outside the off stump and found the ball spinning sharply out of the rough, ending up in the safe hands of Collingwood at slip. The naked eye did not legislate for the possibility that there had been no thick edge – well, not umpire Billy Doctrove's anyway. Television replays showed that Hussey had merely clipped the ground with his bat and Swann had, indeed, found an extraordinary amount of movement off the pitch.

The Australians already felt aggrieved at the dismissals of Hughes (off an apparent no-ball) and Ponting (after Rudi Koertzen chose not to refer Strauss's low slip catch to the third umpire). Ironically, the ICC had only days earlier announced that the referral system trialled in various series in recent months would become standard practice from October onwards. Little comfort for Hussey, while Swann could not have cared less. 'It was the sound, deviation and the fact that it went to slip – and the sheer excitement of getting one past the bat after Cardiff,' he said of his typically enthusiastic appeal. 'If it didn't hit his edge then unlucky to Huss, who is a good mate of mine. But as far we were concerned it was a legitimate catch.'

His tail up, Swann set about tormenting North with changes of pace and flight before sending a faster, straighter ball into his stumps between bat and pad. At times, the turn he produced to right-handers Clarke and Haddin during the remainder of the day was considerable but both were still batting at close of play, the former having made an impeccable century. In the meantime, the experts in press box and commentary booth had been screaming at Swann to get rid of the fielder posted square on the cover boundary and place someone in a catching position on the off side. Such tentativeness, it was feared, could see the Australians get close to making the 209 they still required on the final day. Swann's typically earthy reaction to the game situation was, 'I'm just glad these first two Tests are living up to 2005. The worst thing would be to play in my first Ashes series and it be a pile of shit.'

Flintoff, inevitably, put any English pessimism to rest by dismissing Haddin in his first over on his final day of Lord's Test cricket. Swann joined him in the attack after an hour, with an equally dramatic result. His second delivery, a touch too full, drifted just enough for Clarke to play inside the line. The ball spun back into his stumps, bringing a magnificent innings to a 136-run conclusion. 'He was so quick on his feet and batted so well that it came as a surprise when I got a ball past him,' Swann confessed.

Dragging his creaking knee up to the bowling crease again and again – no one was getting the ball away from him now – Flintoff brought deliveries down the slope to bowl Hauritz and Siddle for his first five-wicket haul at Lord's. Then Swann, having missed a difficult return catch off Johnson, beat the left-hander's swishing bat to knock over middle stump and complete England's historic victory. It was as close to an eruption as the stifling setting of Lord's is ever likely to experience.

'It was a fantastic victory and I'll struggle in my career to have a greater moment than taking the wicket that clinched England's first Ashes victory at the home of cricket for 75 years,' he revealed later. But as much as his own moment of glory, it will be the memory of Flintoff's spell on the final morning that Swann carries into old age. 'Everyone on the field was rooting for him to get his fifth wicket and he refused to let go of the ball until he got it. For him to bowl like that with a wonky knee was extraordinary.'

It might have been Flintoff's match, but Swann's 4 for 87 in 28 overs after his disappointment at Cardiff meant that he was in the thick of it as a participant in the Ashes. It wasn't the Sydney he dreamed of, but it wasn't a bad alternative.

16

POLITICAL GAMES

'I had death threats. I had people saying they were going to rape my wife. But the club refused to let me call the police'
– Jamie Grove

THE VILLAGE OF Exning, on the western edge of Suffolk, sits a couple of well sign-posted left turns off the A14, easily located by the owner of even the most unreliable satellite navigation system. It appears that behind almost every high stone wall lining its roads is a stables or a stud farm, a reminder that Newmarket is barely a decent gallop away. Another right turn, past the equine hospital, and you come to Exning Cricket Club, who play their Two Counties Championship Division One games while grazing cows look up occasionally from an adjoining field.

Unloading his kit from the car boot, Jamie Grove explained why this season had seen him drawn to Exning from nearby Sudbury, for whom he had first played when still in short trousers. 'It sounds daft, but one reason is that to get to Sudbury it is down a lot of winding roads,' he said. 'Exning is a nice straight drive, which makes it much easier for me with my back, especially going home after games when I am bit stiff.'

With time to kill before play began on a late summer afternoon, Grove straddled a boundary-side bench and discussed the route that had brought him to his current cricketing home, via Essex, Somerset and Leicestershire. Any bitterness that might once have existed has subsided over time, but there was no attempt by Grove, an affable and engaging character, to hide the bemusement that has taken its place.

A chronic back condition is only one of the painful legacies of a career that began with a demand to completely remodel his bowling action and ended with death threats after a botched Twenty20 Cup semi-final. In between, there was the disappointment of missing out on the 1998 Under-19 World Cup final, a lack of consistency that he willingly owns up to, and enduring memories of bowling fast at some of the best batsmen in the game. 'I loved having a brand new ball in my hand, looking down the wicket and seeing a world-class player at the other end and thinking, "Right, I have got to beat this bastard." I always believed I could get anyone out, even if someone was hitting me for sixes and fours. It only takes one ball to get somebody out. I loved testing myself against the best players. You won some and, in my case, you lost some pretty badly.'

Born in Bury St Edmunds after his family had moved from Essex, Grove was another cricket club son, packing his kit when he went to watch his father Chris. Grove senior was a former semi-professional footballer with Dagenham who captained Sudbury and wasn't afraid to put his son in the firing line. 'I was playing from the age of three and played my first senior game for the third team when I was seven,' Grove recalled. 'I think I made my debut in first-team cricket when I was 11. I got bounced first ball without a helmet. Dad would be showing us shots in the kitchen every night. If you bowled badly in a game then the meal took three or four hours.

'I always wanted to be an opening bowler. Even though I have always had a wiry frame I was able to bowl quick. My hero was Curtly Ambrose, simply because the guy looked evil. I was lucky enough to play against him once and it was a scary experience. I didn't get on very well at all.

'I was at a state school, so we didn't really play any cricket. But there was a bloke called Rob Blackmore, a farmer who made his own cricket ground, and every Monday night he had coaching sessions. I was down there from the age of five or six. Being in a minor county and not being at a public school made it a bit harder. I got five wickets and 50 runs for Suffolk in an Under-15s game and then got dropped. They brought in a nice little public school boy for the next game.' It was an early taste of the realities of team selection; a sour flavour to which Grove would become accustomed in future years.

Outside of school term-time, Grove was able to switch cricketing allegiance to the age group teams of Essex, which led to a professional contract. When he reported for his first full summer at Chelmsford's County Ground, at the age of 16, a surprise was in store. 'I used to have a perfect side-on action and was able to swing it a lot. My job was always to run up and bowl as quickly as possible and get wickets. On my first day of pre-season they completely changed my action. They made bowl front-on. That has always been a bit of a funny one with me because I had done all that work to get there. Geoff Arnold was the bowling coach and he decided it would be best. They said at some point in my career I might get back problems. To bowl front-on you need to have big shoulders. You have to be a big boy to get some pace because you are not using the twisting of the rest of your body. It changes all your bio mechanics; different angles, different stresses going through your body. I think it hindered me for a good few years and I never quite understood why they did it.

'It was a funny time trying to work out this new action. I lost my pace for three or four months. In the end you kind of work your way back to some kind of compromise. But after a few months I tore the cartilage in my left knee so I missed the rest of the season anyway. I came into my second season as a professional with an action I had never really bowled with.'

Quite apart from the reconstruction of his technique, Grove found himself stepping into a whole new world at Essex. 'I had come from the background of Minor Counties and the difference was unbelievable. Our coach had been a schoolteacher who didn't know anything about cricket but could afford the time on a Saturday afternoon to make sure everything was going smoothly. I got to Essex and there were all these coaches. My first day, I bowled for three and a half hours in the nets. It would never happen now. You get about 20 minutes. And until I did my first twelfth man duties at Essex I had never even seen a game of first-class cricket. I didn't know who anyone was. Walking into a changing room with all these different personalities was a huge shock to the system.'

Recovered from his knee injury and playing regular second-team cricket, Grove discovered the joys of the professional game. 'I absolutely loved it. We had Alan Butcher as our coach and we had a very young team. We would probably lose all but one or two games but we were playing all the 16 and 17 year olds and you were encouraged to just go out and do what you could do. It was fantastic playing on pitches where the ball actually bounced. I was bowling quicker and quicker and although people suggested things that I should do, they always said that if it was going to affect my pace I shouldn't do it. My pace was the thing I had going for me.' It was that speed that attracted the attention of the England management when places for the 1997-98 winter trip to South Africa were being discussed. 'There were some warm-up games and we played against Scotland and a Star of India XI,' Grove remembered. 'We had a big squad and I always felt confident I was going to be around there but I had a shocking game against Scotland. It was one of only two times in my life I bowled no-balls – the other was on Twenty20 finals day.'

To his relief, Grove had done enough to win selection and he duly reported to the warm-up camps at Lilleshall. 'But I had a reaction with my knee after the second fitness test. It just blew up. The medical staff wanted me there but I couldn't do anything. It wasn't a very nice feeling because all the boys would be going off and doing their five or ten mile runs and I was just stuck with the physio. I didn't bowl a ball until we had been on tour for a month.'

After bowling in one warm-up game in Boland, Grove was included for the second Test against South Africa, where his 13 overs produced figures of 1 for 63. 'I did all right – not fantastic – but they were the flattest wickets anyone had ever seen.'

Once the World Cup games began, Grove was in and out of the side, playing in three of the six group games. His best performance was 2 for 23 in a losing cause against Bangladesh and he found himself alternating with Richard Logan for the job of sharing the new ball with Paul Franks. 'Logie had a storming first few weeks of the tour. He was more of a swing bowler and I ran in and hit the pitch, so if it was a quick wicket I would play. It was back and forth and probably up until the Australia game they were still wondering where to go. Then Logie bowled really well – an awesome spell of yorkers. I knew there was no chance of playing in the final then. It hurt more missing out on the Australia game than the final. Once we were in the final then there was no one who was unhappy. We were there and had our chance to get our names in the history books. There was a great team spirit.'

Team coach John Abrahams explained, 'Jamie was quick but more erratic. He was the one you would play against Namibia because he could get them out through sheer pace they wouldn't be used to it. Later on he suffered from not playing first-team cricket. He was a confidence player. If things were going well he was good but it only took a little thing not to go well and he would focus on that.'

Grove agreed that his tour offered a window on his future years in the game. 'Throughout the trip I had good spells, but I didn't ever have what I felt was a really good game. I was slightly inconsistent and that hindered me throughout my career. I got wickets at certain times. It was a difficult tour for me. I went into it injured and had no real practice games.'

Yet there was still plenty of reason for Grove to remember the trip as one of the high points of his cricketing life. 'We went to South Africa with fifteen hundred quid in our pockets, a good exchange rate, and we had a bloody good time; probably too good at times. We were living like kings. There were times when everyone wanted to kill each other, but it didn't happen very often. If anyone was down people lifted them up. But I still don't know how the hell we won the World Cup. We had been playing terribly, but we had some strong characters and everyone backed themselves. We knew we could beat people on our day. The biggest frustration for John Abrahams was that we had a lot people who could bat aggressively and nobody who could bat nicely for 50 overs, apart from Steve Peters in the final. It was all shit or bust, but we ended up winning games because of it. And little things like Jonny Powell's catch against Pakistan when we were struggling changed the tournament.'

Back home in the spring of 1998, Grove was raring to go at the start of a season that would see him break into the Essex first team, taking 3 for 74 and scoring 33 runs in his first-class debut against Surrey. 'By the end of the tour I'd had a fantastic time and was really fit for the start of the season. I remember my debut very well. Nasser [Hussain] gave me the new ball and Alec Stewart was at the other end. He said, "Whatever you do, don't bowl it short and wide." First ball, you just heard it hit the bloody advertising board. I didn't think it was short and wide, but he managed to get a ball from off stump and absolutely blasted it for four. Surrey were the Manchester United of football and I managed to get Adam and Ben Hollioake out within a couple of balls and had Martin Bicknell caught at third man driving. I got some runs, which was quite nice, and hit Alex Tudor and Bicknell for sixes. It was good fun – the sort of thing you dream of.'

Yet Grove was never able to take enough wickets to secure his long-term future at Essex, who released him after the 1999 season. 'At Essex you constantly thought you had cracked it and then you would be out of the team for what you thought was a very stupid reason. We had a pretty hard guy in Keith Fletcher as coach; a hard man and very hard to please. I was bowling quick and swinging the ball and thinking I must be part of the team. But then there is always another person trying to jump over you and Ricky Anderson came in from nowhere and got 50-odd wickets in his first season.

'And you got mixed messages. In my last year I was told, "You have got to bowl as fast as you can, but you have got to bowl line and length on off stump and you have got to swing it away." That was pretty much what you were told every day. It was hard, to be honest. I always felt that as long as I was getting wickets, then conceding runs wasn't a huge issue. I had always been someone who bowled five overs as quick as I could and see what happened. My biggest disappointment with Essex was at a pre-season marine training course at Dartmoor, where I sat down for a talk with Nasser and Keith Fletcher. Keith said I would be playing for England within a year; he would make sure of it. They released me at the end of the year. I played up until I got shin splints that turned into a fracture and then I got released. I saw it coming because if people stop talking to you, you know you are in trouble. I had done well in the second team but when I came into the first team I wasn't getting much of a bowl so I was wondering whether Essex was right for me. It was a funny old club at the time. A fantastic club, but they had an old-school way of encouraging players.'

By the time Essex broke the inevitable news of Grove's release, he knew there was a home for him at Somerset, against whom he had achieved a six-wicket haul in a second-eleven game. 'It was at North Perrott, which is still the quickest track I have ever bowled on. I had just finished bowling and was fielding at square leg when I turned round and saw Kevin Shine, their bowling coach, standing next to me in the middle of a game. He offered me contract while standing there at square leg.'

A five-wicket spell in his opening first-class game for his new county suggested good things to come, but even though Grove's career followed the same pattern of under-achievement over the next two years he looks back at his move as 'the best decision I ever made'. He explained, 'I lived 200 metres from the ground. I used to walk across the river to go to work and get a paper on the way. Even at Championship games you would get a few thousand people and at the one-day matches the atmosphere was unbelievable. The playing side was hard work, but a real eye-opener. You know, we had never been taught what protein was or what carbohydrates were at Essex. They were a hard run club and when you trained you did it 100 per cent, but they didn't know about the things that could make you a little bit better. At Essex we were training really hard but no one ever really told us how to recover.'

After two seasons of being in and out of the first team, Grove was on the move again. This time he recalls it with a heavy heart. 'The biggest regret I have was leaving Somerset,' he said. 'I was playing all the one-day games and a few Championship games. We were second in the table in 2001 and I missed out on getting a medal by one game. I loved Championship games and didn't really like one-day cricket. I was bowling in the indoor nets during a game against Leicestershire. I wasn't playing and Jack Birkenshaw, the Leicester coach, was in there giving some throw downs. Jimmy Ormond was leaving Leicester the next year and Jack said,

"I need an opening bowler. Are you interested?" I wanted to open the bowling and play, so everything looked good. I still had a year on my contract at Somerset, but they were really good about it. At the end-of-season celebrations I was thinking, "What am I doing leaving here?" But I was desperate to play four-day cricket. I moved to Leicestershire and within a few weeks they moved Birkenshaw out of the coach's position and brought in Phil Whitticase. They didn't see me as a Championship bowler so it ended up as a bad move.'

Grove played only two Championship games in three seasons, although in 2002 he did take 17 wickets in the Norwich Union League. 'My first year went OK. I was playing under Vince Wells, who was a lovely guy, but the sad thing was all the politics at the club, which I had known only a little about. I thought players were just leaving to get more money but they lost about ten players in two years and in the end they asked Vince to leave and Phil DeFreitas took over. The less said about that the better. He decided I wasn't the way he wanted to go. It was none of those "face fits" things with him.'

Yet Grove felt that the problems ran deeper than a personality clash with his captain. 'When Jack Birkenshaw left they went from having a huge personality who was running the club, with everything done through him, to Phil as first-team coach. He saw himself more as a manager and the ethos was: if you want coaching, go and ask some of the other players. I had gone from Somerset, where Kevin Shine used to organise net sessions down to the minute, to Leicester, where we had no coaching. We asked if we could get a video camera to film us and they said, "Just go out and bowl in the middle and we will turn the security camera on you." Our bowling lessons consisted of a security camera trying to zoom in from the office and us trying to work out our actions off that.'

The breaking point for Grove, one that he is unable to forgive several years later, was the aftermath of Leicester's appearance at the first Twenty20 Cup finals day at Trent Bridge in 2003. The Foxes were drawn to play Warwickshire, a game they eventually lost when they failed to defend a total of 162. Grove bowled only one over, a disastrous sequence that saw him go for 20 runs, including three wides and three no-balls. It could have been even worse if the free hits he allowed had been punished more severely.

'I hadn't played for about three and a half weeks and had three epidurals in my back. I'd not even been allowed to leave my home. They let me bowl three balls the day before the finals and when we turned up it had been really dewy overnight. You couldn't use the run-ups, so we were bowling off about three paces before play. I declared myself fit and I had an absolute nightmare.'

What happened next still shocks him. 'After that game I had death threats. I had people saying they were going to rape my wife. It was all on the forum on the club website.' Other messages appeared accusing Grove of being drunk in the crowd.

'I wasn't allowed into the ground at Leicester and they wouldn't talk to me. I thought, "This is not for me. My wife – my girlfriend at the time – was getting abused, all over one bad game I had. Fair enough, I probably lost us the game. Twenty an over is not exactly fantastic. I know I completely screwed up. There were 20,000 people telling me that. But I'd helped get us to the bloody finals day. I went to the club office and said. 'I want to call the police because I think this is terrible. But they refused to let me. In the end they said they would put a line on the website saying something like, "We fully back Jamie Grove in everything he has done and he is a professional person." That's all. It was not really the support I was looking for. From that point, I knew I was getting released. I was told that if I wasn't playing then I shouldn't go into the ground. I was having physiotherapy every day but I had to go to the physio's clinic at half past seven in the morning to have it. That is all I was allowed to do. I felt hurt by it all. How can you not back one of your players who is trying his backside off?'

Breaking into a sardonic smile, Grove concluded, 'It was slight victimisation.'

His professional career was at an end. 'I was at an age where, as a fast bowler, you were expected to be winning games. And I'd had enough. I loved playing and testing myself, but all the politics involved? That is not what I do.'

Also, his back problems were getting worse, leaving with him 'irritable leg syndrome', a growth on the inside of the spine. 'If I fall out of my action, it hits my nerve and my legs lose feeling. They can do an operation but there is 60 per cent chance you will end up paralysed. If I'd had physio every day I could have played professional cricket, but I was out of contract so I couldn't afford it. I had some preliminary offers from a few clubs but in any pro sport you need to be 100 per cent in mind and body to be able to train as hard as you need. I didn't have the drive to carry on at that point. I was time to get out there and start working.'

Grove qualified as an engineer and now works in engineering sales. Cricket is fun again, even if a few hours after reliving the ups and downs of his career a last-ball loss against Ipswich and East Suffolk ended Exning's hopes of snatching their league title. Grove took one wicket in his opening spell, but his team allowed the opposition's last pair to score 34 to win the game. On the club's web site a few days later, no one was being threatened.

17

GREEN AND PLEASANT LAND

'The Ashes was probably the best seven weeks of my life' –
Graeme Swann

THE TEN-DAY break between the end of the Lord's Test and the resumption of the Ashes battle at Edgbaston was supposed to allow a period of calm. Yet there was no need for reporters to start scratching around for a storyline to fill the void. The England and Wales Cricket Board obliged by announcing that Kevin Pietersen could no longer hobble through matches on his injured Achilles tendon. He would undergo an operation and miss the remainder of the series.

Ian Bell had been earmarked for Pietersen's place after being named as a spare batsman for the first two Tests, but there was considerable speculation about who was next in line if injuries, form or the need for an extra batter necessitated a new recruit. Having rediscovered his form, Rob Key appeared closer to the Test squad than for several years. 'I thought getting into the World Twenty20 would be a way back in,' he said. 'That is what I had pinned my hopes on. Now there are a few guys out there scoring a lot of runs.'

For a period of a few weeks in mid-season no one was scoring more than Key himself. While the third Test was proceeding to a rain-affected draw at Edgbaston, he was compiling a third century in consecutive LV County Championship games to help Kent, top of Division Two, beat their nearest challengers, Derbyshire. Chasing 318 to win on the final day at Canterbury, Key dominated a big partnership with former England keeper Geraint Jones. Playing shots all round the wicket and hitting 14 fours, he reached three figures out of a score of 167. By the time he chipped a catch to long-off the pair had added 175 in 46 overs and, despite a nervous flurry of wickets late on, Kent completed their fifth win of the season.

Key's performance pushed his Championship average for the season into the mid-60s, similar at that stage to that of Owais Shah. Both men were mentioned by England selector Ashley Giles as being considered for selection. Yet when a batsman was added to the squad for the fourth Test, it was the third man cited by Giles who was given the call, Warwickshire's Jonathan Trott, a South African-born 28 year old with two England Twenty20 games on his record. His selection made it difficult to see where Shah and Key fitted into England's future Test plans. Perhaps Steve James, writing in the *Sunday Telegraph* was correct when he said, 'Shah's time in the game's longest format has, quite simply, passed.'

The Edgbaston Test had been destined for a draw from the moment ugly brown puddles were seen gathering on the outfield the day before the scheduled start. Continuing rain and problems in draining the playing surface meant that the first day consisted of only 30 overs, during which Australia ratted up 126 for the loss of only Simon Katich, victim of Graeme Swann's happy knack of striking in the first over of his spells. Swann should have had an immediate wicket when Shane Watson, given Phillip Hughes's slot at the top of the order, tried a scruffy sweep and was looked upon benevolently by Aleem Dar. But then Katich horribly missed a pull shot, leaving no room for doubt in the umpire's mind. 'I was surprised to get a chance to bowl so early,' Swann admitted. 'I saw Katich shaping up to pull and it skidded on. If it had turned he'd probably have put me away.'

The first two balls of Friday saw Graham Onions trap Watson lbw and bowl Michael Hussey, after which Australia's innings disintegrated. Once Saturday's play was washed out, England found themselves building a lead of 113 on day four. Swann's contribution was a breezy 24, including several boundaries off Mitchell Johnson, and he was back into the attack when Australia reached 44 without loss. Once again, his first over was troublesome, but it was the turn of events after Onions dismissed Katich that gave rise to the hope that England might defy the loss of time and take a 2-0 lead.

Facing Ricky Ponting for the first time, Swann's initial delivery turned sharply from outside off as the Australian captain made his characteristic front-foot push towards the ball, taking his chances with the two men in catching positions. Three balls later, he lunged again and was struck by a ball that would have hit leg stump. He was ruled to have had his pad just outside the line of the wicket. Encouraged, Swann tossed up the final ball of the over and watched it turn like a heat seeking missile between bat and pad to hit the stumps. It wasn't quite Shane Warne's 'Ball of the Century' to Mike Gatting 16 years earlier but it might well have been the ball of Swann's career – making the fifth day all the more anti-climactic.

Swann was inconsistent throughout as Australia lost only three wickets. He was punished for too many loose balls and finished with just that one wicket from his 31 overs as Michael Clarke and Marcus North batted their team to what could even have been a match-winning lead had a day and a half not been taken out of the game. From the various experts came the notion that Swann was striving too hard for wickets on every ball instead of slowly building pressure.

The fourth Test at Headingley found England without Flintoff and, frankly, without much of a clue for the two and half days of action. A batting line-up that looked fragile with the inclusion of Stephen Harmison as Flintoff's replacement, folded twice; for 102 in the first innings and, after being 58 without loss, to 86 for 6 in the second. In between, Clarke and North punished an England attack that proved unable to bowl full and straight. In a reverse of the third Test, it was Clarke who fell in the 90s and North who completed his century – with a leg-side six off Swann – Australia's seventh ton of a series in which England had only one.

Only when Nottinghamshire colleagues Stuart Broad and Swann came together on the third morning at 120 for 7 did England's boisterous fans have any reason to cheer. The pair clubbed their way to a 100 partnership in 73 balls in just over an hour of glorious mayhem in which both umpires were distracted enough to lose count on three occasions of the numbers of balls bowled in an over. Swann had gone out to bat in the second innings without a run or a wicket in the game and with the approach that there were 'two ways to view the day; a lost cause or a chance at immortality'. The padding he wore under his shirt gave him the look of a modern-day Colin Milburn and, for a while, he started hitting like him. Having pulled Peter Siddle over square leg he then took 16 off an over by Stuart Clark with a mix of swing and clips to leg and thumps over mid-off. After Broad's wicket ended the stand at 108, Swann hooked Siddle high into the crowd to reach 54 off 53 balls before being caught behind off Johnson after lunch for 62, the top score in the innings. None of the available technology showed Swann getting anywhere near the ball and any sound that either umpire heard can only have been that of Asad Rauf's mullet swishing against his shirt collar. One wicket later England had lost by an innings and 80 runs, but in a series of vast swings of impetus Swann felt that an important, albeit small, shift had been achieved by England.

'All summer, momentum really did seem prevalent,' he would venture when reviewing the series. 'In the first Test we were outplayed but regained momentum in that last hour and took it on to Lord's. At Edgbaston we started well again, but they got momentum back on the last day and trounced us at Headingley. In that last session, though, Broady and I got back some initiative, even though we got hammered. It was better than meekly subsiding and it really helped going into the last Test.'

THREE DAYS after Headingley, Robert Key found himself at the centre of a lot more attention than he would usually have expected for a Tuesday morning start at Northampton. As he stepped into the sunshine and headed out for the toss, England selector James Whitaker was waiting to shake his hand. Watching his every move from the County Ground press box were considerably more journalists than would normally have watched a Division Two Championship match. When Key chose to bat it meant they would not have to wait long for their story.

The achievement of England's middle order of Bopara, Bell and Collingwood in scoring 16 runs between them in two innings at Headingley had sent speculation over the line-up for the final Test at The Oval spiralling out of control. Everyone who had ever scored a first-class century, it seemed, was being touted somewhere. Those interested merely in stoking up what was potentially the best storyline were banging on about Mark Ramprakash, who since his last Test in 2002 had become the darling of the housewives in *Strictly Come Dancing* and was still churning out the hundreds at nearly 40. The supposedly more knowledgeable experts in the broadcasting world were close to unanimity in calling for Key to take Bopara's place at number three.

His place under no threat, Swann was able to observe the pandemonium with amusement. It was what he had come to expect. 'I knew the nation's eyes would be on the series but I hadn't realised to what extent,' he explained. 'Everyone in the street knew who you were and everyone was talking to you. If you had a good day everyone was patting you on the back and if you had a bad day everyone was questioning what was going wrong. It is just phenomenal the level cricket gets to during the Ashes. You even turn on Radio One, not normally a cricket station, and they had continual updates. They were talking about it on every TV channel. At the press conferences after each day it was just ridiculous the amount of cameras and people in there. I just loved every minute of it. I loved the speculation and hype. It was a crazy seven weeks and so intense. I enjoy sport like that when it is all encompassing.'

At Northampton, Key settled in quickly. As an opener, it was suggested that he could bring solidity to the vital role of coming in for England at first wicket down. Such was the need for those qualities that memories were being evoked of the way in which David Steele, an unheralded county player in his mid-30s, blunted Dennis Lillee and Jeff Thomson in his glorious summer of 1975. On the wicket where the stubborn Steele had played most of his county cricket, Key looked more like Ian Botham when he stuck Monty Panesar's second delivery over the ropes for six. 'It's nice to hear people mentioning my name but the Test is still a few days away, so there is little point worrying about it,' he'd said before his innings.

As his score mounted, Key was clearly having a more comfortable time of it than the father close to the pavilion trying to answer his young son's innocently asked 'Where are the rest of the people?' and struggling to counter comments like, 'It's better on TV. This isn't a real game.' It was real enough for the players under scrutiny in a round of county matches that shaped up, in the minds of the media at least, as a series of unofficial Test trials. Taking lunch with a fifty to his name, Key could have learned of the early dismissals of two other candidates; Hampshire's Michael Carberry, scorer of centuries in four successive games, and Shah, carelessly lbw at Lord's. His own progress continued serenely throughout the afternoon, leaving him within ten runs of a headline-catching century after three hours' batting. But then he missed a drive at a full delivery from Andrew Hall and was out leg before. Three times he swished his bat in annoyance before he reached the pavilion, explaining later, 'You get to 90 and you should go on to get a big hundred.'

Always amenable to the media, Key used the tea interval to answer questions about his potential England selection. 'I've had two decent months and I feel I'm playing as well as I ever have done. It's a funny one really because obviously you think about it [playing for England]. If I do get to play it's just an opportunity. If I didn't get any runs I'd just to go back to county cricket and nothing would be very different really, so there is not much to lose for me.'

Later in the week, Key was out cheaply to a second-innings long hop, while Bell and Trott scored centuries in Warwickshire's second innings at Trent Bridge, where the Friday evening selection meeting was taking place. Before the results of those deliberations were known, though, Key had another important domestic date to fulfil.

Kent were becoming as traditional a part of Twenty20 finals day as Sky commentator David 'Bumble' Lloyd galloping around the field in breathless pursuit of men in foam costumes in the Mascot Derby. Winners in 2007, Kent had been last-ball losers of a pulsating final against Middlesex a year later and anticipated playing a major role at Edgbaston. Before opening against Somerset in the day's second semi-final, Key had said that 'batting first, it is a question of knowing what a good score is', only for the loss of three partners inside the first six overs to make that calculation even more tricky. His own runs came via a thoughtful and well-executed series of shots behind the wicket and, ceding most of the strike to an in-form Darren Stevens, he had reached 34 when he swung at a slower delivery from Peter Trego on the final ball of the 15th over and lost his off stump.

Defending only 145, Key needed his bowlers to perform with discipline and frugality, yet the sixth over ended with the Kent captain looking shaken and powerless as Marcus Trescothick completed a half-century off 27 balls. From then on, the game had an inevitability that even the dismissal of the former England opener couldn't disrupt. 'The most disappointing thing is that on the big day we played poorly,' was Key's verdict. 'You don't mind getting beaten when, like last year, Owais Shah played a fantastic knock, but when you play rubbish you're pretty disappointed. They bowled full and straight and we bowled full and wide at the start.' Kent's misdirection ended up costing them a place in the final, and with it one of the two English berths in October's Champions League tournament in India, where $6 million of prize money would be distributed.

Key's weekend was about to get worse. A phone call from Geoff Miller brought the news that, despite the demands of just about every former player to have been canvassed, the one change to the batting for the final Test was the inclusion of Trott for the struggling Bopara. 'I believe I'm the man to bat at number three,' Key lamented. 'But I got a call to say "You're not in there, but you're not far away. Just keep scoring runs." I've seen a lot of people have a few chances at number three for England and I'd like to have another crack at it.'

Later, he reflected, 'How close I came I will never know. Geoff spoke to me and said they'd had a conversation about me but I needed to go back and make sure I kept scoring runs. If you took out all the media speculation I don't think I would have been that close. I think the selectors would probably have been of the opinion they were going to go with Trotty. There was a bit of a media bandwagon pumping for me but whether that registered on the selectors I don't know.'

Announcing the team, Miller pointed to the weight of runs Trott had scored in county cricket but implied that, in the case of Key and Ramprakash, scoring runs at county level did not really tell them much. The logical conclusion was that runs in the First Division of the Championship carry greater weight – which, you could argue, is one of the main points of having two divisions. Another reason, then, for Key to ensure that Kent, cemented firmly atop Division Two after completing victory at Northampton, didn't stumble on the path to promotion over the last few weeks of the season. 'Division One runs should count more,' Key agreed. 'After playing in both divisions, there is a marked difference between the two.'

GRAEME SWANN had spent a week in which he was supposed to have been playing for Nottinghamshire lying on his sofa with a stomach infection watching old *Star Wars* movies. Having recovered in time to report to The Oval, he found that for the first time since his dramatic arrival in Test cricket not everyone believed that the force was with him. Vic Marks, who knew first-hand the trials of attempting to become a match-winning off-spinner for England, noted that Swann's 'reputation is wilting'. He was not the only commentator to highlight a modest return of only six wickets in four Ashes games, and he added bitingly, 'His batting at Headingley was fun, but irrelevant; his bowling very ordinary. He must be pining for some West Indians up the other end.'

To some, it felt as though his batting was second only behind his much-publicised entries on the networking internet site Twitter when it came to his contribution to the buzz surrounding the series. But unity in the England camp meant than spinners' coach Mushtaq Ahmed retained full confidence in his bowling. Swann was expected to be at the heart of the action when it became apparent that the Oval wicket would be prepared to produce a positive result. 'Swanny is like a soccer striker who wins one out of three games and shares the load for the other games,' Mushtaq argued.

Swann himself was just happy that he was able to venture from his home without having to check first on the availability of public toilets and was relieved that the waiting was almost over. 'It has seemed like forever after what happened at Headingley,' he said, breaking off from the usual battle to ensure that the dressing room iPod was pumping out Stone Roses or Oasis, to the taste of himself, Anderson and Flintoff, rather than the likes of Akon, preferred by the less discerning ears.

Within a couple of hours, it was clear just how big a part Swann might play in the decisive game. Strauss had won a vital toss and as wickets tumbled regularly the experts were up in their seats at signs of the surface's premature disintegration. Swann was caught behind off the final ball of the day but had stuck around in the middle long enough to score 18 and bring up the 300 with a firm drive. Much of his time at the crease, however, had been spent prodding at the surface as if wondering whether it could represent his magic carpet ride to national heroism.

Swann bowled a five-over spell as first change. It brought no tangible reward but offered the encouragement of a big turning delivery past Katich's outside edge and one that veered back through Watson's defensive shot. Australia had reached 73 early in the second afternoon when all hell broke loose. Stuart Broad was the storm bringer, ripping through the opposition batting with pace, accuracy and movement and reducing them to 108 for 4.

Happily for Swann, the umpire posted at the Pavilion End was Asad Rauf, who was under-performing in the manner of the Aussies' top order. Taking the ball as waves of noise crashed around The Oval, Swann tossed it up to North and saw pieces of the wicket fly up as the ball beat the left-hander's tentative prod. With three fielders hunched around the batsmen's feet, Swann fired in a quicker, straighter delivery. The various noises of ball hitting either bat and pad, or both, were quickly drowned by the bowler's appeal and the roar at the sight of the umpire's finger signalling lbw. When some serenity returned to the scene, replays showed that North's rueful smile had been his way of indicating a clear inside edge. One over later, Swann again proved that it is the balls that don't turn that can be the most devastating on a helpful wicket. Katich, playing for the spin, edged thickly on to his pad and into the hands of short leg Alastair Cook. It was 109 for 6; the atmosphere reminiscent of 2005.

Broad bowled Brad Haddin, before Mitchell Johnson twice slogged Swann to the boundary. The spinner's response was to deliver the ball a little wider. Johnson stretched to drive out of the rough, edging to Matt Prior, who held a sharp catch as tightly he himself was then hugged by an ecstatic Swann. Eight wickets had fallen in the session and Broad and Swann led off the team to cheers, hugs and appreciative pats on the backside from Harmison. The innings wrapped for 160 quickly after tea, Asad Rauf granting Swann a bat-pad catch when Stuart Clark was nowhere near making contact.

Despite a flurry of three wickets late on the second day, Saturday found England marching to a lead of more than 400, a perfect opportunity for Swann to play another of the attacking cameos that had become an unexpected feature of the series. After a couple of unsuccessful reverse sweeps he reverted to his more natural method of clean straight hitting, driving Johnson to the extra cover boundary, hitting him square for four more and coming down the track to lift North over mid-on. The admirable Trott continued to proceed almost invisibly towards a debut hundred – scoring only 33 of the 133 England runs in the afternoon session – while Swann smashed consecutive deliveries from North to the ropes on either side of the ground. He then drove Siddle on the up through the off-side for four and went down on one knee to slap the new ball back over the bowler's head. In the next over, having swished and nicked Hilfenhaus just beyond Ponting's reach at slip, he turned the ball to leg to complete his half-century off only 44 deliveries. When he pulled Siddle for another boundary, taking the lead to 498, the crowd chanted, 'Easy! Easy!' An on-drive against Hilfenhaus brought him level with his Test career best of 63, made from a partnership of 90, before he mistimed an attempted hook and skied a catch to Haddin, ending 'my favourite Test innings'.

He revealed, 'Straussy wanted me to go through the gears and not go hell for leather at the start. But I don't really have a gearbox. The sport button on my batting is permanently pushed.' Swann's runs left him fourth in the England averages for the series with a mark of 35, to which he responded, 'I finished one run away from being our joint-third top scorer and I will certainly be reminding the lads about that. I was often able to counter-attack or push along the scoring, which suits my game.'

It had been great fun, but after Trott had been dismissed for 188 and Strauss had declared with a lead of 545, it was time for the hard work to begin. However long Swann played Test cricket there would not be too many occasions when he found himself bowling on such a helpful wicket with such a big total to defend. Certainly not with the chance to be an Ashes winner at the end of it. 'Everything went right for us,' he recalled. 'We won the toss, they didn't pick a spinner because they misread the wicket, and after posting a decent total on the first day there was only going to be one winner.'

This was exactly the kind of moment that Johannesburg '98 had dangled in front of him. Now all he had to do was grab it. As one writer noted, 'He is a showman. Well, this is his showtime.' He had to wait only eight overs to be called to the stage, but although he troubled both openers, he was unable to prevent Australia reaching the close with all wickets intact.

AND SO to Sunday: sun shining, history beckoning and ticketless people milling around outside The Oval, more because of an apparent desire to experience the spiritual elevation offered by such an occasion than any real hope of chancing upon a ticket. An excited impatience accompanied the search for allocated seats and every quick dash to the loo or beer stand before the players emerged. In the England dressing room, according to Swann, the message was, 'Let's not get ahead of ourselves. It is going to be a long slog. If it takes until tea tomorrow then so be it.' But it wasn't, one sensed, enough for this crowd for England simply to win the Ashes. It had to be today, when they could share the moment, have the eyes of the nation upon them and forever recount the story of their day at the cricket. An average audience of almost two million people would be watching live on Sky[3], equally anxious that events were concluded while they were at home watching rather than back at work.

On a pitch that looked like it had been vandalised over the course of three days, Swann took up the attack from the Pavilion End, achieving turn from his very first delivery. But it was again the one that didn't deviate that did the damage. At 86 for 0, the final ball of his second over pitched outside off and went straight on, making it easy for Billy Bowden to dispatch Katich after the ball smacked into his pads. 'The wicket early on settled everyone down,' said Swann, who had impressed observers since his elevation to Test cricket with his ability to make the ball spin even when he fired it in lower and quicker. It was such a delivery that welcomed Ponting to the wicket, the ball spitting back into his pads and prompting another appeal. By the time Watson had been dismissed, one could not help but feel claustrophobic for the out of form Hussey as four close fielders stared him in the eyes and Swann went a stifling 28 balls without conceding a run. His 90-minute spell ended with Hussey edging through the legs of Collingwood at slip.

The afternoon threatened to drift. The stands appeared caught in the grip of characteristic British pessimism and an inferiority complex to the Australians that even 2005 had not fully erased. Swann roused them briefly by catching the edge of Ponting's bat, the ball bouncing off Collingwood's boot and just out of

[3] Sky's 1.92 million for the final day was a considerable decrease in the 7.4 million who watched the climax to the 2005 series on Channel 4, but that's a whole other debate.

his desperate attempt to clutch the rebound. But no one was going to keep Andrew Flintoff completely out of the picture on what was potentially his final day as a Test cricketer. Just when England needed a hero, with Australia 217 for 2, he hurled the ball at the stumps and had Ponting run out by a yard for 66. Ponting dragged himself off, a child being pulled away from the fairground ride because it's time to go home. Bedlam at The Oval became delirium five minutes later when Clarke was thrown out by Strauss after the ball ricocheted to him off Alastair Cook at short leg.

Keeping new batsman North on his toes with changes of pace, Swann saw yet another edge go begging, this one the simplest of the three chances to go Collingwood's way. 'Bowling so much on that last day was fantastic,' said Swann. 'But it was one of those days when it felt like nothing was going to go my way. I beat the bat a lot and had a few catches dropped.' His mood changed in the next over, though, as North aimed a big swipe of a sweep and was too unbalanced to slide his foot into the crease before Prior removed the bails, sending Australia to tea with five wickets down.

A brief break while the new ball was taken, and Swann was soon back in action. Haddin had decided that attack offered the only hope of Australia threatening a total that would have been more than 100 in excess of anything any team had ever scored to win a Test. The Aussie keeper danced down the wicket and tried to swing Swann to cow corner. Strauss, 20 yards in from the deep midwicket boundary, took the catch. Six down, four to go. Enter Harmison, a virtual spectator throughout the match, and three wickets later – including two in two balls – Australia were down to their final man. Swann claimed to have foreseen Harmison's impact on the game, revealing, 'I said to him in the morning, "You have got a role to play somehow; the script is not written yet." Bless him, he came on and took those three wickets and calmed everyone in the ground.'

Swann continued, 'After tea, the game just accelerated. Haddin got out to me and then Harmy got those quick wickets. I was standing at gully and Harmy was running in to bowl and I was thinking, "Please don't finish them off because I want that fourth wicket." The atmosphere around the ground was absolutely electric.'

The crowd could barely contain itself. It was like waiting for the net of balloons to be released at a New Year's party. Swann bowled to his friend and former Northants teammate Hussey, who had stood firm and made a century that had probably saved his Test career. 'I was just trying to get him off strike by letting him have one through the off side so I could bowl at the number 11,'

Swann revealed. 'It just came out perfectly, drifted in and bounced a bit and then the rest is history.'

For the record: Hussey pushed forward, the ball went from bat to pad and looped into Cook's hand. Explosions everywhere. Swann sprinted – who knew where? Arms raised and outstretched, it was like watching Italy's Marco Tardelli after his decisive goal in the 1982 World Cup final. Only when Swann was on his knees could Strauss catch him, beginning an embrace that soon included the entire team. 'The feeling after that wicket was just phenomenal. I was literally running round not knowing what I was doing. I was down on my knees, Straussy hugging me and the boys going crazy. It was a sensational feeling and the noise in The Oval was something I never thought I would experience at a cricket match. It was just superb. To take the last wicket, to be part of history, was phenomenal.'

Ashes duly presented, champagne sprayed and confetti cannons detonated, 'Jerusalem' broke out for the umpteenth time as England's players began their lap of honour, pointing and waving at family members who would soon join them in sloshing their way through the scraps of coloured paper that now covered the playing area. Collared by various interviewers, Swann gushed, 'I have imagined this moment but I never thought I would be this happy in a game of cricket because cricket's rubbish basically, isn't it? But days like today prove that it is one of the best games in the world. This is the best I have ever felt in my life. I don't have kids, so I can only assume it competes with that. I don't know whether to shout, sing or cry.'

Back in the dressing room, the little lad from Northampton who'd turned to spin as a way of getting the ball to the other end of the wicket attempted to take in the magnitude of the achievement he'd been part of and reconcile it with his long-held dreams of Ashes success. The result was an outpouring of emotion. He sneaked into the physiotherapy room to scream.

After the Australian players had visited the England players to sip the beers of shared conflict, the celebrations were able to begin in earnest. This time there would be no Flintoff staggering onto a podium in Trafalgar Square, as in 2005, but Swann did admit, 'Many of us celebrated long and hard into the night and the precise details are a bit of a haze. I woke up face down on my bed, still wearing my cricket whites and stinking of sweat and champagne.'

The headlines, film crews and happy workers that greeted the slowly awakening Swann on the morning after helped to persuade him that the cynics had been wrong in suggesting that the smaller live television audience meant that fewer people in the country were bothered by the Ashes this time around. 'With the football season underway, and after the way we played at Headingley, there was a danger that everyone would forget about the Ashes. But judging by the number of texts I got it is fair to say we were the box office draw. Everyone was rooting for us.'

Most personally satisfying for Swann was the fact that he had so completely stood up to the pressure of expectation; the weight of which no other member of the 1998 junior England team had been fortunate enough to experience in their careers. Robert Key, the only other member of the group to engage in Ashes combat, had never found himself in such a pivotal role as Swann at The Oval. His four second-innings wickets, and eight in the game, had even hoisted him into the top ten in the ICC rankings for Test match bowling – a far cry from the day he missed the team bus on his first England tour. 'I've experienced some dark days in my career when I didn't think I'd get into my county team, let alone play for England,' he admitted. 'But I would take 364 rubbish days a year just to have one like that last day.'

18

JOY AND PAIN

'For two years I had been bowling 34 overs a day in the Essex second team and I was happy, fulfilling a dream. Now I wonder if that's what did it. I didn't bowl for a year and a half' – **Jonathan Powell**

JONATHAN POWELL might have come to terms long ago with the fact that it would be another off-spinner, not him, leading England's bowling attack against Australia, but now fate had managed to interfere with his latest cricketing milestone. He began the 2009 season being appointed captain of Ardleigh Green, the Essex League club he had played for since 2004. Yet by the time Graeme Swann was on his knees celebrating his Ashes-clinching wicket, Powell's captaincy had become as much of a non-starter as a first-class career that had promised so much and amounted to only three matches and a single wicket.

'Work just took over and I couldn't make myself available,' he explained, another late finish having delayed him well into mid-evening. 'Priorities change and by the time it got half-way through the season it was obvious I was not going to be able to play any cricket.' A partner in his own carpentry firm, he added, 'All of our work is in London on new-build stuff. A lot of it has come in and we don't want to run away from it because all paths lead to more work.'

Another who turned 30 during the summer of 2009, Powell has become used to seeing plans go awry. He had begun the winter of 1997-98 being identified as one of the prodigies within the Under-19 squad bound for South Africa. Along with Owais Shah, he had been selected to go directly from the World Cup to the England A tour of Sri Lanka, despite only one first-class game on his resumé. By the time he was back at his home in Brentwood, he was suffering with the injury that would wreck his career. 'Being selected for the A tour was a total shock to be honest,' he admitted. 'I don't think anyone was expecting that. Graham Gooch was the manager and he had captained the side in a few of the games I had played for Essex seconds. He had seen me bowling in the nets and I imagine he wanted to take a couple of youngsters on tour. It was still a complete surprise when the call came.'

Having cut his cricketing teeth at his father's club, Brookweald in Essex, Powell had played age group cricket for his county since the age of 10. He was offered his first contract when he left school at 16, around the time his older brother Mark was playing a handful of games for the county. 'I was always a bowler who batted,' he said, 'but I don't really know why I was a spinner. I think you just turn up one day, find out you are quite good at it, carry on and get some coaching. Spin bowling is something you fall into.'

Having turned professional, Powell immediately began playing regularly for Essex's second eleven. 'It was a bit of an eye opener and, being 16, I was quite nervous but there were a few younger guys in the team who I'd played with a lot so it was not as bad as walking into the total unknown. Pre-season training was quite daunting, mixing with the big stars, but once it got into the season I was nowhere near as nervous.'

Selected for the England Under-19 tour to Pakistan late in 1996, he had the chance to play alongside the likes of Andrew Flintoff, Ben Hollioake and Alex Tudor. Although his bowling opportunities were limited he recalled, 'I was playing a year above myself on that tour and managed to impress a few people. I was considered one of the up and coming off-spinners and I had high hopes of myself.'

The 1997 season brought a first-team debut for Essex in limited-overs cricket and a maiden first-class appearance. The one wicket he took – Leicestershire seamer David Millns – at the cost of 109 runs in a high-scoring draw at Colchester would end up as the only one of his senior career. Having played in two Under-19 Tests against Zimbabwe, Powell was duly selected for the squad to go to South Africa, along with fellow off-spinner Swann and leggie Chris Schofield. 'Swanny was more of an all-rounder, batting in the middle order, while I was predominantly on a tour as a spinner. But we bowled about the same number of overs and I don't think anyone thought of themselves as the out-and-out number one spinner.'

Giles Haywood, who spent much of the tour sharing a room with Powell, recalled, 'Jon was a very relaxed guy; a good, steady cricketer. He wasn't the most prolific spinner compared with Swanny, but he had a bit more flight and guile. That is what they had identified at that time.'

Team coach John Abrahams added, 'As a spinner, Jon's strengths were that he could get it up and down very quickly and would turn the ball as well. He wasn't strong physically, but could get revs on the ball. He was more suited to longer form of game and he could bowl people out.'

The intense preparation period at Lilleshall was a painful experience for Powell. 'We were meeting with former players and had a lot of people giving us information about what to expect, but for me it was the first time I had ever known any kind of injury. I felt a massive twinge in my lower back while bowling in the nets and I tried to carry on. They sent me home to rest about a week before I was due to fly out and said they would have a look again when we got out there. I was on anti-inflammatory tablets the whole time so obviously it was quite serious and maybe I shouldn't have gone. I was struggling to walk because I was in so much pain.'

It might have almost crippled him, but Powell does at least recall the training camp as an important factor in the team's ultimate success. 'We would come up against each other during the season, but we needed that bonding time together,' he said. 'Everyone got on well and was enjoying the cricket. I don't think anyone was unhappy on tour, even those not playing just got on with doing their job.'

Injury meant that Powell's own workload didn't begin until the second Test, where he took one for plenty. After a couple of wickets in the second one-dayer against South Africa, his World Cup performances were more notable for a decent economy rate than his number of victims, which totalled two in six games. The contribution that every one of his teammates has burned into the memory, however, is the spectacular leaping catch on the boundary to dismiss dangerous Pakistani all-rounder Abdul Razzaq in the important victory in the first of the Super League group matches. Powell, who had scored a useful 22 runs of his own, remembered, 'The catch was one of the standout moments of the tour for me. The game looked like it was going to the wire and I was stood literally on the boundary. I thought it was going a mile over my head but I thought I had to make an attempt. I got to it and realised I hadn't fallen back over the line and everyone went mental.

'Overall the tour was obviously a big thing at the time. There hadn't been a youth World Cup for ten years and we were underdogs. We sneaked up quietly and there was a bit of a buzz when we started doing well. But, for me, the main recollection is of being injured. I had a lot of intense physiotherapy and I didn't perform as well as I could. We were just keeping it under wraps and hiding the problem. When I went on to Sri Lanka to join the A team they diagnosed it as the same problem that Mike Atherton had [spondylitis] and said that mechanically my back was all over the place.' Powell bowled five painful, wicketless overs against Sri Lanka A. Studying footage of his action at the time doesn't give obvious cause for alarm, although Abrahams suggested, 'He jack-knifed a bit as he came up to bowl, so we tried to analyse that.'

Powell continued, 'You don't realise you have a back problem until it goes. For two years I had been bowling 34 overs a day in the Essex second team and I was happy, fulfilling a dream, so I wasn't bothered about it. Now I wonder if that was what did it. These days, until you are 19, they manage the number of overs you bowl much better. And you have to be an athlete fitness-wise. That was not the case when I was playing. I basically didn't bowl again for a year and a half. I still get back problems now working as carpenter. I had a lot of physiotherapy, scans, x-rays and acupuncture and tried to change my action so as not to put as much stress on my back.'

At least he managed to score some decent runs while playing as a batsman for the second eleven throughout 1998 and 1999, although his return to the first team for a game against Cambridge University was wrecked by rain. A broken finger further impeded his recovery, as did loss of confidence when he finally had the ball back in his hand.

Essex coach Paul Grayson, a veteran first-teamer at the time, explained, 'Powelly got the yips a little bit with his bowling. He lost a lot of confidence and struggled with his injuries. It was very unfortunate because he could have had a very successful career if he'd had a little more self belief. Generally left-arm spinners are the ones who get the yips; it doesn't happen often to off-spinners. You try to work with them and get their technique back. Sometimes it's a mind thing and maybe you have to get a sports psychologist in to sit down and work with them. But back then sports psychologists were frowned upon a little bit and we as a club never had one. Now, Jonny would be working with one very closely.

'For me, he was probably the most naturally talented out of those Under-19 lads we had at Essex. As a batsman he had a very sound technique and struck the ball well. As an off-spinner he had good control and spun the ball, and was a good athlete as well. In today's game he would be perfect, particularly with the amount of one-day cricket we play. He was a good lad to be around.'

Powell admitted, 'I knew I had a serious problem every time I tried to bowl again. I was worrying about my body. I don't know if it was the injuries in the back of my mind but it was like I had literally forgotten how to bowl. It culminated in my career going downhill very quickly. I didn't really have time to take stock of anything. I lost confidence in my ability and when my Essex contract was up [after 2000] I decided that my body was telling me something. I thought, "I am 21 now and I still have the chance to do something." You see people aged 25 or 26 still going round the counties and ending up on the scrapheap. I decided to get a proper job.'

After three years working for an investment bank, Powell acknowledged that a more robust lifestyle was what he needed. 'I had been looking at the same four walls every day. I am a more hands-on person, so I decided to do a bit of travelling. To finance that I needed to work and get a trade so I put myself through college as a carpenter.'

As the 2009 summer turned into autumn, Powell's girlfriend Kelly travelled to Australia as the advance party in their new life. 'I fell in love with it out there and I am going in January,' he explained. 'I have worked to get my money together and now I think I am going to study again when I get out there. I don't think I am going to survive for long on the tools because of my back so I am going to go to Victoria University and do quantity surveying or project management.'

Powell would be travelling without regrets over the way his career played out. Of all of the members of the 1998 World Cup squad, he probably fell shortest of the predictions being made for him as he and his young teammates headed out to South Africa. Yet he concluded, 'For the first three or four years you do wonder why it is not you out there and think, "Bloody hell. Where did it all go wrong?" But then other priorities come along and your life starts again. Now it's nice to see guys like Swanny out there and to look back and say that you played with them.'

19

ONE-DAY BLUNDERS

'England like Owais Shah because he hits the ball in unusual areas. The only problem is his brain is often in unusual areas too' – cricket writer and former England international **Derek Pringle**

THERE IS a tradition in Karachi, the city of Owais Shah's birth, that you never ask someone where they are going when they leave the house because it is considered bad luck. As the seven-game series of one-day internationals against Australia unfolded, the sequence of calamities dogging the Middlesex man suggested that someone must have posed the question as he'd set off to rejoin the England squad.

Before the matches even began, it was his challenge in a kickabout at The Oval that had led to a knee injury to young Kent batter Joe Denly, who would miss three games as a result. 'Owais will probably feel bad about it because it was a bit of a clumsy challenge,' said captain Andrew Strauss. 'We have a "no tackling" rule, but I'm not sure it was heeded.' A day later, Shah was batting fluently when he trod on his stumps; in the second game at Lord's he was horribly run out in a mix-up with Paul Collingwood. Game three saw him given out lbw to a ball that was missing the stumps. In the fourth he was well set again before holing out to a full toss that should have been called as a no-ball for being above waist height.

By the time the series plodded to its conclusion – with England saving themselves from a 7-0 humiliation by winning the final game in Durham – Shah was still without a big score. It was not what had been expected of a player who, in the absence of Kevin Pietersen and Andrew Flintoff, both injured, and Collingwood, rested for three games in mid-series, was a senior figure in the side and considered overdue in his deliverance of match-winning contributions. 'I like to feel that I am in that mindset regardless of KP and Fred,' he said before the series, hopeful that weight of runs would push him back into Test contention.

He had been eliminated from selectorial discussion prior to the decisive fifth Ashes Test after a run of low scores that were more meaningful than a brilliant 40-over century at Kent. An interesting perspective, however, was offered by his Middlesex teammate Nick Compton, suggesting Shah had been victim of old preconceptions. 'Owais has seemingly been discarded,' he said. 'Yet since he was dropped by England I have witnessed the extraordinary amount of work he has put in to correct his cramped appearance at the crease. His recent innings have been a revelation, which suggests that the selectors either haven't acknowledged his transformation or that nothing he now does could overturn what I see as a callous categorisation. I have never seen him hit the ball so well.'

Naming the one-day squads to face Australia and compete in the Champions Trophy in South Africa immediately afterwards, national selector Geoff Miller described Shah as 'an international quality batsman'. He looked it in the opening game of the NatWest series; aggressive from the first ball and punishing Brett Lee on both sides of the wicket. 'The clash with Joe didn't affect me when I walked out to bat, but it did in other ways,' Shah said. 'I struggled to sleep that night because I was concerned about causing him serious harm, even though I made sure when I went out to bat I didn't carry any baggage with me.'

He'd just pulled Mitchell Johnson for four to reach 40 when he jumped back too far in trying to repeat the shot and stood on his leg stump. In the next game, with England making another unsuccessful pursuit of a modest Australian total, he had advanced purposefully to 12 when he and Collingwood did a dance of death shortly after setting off for a quick single and was barely in the frame when his stumps were broken.

By the third match, at Southampton's Rose Bowl, and the fourth, back at Lord's, his batting had become tentative. England's desperation and his own need for a decent contribution had apparently choked the confidence from his stroke play. As he returned scores of 8 and 39, the press box began accusing him of being too concerned about his place in the team, which was perhaps excusable given that they'd been suggesting he was playing for his career. Nasser Hussain had gone as far as saying that Shah risked becoming an unpopular player inside and outside the team. 'He frustrates management more than any other England player,' he offered. 'And the trouble is, he's proving them right. He can hit sixes, reverse sweep, play spin and fast bowling. But he can't run and that becomes a virus because everyone starts talking about it.'

Shah doesn't believe his running is quite the issue that others would make it out, but along with the fielding, the cramps, the nerves and all those other sticks he has beaten with over the years, he has to accept it. 'The running was one of those things,' he shrugged. 'When you're low on confidence, you might be a bit tentative, things like that happen. I don't personally think there is a problem, but I have had shockers. I'm not a perfect cricketer; I'm a human being. I make mistakes and then I do something good as well. That's just part and parcel of playing cricket.'

A couple of unconverted starts and another single-figure dismissal in the final game meant that he might well have been left out of the squad for the Champions Trophy had tournament regulations not required the 15-man party to be named before the Australian series. Such was the rapid-fire nature of the international schedule. Already, the Ashes seemed a long time ago. There had been much criticism of the unseemly haste with which the England players had been forced into their new red one-day outfits after that triumph. Two days after victory in the fifth Test they'd flown to Belfast for a warm-up game against Ireland, who almost pulled off a shock win.

'It was the only disappointing thing about the summer,' Graeme Swann suggested. 'I believe that you should celebrate your victories as hard as possible but that wasn't able to happen because of the scheduling. They have to fit in those games. It would have been nice to have celebrated, especially for the players, and I don't think it was a surprise that everyone was so burnt out during the one-dayers.'

Swann had been left out in the middle of the series, when Adil Rashid was preferred as the one spinner. But England's schedule of home internationals ended as it had begun in the Lord's Test back in May – with a man-of-the-match performance by the off-spinner. Bowling with flight and enjoying the grip offered by the Chester-le-Street pitch, his figures of 5 for 28 were his best for England in limited-overs cricket and saw Australia bowled out for 176. He beat the bat to hit the stumps and got enough turn to bring his close catchers into play with leading edges, celebrating bowling Brett Lee for his fifth wicket by copying the fast bowler's little celebratory jump and hitch kick. 'Steve Harmison told me it would turn,' he said. 'It was nice to see it go early and absolutely gripping. It was a tough series because we were thoroughly outplayed and it was important we got something out of it.'

A ONE-SIDED series, with barely a single gripping finish, was not what the 50-over format needed after a summer in which it had been at the centre of debate over the structure of English domestic cricket. As the summer progressed it had become clear that plans for the second Twenty20 tournament – the proposed P20 league format – were limping along even more precariously than England's middle order. Just as Kevin Pietersen was going under the knife in mid-season, the ECB took the scalpel to the new competition, which had been earmarked to replace the doomed Pro40. Observers who had feared overkill in the shortest form of the game celebrated, along with coaches who wanted more preparation time in a less-crowded schedule. With a bit of due care and attention English cricket might emerge with its most judicious playing calendar for a good many years.

In the 2009 *Wisden*, Scyld Berry had argued that the existence of four competitions was 'the biggest single reason why England alone among the major Test playing countries have never won a global one-day tournament'. English counties would now compete for only three trophies for the first time since before the introduction of the Benson and Hedges Cup in 1972. Of course such rationality was, according to many, merely the by-product of the demise of the additional 20-over event rather than its cause. Prominent in the decision-making had been the growing awareness that, due to a combination of scheduling difficulties and lack of major sponsorship, there was little prospect of attracting the vast number of international (specifically Indian) players that would make the second 20-over tournament a viable property for the international (specifically Indian) television market. It was obvious that this particular goose would not only fail to lay its golden egg but could potentially bring down the nest in which the Twenty20 Cup had made a successful home.

Instead, the Twenty20 Cup, rebranded as the T20, would now be spread throughout the summer, protecting the pre-eminence it had enjoyed since its introduction in 2003. The two-division LV County Championship would remain unaltered and the third tournament, assumed initially to be the 50-over Friends Provident Trophy, would be played a little later, freeing it from the shackles of the damp spring weather. A few days later, however, a further announcement identified the third tournament as a version of the old Sunday League, although in what format was anyone's guess. Following a period of further discussion with the counties and debate in the media, a 40-over competition was decided upon. The Pro40 is dead; long live the, er, ECB 40 League. England's cricketers, and those who wished to become so, would therefore have no domestic 50-over games in which to prepare themselves for the format still used in one-day internationals and for which World Cups were confirmed and planned for 2011 and 2015. The compromise was that the tournament, featuring three pools of seven teams plus semi-finals and a final, would feature ODI-style powerplays.

ECB chairman Giles Clarke explained, 'Directors of cricket and coaches reported through their county votes that the leading one-day team in world cricket, South Africa, does not mirror 50 overs at domestic level and that, provided powerplays and fielding restrictions were the same as the international format, the skills required were very similar.'

It emerged, however, that those within the ECB responsible for the England team had understandably fought for the retention of the longer game, only to lose out to the counties, who found the 40-over game a more saleable property at the gate. Those critics who frequently complained that the counties wielded disproportionate power considering their dependence on the England team had a field day. Even selector Geoff Miller aired doubts about his bosses' decision. 'If all we are playing is 40-over cricket then I have a problem with that,' he said. 'I am looking at it from a cricketing point of view. I understand there is a financial point of view as well. My job as national selector is to win cricket matches and if we do that it makes money along the line. We have always said we want to county cricket to mirror international cricket. If you're not playing the 50-over format it is going to be a little bit of a hindrance coming in.'

The players were caught in the middle. 'It's a bit of a strange one really considering we are still going to be playing 50-over cricket internationally,' said Shah. 'It's a big decision and we just have to get on with it, but it does seem a little bizarre that we won't be playing 50-over games domestically. Trying to prepare for a 50-over international game, it would be nice to play it for your county, but so be it. As players we just have to move on and get on with it.'

Paul Franks, the PCA representative at Nottinghamshire, was a little more forceful in his comments. 'We were asked about the 50-over game but our thoughts don't go anywhere,' he argued. 'The ECB's main baby, the Twenty20, has been taken over by India with the IPL and the Champions League, so it seems that we are trying to catch up and do something different. OK, well consult the players first because we have to do the job. One or two people are trying to be a bit ingenious and come up with something they can leave their stamp on. Well, let's have a period of due diligence first.'

Midway through the Australian one-day series, it emerged that the 50-over decision was merely the latest with which the PCA took exception. It even proposed that a new body, the Professional Game Board, should make such decisions to ensure a balance between cricketing and commercial considerations. PCA chairman Vikram Solanki, the Worcestershire and ex-England batsman, urged the ECB to consult the players more widely in the meantime. A statement from the players said, 'Of particular concern is the dismissal of player views and the recommendations of the ECB Cricket Committee that a 50-over competition be retained.'

Stephen Peters, the players' representative at Northamptonshire, said, 'The PCA has done a lot to get the players a say, but there are still too many things where we are asked for our opinions by the ECB and they head off in their own direction.' Earlier in the season he had pointed to the decision to trial a different ball, manufactured by Tiflex, in Division Two of the Championship, in spite of players' reservations, as an example.

Damningly, a poll of cricketers shown to the *Sunday Telegraph* reportedly revealed that only 11 per cent retained faith in the ECB. 'I wasn't one of the 11 per cent,' continued Franks. 'I know there is a huge amount of disappointment about how decisions are being taken. Some of it is baffling and the players don't understand. Most of the decisions affect the players but not the guys making them; they just push their pens around their desk. The players are all for better competitions, but there is little communication of the players' voice to the ECB.'

Franks also cited the Memorandum of Understanding between the ECB and counties, which would reward teams financially for playing younger players. 'I am disappointed with certain things, particularly the MOU. I am all for playing young players, but they have got to be good enough. Would it happen in Australia? We have belittled the quota system in South Africa for a number of years and said it was wrong to pick players based on race and now all of a sudden we become ageist. Certain counties will try to fill their boots. Why should a player aged 31 or 32 be eased out of game? That is not right. If a young player has long-term potential then I am all for it, but not just giving them an opportunity before they are ready.'

OPPORTUNITY WAS on the mind of Owais Shah during the flight to South Africa for the eight-nation ICC Champions Trophy. It was another chance for England to win their first senior global trophy; and a possible final opportunity for him to identify himself as an indispensible member of his country's one-day middle order. If he, like others, sensed that his place on the plane was down to those tournament regulations, then team director Andy Flower did little to reassure him when asked if he knew his best eleven. Pointedly, he said, 'We know our best team from the squad we have.'

Back at the Wanderers in Johannesburg, where he had lifted the Under-19 World Cup, Shah was restored to the number three position as England chased only 213 to win on a green and bouncy track in their group game against much-fancied Sri Lanka. After the loss of two early wickets, Shah approached his work like a Test match, while a reinvigorated Paul Collingwood counter-attacked against the swinging ball with a swift 46. Eoin Morgan made an inventive half century, while Shah continued his anchor role, manoeuvring the spinners and occasionally freeing himself, driving Mendis and Muralitharan for fours and swinging Kulasekera nonchalantly over mid-wicket for six before edging a catch on 44.

An unlikely victory meant that a repeat performance against South Africa on a more batsman-friendly surface at Centurion would secure a semi-final position. It was to be the day when, after a year of frequent frustration and underachievement in the West Indies and around England, Shah delivered his finest-ever innings for his country. A stunning assault brought him 98 off 89 balls, probably the best one-day knock by any England player for more than a year, and the catalyst for what captain Andrew Strauss described as 'the best England batting performance I have ever seen'.

Batting first, England had made 49 off the first 10 overs before Shah made his dramatic entry, warming up by picking up a ball from Albie Morkel from outside off stump and dropping it over the deep square leg boundary. The tentative and tense figure of the previous few weeks had clearly been left behind in England. This version of Shah launched into the bowling with no fear of the consequences, an exquisite on-drive off Morkel and an open-faced dab against Johan Botha accelerating his scoring. His only moment of discomfort was when he had to bail out against a Morkel beamer, but a driven boundary and a single took him to 50 off 63 balls.

And then things really got interesting. He swept J.P. Duminy low over square leg to bring up a century partnership with Collingwood, skipped down the wicket to deposit Roelof van der Merwe over long off and disturbed the sunbathers on the grass bank behind the leg-side fence with another huge six off the same bowler. Morkel was hoisted into the crowd again and when Dale Steyn rejoined the attack, Shah pulled him viciously for his sixth maximum and put the next ball away for four. He had gone from 53 to 95 in only 14 deliveries.

'I didn't think I was playing for my career,' he recalled. 'As far as I'm concerned I try to play every game as if it's my last. Even against Sri Lanka, I felt that the correct to do was bat through and try to see us home. Against South Africa it was different conditions and I decided to take the attack to the bowler and it came off. It was one of my best innings for England. I faced a few balls and didn't feel like the pitch was doing much laterally. I backed myself to play a few shots. I never doubt myself, never will. If I doubt myself there is no point me going out there to play.'

Having got to 98, Shah's momentum was stalled by a drinks break and Collingwood playing out a tame over. He had not faced for almost ten minutes when he aimed to turned Botha to the leg and a thick edge looped off his pad into Mark Boucher's gloves. He'd missed out on a second one-day international century, but Collingwood's 82 and another delicious half-century by Morgan produced a score of well over 300. It was too much for the home country, despite their raucous support and a battling century by captain Graeme Smith, horribly dropped by Shah in the 80s and eventually caught by the same man for 141. It had been a triumph for the 50-over game and redemption for Shah, named Man of the Match. 'Owais played an absolute gem of an innings,' said Strauss, while even the journalists who had been calling for Shah's execution from the team spent the next couple of days in raptures.

'I feel really good about my game. I have been striking the ball well for a couple of months,' Shah told his new admirers. 'We got smashed by the Aussies and I think the team was low on confidence, but when you start a tournament like that with nothing to lose you can be dangerous. We owed the bowlers a couple of decent performances with the bat.'

In a meaningless final group game, England were soundly beaten by New Zealand, with Shah's aggressive approach seeing him an edge a heave at Shane Bond to the keeper on three. Australia were waiting in the semi-final, as dominant as they had been in England. This time, Shah made a second-ball duck when caught down the leg-side off Lee and unbeaten centuries by Ricky Ponting and Shane Watson overhauled an inadequate total. It had not taken long for the cricketing world to return to the normality of the previous few weeks.

Graeme Swann reflected, 'After the one-day series I think everyone had had enough of cricket, but the Champions Trophy, in a new country and new atmosphere, was really enjoyable. Obviously winning those first two games and getting to the semi-final was a good effort, but it was just a shame the way it finished. I don't think in our heart of hearts we thought we were good enough to win it, but it would have been nice to get to the final and then anything could happen.'

20

THE END OF DAYS

'There are guys who will sit on their arses and live the life of a rock star, and there are guys who are so proactive' – ECB Lifestyle Adviser **Ian Thomas**

WHILE ENGLAND'S one-day team was stumbling through its late-season assignments, the domestic season tip-toed quietly towards its conclusion. Without the dramatic conclusion of 2008 – Durham having already wrapped up a second consecutive LV County Championship – and with attention focused on the national team, it was hardly a resounding finale. For the players, it inevitably represented a time of reflection and judgement, based on performances and averages, and cold assessment about the current and future status of careers.

The last round of Division One matches saw Nottinghamshire clinch second place, for which they received £225,000, more than double the amount paid to the previous year's champions. National commitments meant Graeme Swann had not played a four-day game for the Trent Bridge team since April, while Paul Franks finished the season with only four Championship games to his name. In the last of those, against Yorkshire in early September, he contributed three wickets in each innings and a half-century, only to be struck down by injury for the second time in the season.

'It was mostly a frustrating year,' he concluded. 'I got a stomach strain just before the Twenty20 and that was disappointing because I'd been earmarked to play a big part in that. It was the same again when I got back in the Championship team towards the end of the season. I had a badly broken hand and that wiped out the last month. I got six wickets against Yorkshire, bowled 50 overs in the match and batted well and I was looking forward with genuine optimism to the rest of the season. I'd worked hard to gain an opportunity and I then had my opportunity taken away.'

Franks's left-handed batting retained its potency throughout the season, particularly at club level, where he scored more than 600 runs at an average of almost 79 for Farnsfield in the Nottingham Premier League. And the retirement of Mark Ealham at the end of the season gave him a clear goal for 2010, with the role of veteran all-rounder apparently there for the taking. 'Mark's been a fantastic servant and it's not an envious task to fill his boots. But I have been around for a while now and I can be a sounding board for younger players, trying to help them along. In the end, though, it's about me. My place in the team revolves around my form. I am not asking for any favours and if I am playing well I will get the rewards.'

Already Franks is planning to extend his role as an on-field stalwart into a more formal coaching role, although he said he planned to keep playing 'for a few more years yet'. Known in the Notts dressing room for sharing an encyclopaedic knowledge of cricketers with coach Mick Newell, he continued, 'I have been working through my level three coaching course and I do have massive interest in the game as a whole. I don't think I am going to walk away from the game because I think I have plenty to offer. I have learned a lot from some great coaches, like Dennis Lillee and Peter Moores.

'At various stages of my career there have been people who have ignited things within me. My first coach at Nottinghamshire was a bloke called Stuart Burrows. He was fantastic because he made the game very simple and enjoyable and he tried to emphasise a work ethic that still remains. He is still at Trent Bridge and I talk to him regularly. He has an ability to keep you grounded, whether you have succeeded or failed. In the pro ranks, Mick Newell has been there since I started: colts coach, second eleven coach and now first team. We have evolved and grown together and I trust him implicitly. I think he trusts me; he knows what he is going to get and we have an understanding of what we give each other.

'Those guys gave me an understanding and grounding in the game. They kept it simple and didn't try to turn it into nuclear physics. It is important that we as players have a clear idea of what they want from us, and what we want to get out of the game. I am still learning and further down the line I would like to think I can pass on some knowledge to younger players.'

In Division Two, Kent captain Rob Key was presented with the winners' trophy after the penultimate game of the season against Leicestershire at Canterbury, where there was a muted air to the proceedings. Partly it was because the title had not required any last-match heroics, but also Key explained, 'We have to recognise that this is only for the Second Division. There are, by definition, nine better teams in the County Championship than us. But we have done what we set out to do, and it is still an achievement to be proud of, especially given the hard work that goes into winning. We have won eight games, with one match still to go, and we feel we deserve to finish on top. After the disappointment of being relegated last season we were all determined to get back up at the first attempt. The hard work, though, starts now.'

Key's own season had witnessed a remarkable reversal in fortunes. Having been unable to hit the ball off the square for three months, he eventually averaged over 58 in the Championship and comfortably passed 1,000 runs, including four centuries. As the season had neared its conclusion, speculation increased that he would exchange the challenge of leading Kent in the top flight for the fat salary and batsman-friendly wickets on offer at Surrey. Key insisted, though, that he was never formally approached by any other teams. Within a couple of weeks, the gossip was halted by an announcement that he'd signed a new contract and been reappointed captain for 2010. 'I will always be committed to trying to win trophies and bring success to the club,' he said. The county's chairman of cricket, Graham Johnson, even paid tribute to the manner in which Key had conducted the negotiations, saying, 'He was open and honest throughout and brought a sense of fun to discussions.'

As someone who has a realistic view of the standards in the lower division, Key always seemed like a long shot to move to The Oval, especially as he still harbours England ambitions. 'A few years ago people probably thought I was done from the England set-up but I managed to force my way in through weight of runs in 2004, so hopefully I can do that again next year,' he said. 'I think there was a feeling that people couldn't come out of county cricket and score runs at the highest level, but Jonathan Trott scoring runs in a massive Test match has hopefully proved to the England set-up that people can do it.'

Meanwhile, Surrey, one of the country's richest clubs, remained stuck in the lower reaches of Division Two after their first season under new supremo Chris

Adams and an all-star coaching staff that included Graham Thorpe, Alec Stewart, Martin Bicknell and Ian Salisbury. Leg-spinner Chris Schofield had not produced the haul of wickets in the second half of the season that might have been expected as playing surfaces became drier, although good form with the bat had included his first century in first-class cricket; an innings of 144 against Essex. 'I have got a two-year contract, newly signed, and the club have been happy with what I have done this year so they see me having a future here,' he said. 'I am only 30 and I have an opportunity to go on for another five or six years at least.'

An unexpected, yet familiar, teammate had pitched up at The Oval for the final couple of weeks. Richard Logan's season with Berkshire had been a personal success with both ball and bat. In six Minor Counties Championship matches, he'd taken a team-high 34 wickets at a little over 20 and scored 381 runs at an average above 66, hitting three half-centuries along the way. 'As a team we struggled a bit and were slow out of the box, but towards the end of the season we hit our straps,' he recorded. 'I was pretty happy with how well I did, although I was a bit like the team in that it took a while to get going. Towards the middle of the season I was bowling well.'

With the season taking its toll on Surrey's bowlers, Logan was invited to take his boots along to The Oval. 'Richard Johnson, our coach at Berkshire, has a few contacts and spoke with Griz [Adams]. They were keen to see me bowl.' After taking six wickets in a second-eleven game, he had a couple of wicketless Pro40 matches and a return of 2 for 101 against Glamorgan in the Championship. 'I got a bit of a go and did OK,' he said. 'Nothing massively to write home about.' No offer of more permanent employment materialised, leaving Logan preparing for a second season with Berkshire, although he added, 'I am training a lot and am in good shape if anything comes up.'

Meanwhile, his venture with the League Cricketers' Association was moving forward, even though it had not hit the membership target he'd outlined earlier in the season. 'It's taken some time to get going but we now have plenty of things in place and are getting a few more business partners. We are getting advertisers for a new online magazine and are planning more matches and a tour in 2010. We have come a long way in a year so we are pretty happy.'

Further up Division Two, the battle for the promotion behind Kent boiled down to Essex or Northamptonshire. Once Northants had won their final game at home to Leicestershire inside three days, Essex needed to win at Derbyshire to steal second place. The home team could have batted out the final day for a draw but instead the Northants players watched with an increasing sinking feeling as the two teams contrived a declaration in which Derby, somewhat generously, set Essex 356 to win at a little under five an over.

Graham Napier sat padded up in front of the pavilion, ready to bring his big hitting to bear late in the innings. After his defining Twenty20 performance a season earlier, his batting, especially in limited-overs cricket, had been rather anti-climactic, although an average in the high 30s in the first-class game was more than adequate for a number eight. A bowling return of 29 first-class wickets might have been modest, yet an average of around 34 was lower than the career mark he had carried into the season. The retirement he'd been considering 18 months earlier remained far from his thoughts, replaced by a plan to remain in contention for an England selection. It would begin with a winter playing in New Zealand for Central Districts.

'Over the course of the season there has been a consistency to my game with bat and ball, without quite going on to hit the big scores or take big-wicket hauls,' he said as the campaign came to a close. 'I'm not in the [England] frame right now but I'm determined to keep going out and maintaining a decent level of performance with the intention of making it to the highest level at some point. It's a great bonus to be wanted by an overseas team during the winter.'

At Derby on the last day of the season, he was not needed after all. Needing 100 off the final 16 overs, a century by Ryan ten Doeschate eased Essex home with five overs to spare. After a season of toil, Northants had been denied the biggest reward by an artificially-induced run chase. The response of their coach, David Capel, was admirably philosophical. 'We have to accept it and move on. It was probably quite a generous declaration given that Essex were facing tired bowlers and, in hindsight, it might have been better if Derby had set them 420 or 450 because Essex still had to try to win it. But we had chances against Surrey and Essex to put ourselves in the position where the Derby match shouldn't have mattered. I don't blame Derby, they were looking to win that game too and they did what they thought was best for them.'

Stephen Peters, therefore would miss out on the opportunity to test himself against First Division bowling after a season in which he had averaged nearly 44 in first-class games, topped 1,000 runs for only the third time and scored his habitual three centuries. 'I'll keep playing until they get fed up with me,' he said. 'If I am still scoring runs and playing well I will keep playing as long as I can.'

His involvement with the Professional Cricketers' Association as the Northamptonshire representative has, however, given him an idea of where he wishes his career to take him once the runs dry up for good. At the beginning of the season he had stood for the post of PCA chairman, losing out to Worcestershire's Vikram Solanki, but he still feels a pull towards cricket administration. 'That is of interest to me. I believe strongly in the PCA and saw running for chairman as a good opportunity to further my career in that field. I am lucky that I liaise very well with the club here and the chief executive has me involved in heads of department meetings.'

Discussing his approach to the election, he explained, 'I would have looked to continue the good work of the PCA, which has grown dramatically over the past ten years. I worked on my character as I get on with most people and know most guys in the game. That is where some of my strength lies. I am open to listening to everyone; old players and young.'

Most players agree that the work of the PCA has assisted them in the personal deliberations that they have to face up to at the end of every season, especially with each year that passes from the age of 30 and above. A typical situation is that of Schofield, who hopes to remain in the sport beyond his playing career. 'I think that is definitely going to be an opportunity because I know that, with the PCA, there are a lot of offers, like coaching courses and umpiring courses. They are crying out for young umpires, so that is something to look at.'

Ian Thomas, an ECB/PCA Performance Lifestyle Adviser, explained, 'We are arranging one-day taster courses ranging from plumbing, tiling, managing your property portfolio and starting up your own business, as well as looking at opportunities within cricket.'

But, as the experiences of the World Cup team of 1998 demonstrate, it is not just the 30-something veterans who are faced with the transition out of careers as a professional cricketer. 'For a younger player it can be even more difficult, especially if you have never really found out how good you are or had the opportunities you want,' said Thomas, whose own career with Glamorgan ended at the age of 25. 'If you are younger it is harder to accept that your career might be over because people will offer you trials and give you that hope. At some point a player makes a call to keep throwing his hat into the ring or call it a day. Some will decide they weren't enjoying it or are not good enough, while others will try for a bit too long. The most important thing is for them to know that if they do want support then it is available, whereas in the past that support wasn't there.'

More than two-thirds of players are reported to be accessing ongoing PCA support throughout their careers, and the organisation hopes that it becomes a natural extension for those men to turn to them for advice when the day of judgement arrives. 'It could just be somebody to talk to or actual functional stuff, like finding courses or sourcing work placements,' said Thomas. 'All the county academies use us now. It is a compulsory part of their development.'

Those initiatives have become even more important due to the evolution of players' contracts. The days when players spent the winter in alternative employment, earning their winter wages and preparing for later life, are pretty well gone. Thomas continued, 'When I was playing for Glamorgan there was a bit of that. I worked as a sales rep in the winter, but that disappeared in the last couple of years with the introduction of 12-month contracts. Now players are off in October and are back in November. Guys having to find alternative employment is disappearing. The Indian Cricket League was a big driver in that because the ECB and the clubs wanted players on year-round contracts so that they didn't go and play in unsanctioned tournaments.'

Unsurprisingly, Thomas reported that some players begin planning their futures as soon as they arrive in professional cricket, while others prefer to pretend that their bodies, and their skills, will last forever. 'There are guys who will sit on their arses and live the life of a rock star, and there are guys who are so proactive. Mark Wallace, for example, the Glamorgan wicketkeeper, has qualified as a sports journalist. He is at top of his game but he is being proactive. The PCA offers an education fund, where we pay for half of any course the players want to do, and we provide a personal adviser. You are not going to catch everyone, but you hope you can make things easier.

'Others are in the bubble of cricket and just want to train and it is easy not to look ahead when you are concentrating on your cricket, putting your life and heart into developing your game. We try to make players aware that you can do both: focus on your cricket and also create that Plan B alongside your career. And if you plan for your future instead of ducking your head in the sand I think it helps your game.'

The summer of 2009 provided one particularly stark reminder of what can happen to a professional cricketer when his post-career life descends into chaos and becomes prey to undesirable influences. Former all-rounder Chris Lewis, a member of the inaugural England Under-19 World Cup team and veteran of 32 Tests, was jailed for 13 years after being found guilty of smuggling cocaine into the country, a case that Thomas felt highlighted the need for even the top bracket of cricketers to have some kind of future life plan in place. 'It is an extreme example, but it highlights what can happen. He was a quality player and played Test cricket for several years, but what has he done since he finished playing? I think a lot of his time was spent around the periphery of the game and if he hasn't had a career to transition into and a plan to follow then it shows how easy it is for people to make mistakes.'

The two subjects of this book who spent 2009 in international cricket have both begun looking ahead. 'I have been thinking about it for a few years,' said Owais Shah. 'I don't know when I will retire, but I am thinking about what line of work I am going to get myself into. Cricketers can retire anywhere from 35 to 45 so I am putting some stuff into place, doing maybe a bit of property stuff, which interests me a fair bit.'

Continued good performances in an England shirt should leave Graeme Swann in position to capitalise on an elevated profile and an engaging personality. 'I am not a person to plan for the future,' he admitted. 'Hopefully cricket has opened some doors and I would like to work in the media. It is a good crack, good money and I enjoy it. I like being on camera and I love being on the radio. Maybe I'll get Chris Moyles off Radio One. I don't want the whole of my life to revolve around cricket. I love the game but I don't just want to be doing cricket when I am 70 years old. I would like to have other facets to my life. I absolutely adore music and I love writing so maybe I will be a musician who writes. I wouldn't mind being an MP at the moment because you have a great living on the side stealing from the tax payer.'

It is that kind of wise-cracking personality that makes Swann a natural to follow another cheeky-chappy spinner, Phil Tufnell, into the world of celebrity reality television. 'I wouldn't put that past me. But I would rather do the dancing than the jungle because I can move. I couldn't eat kangaroo bollocks. I remember seeing Tuffers eat a cockroach for a pint of beer. Fuck that. I would be running a mile.'

21

THE BOYS OF 2010

'We want hardened men, not little fat boys' – England team director **Andy Flower**

THE ENGLAND and Wales Cricket Board is clearly not short of budget for framed photographs at its National Cricket Centre. Lining most available wall space in the offices and the nets area at Loughborough University are shots of key moments in the international careers of those players who have passed through the centre's doors; everything from Rob Key scoring a double-century at Lord's to Graeme Swann celebrating one of his recent crop of Test wickets.

The gallery made for an imposing audience as, late in the 2009 season, the best of the country's young players were put through their paces at the ECB's newly-instituted Cricket Talent Tests. As Dave Houghton, the former Zimbabwean Test captain, fed balls into a bowling machine and barked instructions about where they should be hit – "Mid-wicket! Square leg! Third man!" – the likes of Andrew Strauss and Andrew Flintoff looked down in judgement, along with the various clipboard-carrying ECB staff.

At the lockers where they had changed into their gear the players had found a further reminder of the footsteps in which they trod, each hook bearing the names of those who had occupied the places during winter training camps over the previous decade. An introductory DVD message from England team director Andy Flower had informed them, 'We want hardened men, not little fat boys.'

The ECB acknowledges that the initial factor in ensuring that Under-19 internationals advance satisfactorily towards senior representative cricket is getting the selection of the youngsters right in the first place. In his role as the ECB's Head of Science and Medicine, Simon Timson, a former athlete and bobsledder who was previously performance director for Great Britain's bob skeleton Olympic team, is responsible for implementing the necessary scouting, testing and development programmes. He clearly enjoys his work. 'The first thing is talent identification,' he said, needing little time to warm to his subject. 'If you identify the right players for the right development programme you minimise the potential for what I would call talent attrition; that is, players dropping out at different stages.'

It is, of course, easier said than done, particularly in a country where most youngsters play their cricket alongside, or behind, football. Timson's charts and statistics tell him that for someone to reach full development in a skill they need 10,000 hours of deliberate practice. A child footballer who plays at the top available level and goes into a club academy has probably reached that target by his early teens. 'Cricketers take longer because of other competition for their time,' Timson added.

It explains why Pakistan and India, where cricket is king and the 10,000-hour threshold is reached early, can frequently offer senior places to players such as Mohammed Aamer, who had barely turned 17 when he opened the bowling for Pakistan in the World Twenty20. And why the technically advanced Owais Shah was regarded – and still is – as one of the most talented players ever to have played for England at Under-19 level. 'In places like India and Pakistan cricket is played non-stop,' said Shah. 'Kids growing up in the western countries, as I put it, have other options, like football and rugby, and so many more facilities. In the sub-continent you don't have so many facilities for other sports and the conditions are not great, so you stick to cricket. Every kid is playing on the street corner. The sport is encouraged by your parents.'

It means that identifying young talent in England remains an inexact science, and explains why the Talent Test was designed following Timson's visit to the annual Scouting Combine staged by the National Football League in Indianapolis. There, the best college players in the United States are put through a series of rigorous physical and mental challenges to test their readiness for professional American football. Similarly, although dealing with a younger age group, the ECB's version aimed to shrink the margin for selectorial error. David Graveney, former chairman of selectors and now National Performance

Manager, said, 'It is not a perfect fit but the principle is the same. We don't have any organised national data on the Under-16s so we are taking the principles of the NFL combine and applying it to that group There is plenty of evidence that county academies have selected one group one year and have changed to another group the next year, which would indicate that their selection process is not as good as it could be. My brief is to work with academy directors from Under-13s through to Under-19s and to judge how efficient academies are, so the process they use to identify talent is a key area.'

Timson continued, 'You need a strong understanding of what you want: a clear talent profile that shows what you are looking for at ages 14, 16 and 18 – technically, physically, in decision making, mental toughness and all the different lifestyle factors. That means there is less risk of picking the wrong people. Injuries are inevitable and people will fall out of love with the game or have other pressures in their lives, but you can minimise the risk.'

While, academically, many experts have sought to lessen the burden of be-all and end-all exams, the philosophy of Timson and the ECB is to apply more pressure at an early age. After all, cricket, unlike other professions, is one where you face a public examination on every delivery. 'Something like the Cricket Talent Test is important because it proves whether you can prepare and come and perform on any given day,' Timson said. 'That is a key attribute; the mentally tough cricketer has it. It is the essence of sport. Can you do it when it matters? If a player walks out in a World Cup semi-final with 40 needed to win, is he going to have the temperament to guide a team home? Tests won't tell us completely but will help build a profile. You can select someone for a programme knowing they are mentally tough or, with your eyes open, knowing there are areas to work on. We will understand how can we support and help. It might be the forward defensive, or dealing with mental pressure.

'Our 21st century does everything to take pressure off us and make life comfortable. We face less pass-or-fail situations. But one of best ways to make young players perform under pressure is to have consequences in the training environment.' Such measures at the ECB's various junior training camps include doing the washing up, sitting out a practice session or additional physical training. If it sounds like being in the army then that is deliberate. 'A lot of it comes from military training,' Timson added. 'We have involved a retired head of recruitment and development for the SAS, and military psychologists. The players have responded to it. They ask what the objective is and what happens if they fail. They now say they want to be under pressure.'

Sadly, the vision of Kevin Pietersen collecting the dirty dishes because he dropped a catch in training was removed by Timson's explanation that such methods are not used at senior level, but they remain a vital part of the programme for talented teenagers. 'The time you learn about them properly is when they are in competition. You never know until you put them in that situation. But you can hone it down to a small number you are fairly certain will respond positively.'

Timson acknowledges it will take a few years of trial and error before there is enough evidence to fully evaluate such testing and trials. 'We are just starting; working out what the different variables are that we can test. What can we do to track the players who are successful and those who are less successful and try to identify the factors that discriminate between them? That will allow us to refine things so that, in four or five years, we can say that this set of tests can give us a reasonable idea, along with performance data at county age group cricket, of whether these kids are going to go on and make it. If we see a set of traits that those who make it all seem to have, we can zero in on those traits. It is something totally new in cricket so it is an experiment.'

English cricket has never enjoyed a reputation for radicalism and Graveney pointed out, 'It is always a challenge to get people to buy into a new culture. This is new territory, but it is necessary for the performance department of the ECB to be able to judge how players are being developed. It is an exciting time.'

Asked whether the scientists are taking over from the batting and bowling averages, Timson stressed, 'This is not the only part of selection. We will be scouting, watching performances and getting a raft of additional information. The number of runs and wickets is still the first thing we will examine – at the highest possible level you can assess a player in each age group. Then the skill tests, physical tests and psychological tests tell us if they have the character and attributes to make the most of that talent.'

Northamptonshire coach David Capel has seen close-up several of England's junior team of '98 – and many of their successors – battling to make the grade over the past decade. During 2009, his county had David Willey, son of former England batsman Peter, in the Under-19 team. As a county coach he fulfils an important role in the development of promising teenagers and his view of what is needed above all else is, 'Awareness, maturity and understanding of how important it is to get a balance in everything.'

He continued, 'If you have a sharp focus and want to get there, then often you do. There are benefits in being able to make sacrifices. The extreme case of that was Geoff Boycott, who was almost obsessive, and I look at guys like Graham Gooch, players who have put a lot into their game. You need to add that to getting the right kind of advice, coaching and support at the right time. Some of the most successful young people are the ones that seek knowledge from the old sages and have a little bit of humility. I think it is partly a cultural thing. If you have an environment that helps that aspect then you are fortunate, but you need to be the sort of person who can see what you need to do and be aware of the distractions. Our goal at Northampton is to create an environment where we can help people to prioritise, to pick out the things they need to do and help them be organised as professionals. We want them to recognise their opportunities and make the most of them.'

A traditionalist who would, you suspect, approve of the military methods being employed by the ECB, Capel believes, however, that the nature of the world in which players are growing up makes it more difficult to predict results, even with a scientific approach. 'At times it is disappointing that players have not kicked on and become as good first-class players as you would have liked. They have not grown up quickly enough. My thought it is that it is a reflection of society and mirrors what is going on generally with the younger generation.

'When I was coming through as a 16 to 20 year old, at the end of the day's play you talked to the opposition and senior players and learned from them. I don't think that happens now. Players get away from the ground and do their own thing and when they get their days off they are out until three or four in the morning. For people between 18 and 28 to feel normal and socially accepted that is what they do. People in general are not settling down and marrying as early. I look back at people like Ian Botham and myself. It was not unusual to be married by the time you were 22 and have children by 25. That doesn't happen very often now. The majority of my group here are not thinking of having children before 30. When there was a wife and children, responsibility and maturity came with it.

'There is a bit of a snake pit out there for young players. Some do it well and come through, like Ravi Bopara and Alastair Cook. But, as people, I still don't see them being as mature as many of the generation I came through with. We were like old men compared to today's players. We all looked 40. We were a more life-hardened set of people. Many had been labourers since 16 years of age and by the age of 20 were more advanced as cricketers than the 23 year old of today.'

Capel's comments hint at something of a vicious circle. The ECB, rather than sending its young players out into the wider world for an extended period before they devote themselves to cricket, is increasingly throwing its protective net around them at a younger age. It might help to identify talent earlier but, if Capel is right, might it not retard the development of the individual? As C.L.R. James famously pointed out when asking 'what do they know of cricket who only cricket know?', the nurturing of the human being cannot be divorced from that of the cricketer. And, anyway, does the game benefit if articulate and amusing players like Graeme Swann disappear under a conveyor belt of mono-syllabic Premier League soundalikes.

The ECB is aware of such pitfalls, of course. It is where its partnership with the Professional Cricketers' Association has one of its most important roles to play in the coming years. Not only must they seek to produce well-rounded, socially adept cricketers, but also ensure that those who will inevitably fall by the wayside at some stage of their careers are not left high and dry like so many young footballers, courted by the big teams from the age of 12 and discarded at 16.

Performance Lifestyle Adviser Ian Thomas explained, 'The ECB are every keen to get guys from earlier ages up to the required standard. It is a change of policy and the support we give might need to be greater. Part of our role is working with the academies and educating young players on the various aspects of being a professional cricketer; from time management, to organisation and communication skills, media training, image and press management. Within the academy environment there is a trend that a lot of guys at 18 choose not to go to university but go into cricket full-time. In their contracts we want personal development time to be allowed so that coaches free them up for a day a week to go to college or do work experience. If it is all cricket, cricket, cricket then they are not preparing them for that transition out of the sport, whether that comes at 20, 26 or 36.'

The question of how well county cricket prepares players for a successful passage from Under-19 to senior international is another that is never far from the surface. The selection of South African-produced Jonathan Trott for the final Ashes Test highlighted, in many people's view, the weakness in the English system.

Capel suggested, 'There seems to be greater maturity collectively in Australian and South African teams over the years. Any 19 year old who has been with Young England would be a professional cricketer here, being paid at a certain rate. It is almost like having made it; you have your money and there is a bit of a social scene that goes along with county cricket. Having represented Australia at 19 years of age, I wouldn't be surprised if those young cricketers are still not being paid to play. They are thinking about what they need to do to get into the Sheffield Shield. It keeps them hard, keeps them pushing forward and with a sharper focus.'

Capel's comments would appear to offer a juicy half-volley to those who say that county cricket is too soft and employs too many players. But he quickly clarified his position by adding, 'It is not that there are too many jobs in county cricket.' Rather, he believes that a greater respect for the hierarchy for the dressing room would benefit the younger generation. 'They should be made to work bloody hard to get into the top tier and should revere and respect the legacy that has been left behind. No one has a God-given right to be a professional or a first-team player.'

In summary, Capel warned, 'Some players expect everything, blame everyone and do nothing to improve themselves. What I have seen is that those who are the opposite – who have expected nothing, blame no one and done something – are the ones who have kicked on and maximised their potential.'

At Kent, skipper Robert Key saw young batsman Sam Northeast make encouraging progress during 2009 both in the county team and in the colours of England Under-19s. But he pointed out that the speed of development of such players can owe a lot to location. 'It does often depend on what county you are at,' he said, recognising that the current domestic structure does not always help smooth the path for a fledgling professional.

'When I started it was one division and the counties were not under so much pressure, so they could play a young guy. Nowadays, with promotion and relegation, teams will go with the tried and trusted players. But if you are at a county like Leicestershire in the Second Division there is a far better opportunity because the quality players aren't throughout the county system the way they were ten years ago. You might even get a situation where more of the players from my Under-19 team might have been able to hang around longer with a Second Division team than a few years ago. With two divisions the talent is more focused on the First Division clubs. So there may not be as many opportunities in a team like Durham but there are in the Leicestershire team. Ultimately, though, the good players who can deal with the pressure will come through wherever there are.'

As Timson, Graveney and others at the ECB continue their search for clues to a player's potential it is interesting to examine how much the progress of the careers of the Under-19 team of 1998 could have been foretold by their performances at that level. The exercise is instructive rather than conclusive but does at least suggest a pattern that emphasises the importance of those games as a step on the development and assessment path.

Of the batsmen, it is the three who had the highest averages in Under-19 Tests (Shah 58, Key almost 50 and Peters 43) who have had the longest first-class careers. Yet just below that threshold, Michael Gough's mark of over 40 was perhaps enough to hint at a more than materialised. The earliest two casualties, however, were Ian Flanagan and Giles Haywood, whose Test averages of 18 and 10.55 were by far the lowest. That wicketkeeper Nick Wilton's lack of batting expertise would work against him might have been evident in an Under-19 average of 15 in both Tests and one-day games.

Among the bowlers, Graeme Swann was a consistent performer, his 26 youth Test wickets costing only 23 apiece and his batting achieving an average of 32, while Franks averaged 32 with bat and 22 with the ball. Graham Napier had limited opportunities at Under-19 Test level but was a solid one-day performer with a bowling average of 26 in 12 matches and an economy rate of four and a half – a reasonably accurate gauge of what was to come in later years. Seamer Richard Logan did well enough for the youth team, taking 20 wickets at a little under 30 in seven Tests before embarking on a first-class career that eventually extended into 2009. Meanwhile, Jamie Grove, an early loss to the professional game, had taken only seven wickets at more than 51 in four Tests. The only clear-cut anomaly in the group is Chris Schofield, still going strong after picking up only five wickets in youth Tests at a cost of more than 80 each.

Another of Timson's favourite statistics is the historical data he quotes on the typical path of a first-class career. 'We know that the best players reach the top ten in the world by the age of 27. They have made their international debut by 23 and their first-class debut by 19, so we are trying to drive a pathway that might help people hit those milestones.'

All 14 players in England's 1998 youth World Cup squad achieved the earliest of those targets and five hit the timeline for their international debut. Given that Timson's target is for 15 per cent of the current Under-19 internationals to become senior England players it sounds like a good conversion rate. But of the nine who failed to make the 23-year-old cut-off for a full England appearance, six were already out of the game or in their final professional season by that age. And no one has enjoyed a run in the Test team longer than the one Swann embarked upon in 2009.

Timson acknowledged the importance of the ECB and the counties being aligned in player development objectives. 'We all have to have one goal: that is producing as many players as possible who can perform at world-best level. That will benefit everyone. The more players in county cricket playing at a high level, then the more competition for places there will be to drive up standards. David Graveney and John Abrahams have done a great job in building partnerships with counties and getting them on the same page. It is a common goal. If England cricket is flying, then county cricket is doing well.'

The aim, then, is to avoid situations like those of Stephen Peters and Michael Gough, who both felt they were left without off-field mentoring at important stages in their careers, and Shah, who recalled the extent to which he was left to fend for himself when he was advancing from the Under-19s into full-time county cricket. 'There wasn't much help here at Middlesex. You had a second-team coach and you had a first-team coach. Looking back on it, I didn't have the right advice and nor did a lot of guys. You don't know what to do; one week one thing might work and the next week it wouldn't.'

And he added damningly, 'I haven't yet seen a 19 year old come into county cricket and tear it up yet. If there is one tell me. So nothing has changed.' He suggested that part of the problem is that the guidance given to young players focuses too little on the mental approach to the game. 'Coaches are all for looking at technical stuff, but I would say 80 or 90 per cent of the time it is upstairs. How is that guy feeling? When you are 20 and you are required to be performing day in and day out, but you aren't, it is not necessarily your technique. It is your mindset because you don't really know how to cope with performing every day and you put too much value on every time you bat.'

It is the kind of pressure to which players such as Flanagan and Wilton have admitted they succumbed. Shah continued, 'You think, "Oh, my God. I have failed again." Well you are going to fail. Percentage wise if you are performing 75 per cent of the time you are doing very well. Angus Fraser told me that he had more bad days than good days and he was a bloody consistent performer. But you don't realise things like when you are young. You are never told things like that in depth. That is important as a youngster coming into the game.'

Discussing the fortunes of the players in England's victorious Under-19 World Cup team it is tempting to say that those who did not achieve rewarding professional careers were those held back by issues of the mind rather than technique. Mental factors are, after all, greater in cricket than many other sports because of the slow pace of the game and the time available for participants to brood and think about the next ball, the next shot, rather than being carried along by the more instinctive, continuous flow of, say, football.

Nevertheless, in the cases of Wilton, Haywood and Flanagan, rejected early by their counties, they admit simply to not being good enough in important areas of the game. They would argue that all the psychological mumbo jumbo in the world doesn't change that fact. But, on the other hand, why did Peters did not kick on after being more successful than anyone in the youth World Cup? Why does Shah, the flashing bade of that group, remain such an enigma.

A common question asked of me during preparation of this book has been, 'So, what conclusions have you drawn?' Sadly, there is no magic bullet. Those responsible for developing teenaged cricketers, and those writing about the young players of the past and future, will be left making their guesses. As long as the game is played by humans – any two of whom will react completely differently to external influences such as injury, pressure, success and setbacks – then books such as this can draw no definitive conclusions, merely offer individual case studies.

And, as Simon Timson said, 'Whoever designs the test that tells us completely about things like mental toughness will be a millionaire. I don't think anybody has the answer.'

IT WAS early evening, the middle of October, and cricket was the furthest thing on Graeme Swann's mind as he crammed clothes into a holdall ready for his stag weekend. 'We're going to the Stuttgart Beer Festival,' he explained. 'Hope to get back on Sunday!' The naming earlier in the day of the England Test and one-day squads to tour South Africa during the winter had completely passed him by. 'To be perfectly honest, I haven't seen or heard anything. I know I am in but I've no idea about anything else.'

The biggest headlines he'd missed were the Test party's inclusion of Sussex all-rounder Luke Wright, the exclusion of Stephen Harmison, and the dropping of Owais Shah from the limited-overs squad. The recall of a fit Kevin Pietersen and promotion of Ashes hero Jonathan Trott might have been expected to threaten Shah's place in the first eleven, but few foresaw the selection of Essex opener Alastair Cook leaving him stuck at home completely.

Having learned of the demotion of both Shah and Ravi Bopara, Swann commented, 'Our one-day form has not been great and it was inevitable that they were going to make changes. It is probably hard luck on those guys, but I don't think anyone has performed that well over the last couple of years to definitely claim a place. It's pretty harsh because Owais batted beautifully [against South

Africa] but they are both class players and they will definitely have another part to play in English cricket in the future.'

At the time of that innings of 98 in the Champions Trophy, Shah's missing two runs seemed insignificant. Now they loomed large. Would England really have dropped their sole one-day century-maker of the summer only two innings later? Even without the three figures to his name, Shah had been 'extremely disappointed' when he received the news while preparing to play for the Delhi Daredevils in the Champions League Twenty20 tournament in India. After all, earlier in the year hadn't he commented that 'if I have two bad one-day games I don't get dropped'?

'I feel I performed reasonably well in helping England to get to the semi-finals of the Champions Trophy, but I was overlooked,' he said without any attempt to hide his displeasure. 'I was told I haven't performed consistently enough. I thought I was playing well. I had a decent series against the West Indies in England. Sure, I didn't have a great series against Australia, but I was hitting the ball reasonably well. I was really confident, especially after performing well against South Africa. I feel I'm playing well and have plenty to offer the one-day team. I still felt I wanted to be part of the set-up because of my experience but this doesn't mean I am going to rule myself out of playing for England. I feel a bit hard done by but I have to crack on and try to do what I can to get back in the team.'

Shah's sentiments echoed those he had made after his demotion from the Test team, and once again he was left lamenting, 'I guess I just have to wait and see what direction the selectors go.' With his 30th birthday behind him, it appeared entirely possible that he might now be marooned permanently down a path the selectors no linger wished to travel. It seems as much an indictment of English cricket attitudes as of Shah's own inconsistency and ability to infuriate.

An interesting defence of the player was offered by *The Wisden Cricketer*'s Rob Smyth, who suggested, 'There is something peculiarly English about the rejection of Shah. Only in this country could Alastair Cook be preferred in a one-day squad. For decades, English cricket has looked longingly from its dreary two-up, two-down and marvelled at how the rest of the street lives, how they embrace life in such an unfettered, stylish way. Yet whenever England are invited over the road, they prefer to stay at home.'

Smyth went on to suggest that 'the career of Shah is a perfect study in how to completely waste a truly unique talent'. Pointing out that he clearly does not conform to management's idea of what an England player should be, he continued, 'With the bat, Shah does everything England don't do in one-day cricket. He hits sixes, huge ones too. He has a force that, at its strongest, cannot be contained. Dropping a player like Shah, who has averaged 35 with a strike-rate of 82 over a two-and-a-half-year period, is the sort of decision that only very good teams should have the right to take.'

For those who are fans of the Middlesex man – and although there are many, they are obviously not in positions of influence – Smyth's article was as pleasingly punishing in its execution as those six sixes Shah belted at Centurion. He concluded, 'Shah has been treated like dirt. England may now have washed their hands of him, but the stains of a wasted talent will always be visible.'

As his year of unfulfilled promise drew towards a close, Shah was not about to write himself off, insisting instead that he could still improve as a batsman. 'Definitely. You go back to Mark Ramprakash. He is the most consistent batsman in England and for the last four or five years he has been phenomenal. If you can reach that sort of consistency level at that age then you are doing all right. We can all take a leaf out of his book.'

Swann, then, was the last man standing – the only one of the 14 junior players who triumphed in South Africa in 1998 to be making the latest trip as a member of the full England team. For now, though, with his winter of cricket having been confirmed, he was eager to savour whatever time away from the sport that he could get. The chaotic modern calendar was reflected in the timing of his stag weekend a full three months prior to his marriage to fiancée Sarah in January, which itself would be fitted in between tours to South Africa and Bangladesh. 'It's the only free time in our winter schedule,' he explained. 'It's been such an incredible, enjoyable year, but to get my feet up and not have to get my cricket kit on first thing in the morning and go training is nice. The Ashes seems like ages ago now.'

Yet Swann had spent long enough wading through county cricket on his way into the England team, and seen enough of his fellow young hopefuls and recent teammates stumble and fall, not to lose sight of the privileged life he was now living. 'This is our lot, but I much prefer it to not being in the team. You just get on with it and make sure every day is as special as the last one. If you start thinking about how tired you are then you start taking cricket for granted and that is dangerous. I am not going to complain.'

He paused, as if having another of those 'pinch me' moments of the remarkable past 12 months. 'This is still the best job in the world.'

APPENDIX

THE BOYS OF '98 IN FIRST-CLASS CRICKET

1 January-31 December 2009

PAUL FRANKS (Nottinghamshire)

Batting	**M**	**I**	**NO**	**Runs**	**HS**	**Avg.**	**100s**	**50s**
First Class	5	6	0	201	64	33.50	-	2
One-day	11	7	3	150	50	37.50	-	1
Twenty20	5	2	0	1	1	0.50	-	-

Bowling	**O**	**M**	**R**	**W**	**BB**	**Avg.**	**Econ.**	**5wkt**
First Class	125	34	396	11	3-52	36.00	3.17	-
One-day	45.3	0	257	1	1-51	257.00	5.65	-
Twenty20	11	0	99	1	1-9	99.00	9.00	-

ROBERT KEY (England, England Lions, MCC, Kent)

Batting	**M**	**I**	**NO**	**Runs**	**HS**	**Avg.**	**100s**	**50s**
First Class	19	32	5	1,374	270*	50.89	4	5
One-day	9	9	0	170	44	18.89	-	-
International T20	1	1	1	10	10*	-	-	-
Other Twenty20	10	10	2	224	58*	28.00	-	1

Bowling	**O**	**M**	**R**	**W**	**BB**	**Avg.**	**Econ.**	**5wkt**
First Class	22	5	59	1	1-14	59.00	2.68	-

RICHARD LOGAN (Surrey)

Batting	M	I	NO	Runs	HS	Avg.	100s	50s
First Class	1	2	0	6	6	3.00	-	-
One-day	2	1	0	5	5	5.00	-	-

Bowling	O	M	R	W	BB	Avg.	Econ.	5wkt
First Class	30	6	101	2	2-101	50.5	3.37	-
One-day	12	1	74	0	0-33	-	6.17	-

GRAHAM NAPIER (England Lions, Essex, Wellington, Mumbai Indians, Central Districts)

Batting	M	I	NO	Runs	HS	Avg.	100s	50s
First Class	10	16	6	348	64*	34.80	-	2
One-day	28	26	2	593	77	24.71	-	3
Twenty20	16	14	1	126	47	9.69	-	-

Bowling	O	M	R	W	BB	Avg.	Econ.	5wkt
First Class	271.2	55	1,007	29	4-32	34.72	3.71	-
One-day	230.3	15	1,255	41	4-33	30.61	5.44	-
Twenty20	56.1	1	411	25	3-21	16.44	7.32	-

POSTSCRIPT: Graham Napier ended 2009 by playing exactly the kind of innings that people had been waiting to see ever since his magnificent night at Chelmsford in June 2008. In his third match for Central Districts in the imaginatively-named New Zealand Cricket One-Day Competition – the country's 50-over tournament – he smashed an unbeaten 73 off only 29 balls to beat Northern Districts. Having gone out to bat with his team needing 82 runs off less than eight overs he blasted five sixes to see his winter side home with 15 balls to spare. His half-century, reached in 20 balls, was the second-fastest fifty in the history of New Zealand domestic one-day cricket.

STEPHEN PETERS (Northamptonshire)

Batting	M	I	NO	Runs	HS	Avg.	100s	50s
First Class	14	25	1	1,050	175	43.75	3	5
One-day	8	8	1	148	69	21.14	-	1
Twenty20	2	2	1	61	61	61.00	-	1

CHRIS SCHOFIELD (Surrey)

Batting	M	I	NO	Runs	HS	Avg.	100s	50s
First Class	14	21	3	644	144	35.78	1	3
One-day	16	14	5	276	66	30.67	-	1
Twenty20	9	7	0	66	17	9.43	-	-

Bowling	O	M	R	W	BB	Avg.	Econ.	5wkt
First Class	363.3	35	1,357	22	5-40	61.68	3.73	-
One-day	129.4	2	573	25	5-32	22.92	4.42	-
Twenty20	34.5	0	298	12	3-21	24.83	8.56	-

OWAIS SHAH (England, Middlesex, Delhi Daredevils)

Batting	M	I	NO	Runs	HS	Avg.	100s	50s
Test	4	6	0	133	57	22.17	-	1
Other First Class	9	17	2	600	159	40.00	2	1
ODI	19	18	0	546	98	30.33	-	3
Other One-day	10	9	1	451	130	56.38	1	3
International T20	7	6	0	112	38	18.67	-	-
Other Twenty20	10	10	2	254	61*	31.75	-	1

Bowling	O	M	R	W	BB	Avg.	Econ.	5wkt
ODI	12	1	53	4	3-16	13.25	4.42	-
Other One-day	3.2	0	11	4	4-11	3.75	3.30	-

POSTSCRIPT: Having been dropped by England, Owais Shah at least finally got to wear the shirt of the Delhi Daredevils when he reported to his Indian Premier League employers for the inaugural Champions League in India. Clearly popular with the Delhi fans, observers noted the relaxed air Shah bore throughout the tournament, where the absence of other overseas signings AB de Villiers and Daniel Vettori ensured that he was more than the mere observer he'd been during the earlier IPL campaign. Although Delhi failed to advance to the semi-finals, Shah had the consolation of being named Man of the Match in their last game against the Cape Cobras after making an unbeaten 39 on the bowler-friendly Delhi wicket.

Shah ended the year by boarding the plane for his stint with Wellington in New Zealand's Twenty20 tournament. Already in action in New Zealand's domestic season was Ravi Bopara, the man who had replaced him as England's number three and subsequently, too, been discarded. Meanwhile, the man whose Test place Shah and Bopara had taken, Ian Bell, was fully back in the fold after scoring a century in the second Test in South Africa.

GRAEME SWANN (England, Nottinghamshire)

Batting	M	I	NO	Runs	HS	Avg.	100s	50s
Test	12	14	3	452	85	41.09	-	4
Other First Class	4	4	0	52	26	13.00	-	-
ODI	14	9	2	81	18	11.57	-	-
Other One-day	2	-	-	-	-	-	-	-
International T20	5	2	0	5	5	2.50	-	-
Other Twenty20	3	3	1	97	90*	48.50	-	1

Bowling	O	M	R	W	BB	Avg.	Econ.	5wkt
Test	518	111	1,508	54	5-54	27.93	2.91	4
Other First Class	102	18	306	6	3-53	51.00	3.00	-
ODI	70	1	340	11	5-28	30.91	4.86	1
Other One-day	13.3	2	39	5	3-24	7.80	2.88	-
International T20	18	0	135	5	2-28	27.00	7.50	-
Other Twenty20	12	1	81	4	2-9	20.25	6.75	-

POSTSCRIPT: Graeme Swann's remarkable first full year of Test cricket continued right up to the moment when he took the final wicket in England's victory in the second Test against South Africa in Durban on the day before New Year's Eve. Not only did it give England a 1-0 lead; it brought him his second five-wicket haul in consecutive games and earned him a second Man of the Match Award of the series.

In the first Test at Centurion, the tourists had escaped with a draw after a final-session batting collapse. Yet it was Swann who had given the outstanding individual performance at the ground where, on his first senior England tour in 1999, he had turned up late after missing the team bus. Having taken 5 for 110 in South Africa's first innings, he proceeded to turn the game on its head with a joyous 81-ball innings of 85, the highest score by an England number nine for three decades. This time, you suspect the bus would have waited had his alarm malfunctioned.

At Kingsmead in the Boxing Day Test, he took four more wickets when South Africa batted first and then chipped in with 22 rapid runs as England built a commanding lead. It was his two wickets before tea on the fourth day that hastened South Africa's descent towards 133 all out, and his fifth wicket that wrapped up a win by an innings and 98 runs. By the end of the match Swann had become the first England spinner in history to take 50 Test wickets in a calendar year and elevated himself to third place in the ICC's world bowling rankings. For good measure, he had taken a wicket in the first over of a spell on a remarkable five occasions in the series. All that was left for former England off-spinner Vic Marks to remark as the year closed was, 'Where will it all end?'

MINOR COUNTIES CRICKET 2009

RICHARD LOGAN (Berkshire)

Batting	**M**	**I**	**NO**	**Runs**	**HS**	**Avg.**	**100s**	**50s**
MCCA Trophy	3	3	1	94	64	47.00	-	1
MCCA Championship	6	10	5	331	87*	66.20	-	3

Bowling	**O**	**M**	**R**	**W**	**BB**	**Avg.**	**Econ.**	**5wkt**
MCCA Trophy	30	2	198	4	2-53	49.50	6.60	-
MCCA Championship	192.3	40	691	34	8-56	20.32	3.58	2